AF743471

St. Mary's College

Strawberry Hill

MONSTRA TE ESSE MATREM

Library

BETWEEN TWO WORLDS

Politics and Economy in Independent Ireland

BRIAN GIRVIN

BETWEEN TWO WORLDS

Politics and Economy in Independent Ireland

Gill and Macmillan

Published in Ireland by
Gill and Macmillan Ltd
Goldenbridge
Dublin 8
with associated companies in
Auckland, Delhi, Gaborone, Hamburg, Harare,
Hong Kong, Johannesburg, Kuala Lumpur, Lagos, London,
Manzini, Melbourne, Mexico City, Nairobi,
New York, Singapore, Tokyo
© Brian Girvin 1989
Print origination by
The Type Bureau, Dublin
Printed by
The Camelot Press, Southampton

All rights reserved. No part of this publication may be copied,
reproduced or transmitted in any form or by any means,
without permission of the publishers.

British Library Cataloguing in Publication Data
Girvin, Brian, *1950–*
Between two worlds: politics and economy in independent Ireland.
1. Ireland (Republic). Economic conditions, history
I. Title
330.9417
ISBN 0-7171-1545-3

WITHDRAWN FROM
St Mary's University College
Twickenham
London
ST MARY'S COLLEGE
180537
STRAWBERRY HILL
330·9415 GIR

For Steve McCarthy,
the best of friends

Contents

Abbreviations

ACC	Agricultural Credit Corporation
CIO	Committee on Industrial Organisation
CTT	Coras Tráchtála
DEAC	Dollar Export Advisory Committee
ESB	Electricity Supply Board
FII	Federation of Irish Industries
FSI	Federation of Saorstát Industries
FIM	Federation of Irish Manufacturers
GATT	General Agreement on Tariffs and Trade
ICC	Industrial Credit Company
IDA	Industrial Development Authority
IMF	International Monetary Fund
ITGWU	Irish Transport and General Workers Union
ITUC	Irish Trade Union Congress
ITO	International Trade Organisation
NDF	National Development Fund
NLI	National Library of Ireland
OEEC	Organisation for European Economic Co-operation
PDDE	Parliamentary Debates Dáil Éireann
PRO	Public Records Office (London)
SPO	State Paper Office Dublin
UCDA	University College Dublin Archives Department

Preface

The main argument of this book is contained in the title. The two worlds are those of the liberal democratic industrial states most representative of Northern Europe and the developing (and often undemocratic) states of the Third World. The dichotomy between these two forms is sharp, particularly given the vast differences in wealth, education, and economic opportunities. Ireland does not fit easily in either category; it is not an underdeveloped economy, but neither is it an advanced industrial society. This study suggests that Ireland can be more accurately categorised in terms which place it somewhere between these two poles; it is a liberal democratic state with a developing, though not advanced or mature, industrial economy. Consequently Ireland can be more accurately compared with states such as Greece, Spain or Turkey.

If Ireland's failure to attain industrial maturity to date is accepted, then many of the current difficulties facing its economy become more explicable, if not any more amenable to solution. The current recession can be attributed partly to external exigencies, but the nature of Irish society also prevents resolute action to offset these external disadvantages. There is a continuing tension between tradition and modernity with the former frequently neutralising the impact of the latter. The main emphasis in this book is on the period 1922-1966 in the belief that the policies followed during the first forty years of independence continue to affect the environment within which policy is formulated. The substitution of free trade for protection during the 1960s and entry to the European Community did not remove the obstacles to self-sustained growth. These changes provided opportunities which were not necessarily availed of. Indeed it can be argued that self-sustained growth continues to be an elusive goal for reasons identified in this book.

While writing this book I have been fortunate that many people willingly helped to smooth the way towards its completion. It would never have been written in its present form without the cooperation of several government departments. The research was carried out at a time when much of the relevant material was still held by the respective departments. Therefore I have been heavily dependent on the goodwill of the ministers and civil servants for permission to consult these materials. These facilities were always provided and I am happy to acknowledge the assistance provided. Given the circumstances I willingly signed the Official Secrets Act, but at no time have the departments obstructed my wish to publish material from the sources provided to me. I am particularly grateful to the Ministers for Industry and Commerce, Finance, and Labour for access to their files. At the Department of Industry and Commerce I owe a special thanks to Margaret Hannick, who went to endless trouble to locate files which I sought or to identify material which might be of help to me. As this book concentrates mainly on Industry and Commerce her help was of primary importance. At the Department of Labour Alfie Duggan and his staff provided me with a considerable body of material on industrial relations. Dr Patrick Honohan at the Department of the Taoiseach helped to locate material on a number of occasions which proved very useful.The Department of Finance very kindly provided files which expanded the sources already used. Mr Liam Connellan, the Director General of the Confederation of Irish Industry, granted me permission to consult the minutes of the various industrial organisations which are in the possession of the CII. I am very grateful to these organisations and individuals for their help and their permission to consult and cite these materials.

The State Paper Office is the repository for the files of the Department of the Taoiseach. These materials were a primary source for this book. The staff, who work in rather cramped conditions, were uniformly helpful and friendly during my many visits to the office. The experience of working there was an enjoyable one, perhaps a consequence of its size and the resultant intimacy.

The written record is often deficient or inadequate for the historian's purposes. I supplemented the archival record by interviewing a number of people involved in various aspects of policy making. I would like to thank Patrick Lynch, Kevin McCourt, Sean O'Gorman, J.J.Walsh and T.K.Whitaker for agreeing to speak with me about their involvement in Irish policy making and for being so forthcoming on all occasions. I regret that the only failure in this method of approach occurred when I sought an interview with Sean MacBride.

I have benefited from the active interest which Professor Joseph Lee took in this project. He supervised the thesis on which it is based. His careful comments on various drafts improved the quality of the book and often forced me to redefine my argument in response to his queries. His knowledge of twentieth century Ireland is extensive and I have found much in his own writings which opened up avenues for analysis. Over the years Professor Lee has supported me in my academic work and encouraged me to advance along whatever idiosyncratic path I was exploring at that time. I joined his staff at the Department of Modern History in University College, Cork while preparing this book, an environment most congenial to such work. Professor Lee has helped me in so many ways that my gratitude is considerable. I would like to take this opportunity to thank him for this support and encouragement.

During the final preparation of the manuscript Fergal Tobin at Gill and Macmillan was extremely helpful particularly in resolving the inevitable tension between the demands of the author and those of the publisher. Mrs Norma Buckley and Ms Margaret O'Connell typed various drafts and led me through the obstacles present in a new word processing system.

This book would not have taken its present form had I not been influenced by Bill Warren. I met Bill some sixteen years ago and between then and his tragic death in 1978 we became friends. He very quickly shattered my naive illusions concerning the nature of modern capitalism, the place of imperialism within that system, and the dynamics of change in the contemporary world. Bill's strengths were his strong sense of iconoclasm and his ability to translate that into a coherent intellectual view of any given question. I welcomed this approach to politics which at that time was fairly unusual, though not entirely absent, among most strands of Marxism in Europe. His death robbed the socialist movement of a fine intellect which, given the crisis it is now in, would have been of immense value.

My father Brendan Girvin has always supported me in my study and research from the moment I gave up a ‘secure’ job to attend university. I always feel that he was somewhat sceptical about my decision to do so and concerned that the outcome might be negative. I would like to thank him for all his support and hope that the publication of this book persuades him that the effort was worth it. Clare Crowley read an earlier manuscript in full and offered many suggestions which helped to improve the final work. I will always be grateful for her support at that time; without it it is unlikely that I would have persevered.

My main debt both intellectual and personal is to Steve McCarthy. Over the years Steve's friendship has meant more to me than any other personal relationship; even when we do not see one another for a considerable time the closeness is always there. His strength has kept me buoyant at moments of crisis. In addition to this Steve has given me hospitality when I arrived in Dublin to carry out research (it also included carrying out the foundations of his house in a wheelbarrow during one cold winter). For many years we have argued about the nature of modern Irish society and some of Steve's insights have probably been incorporated into this book though they are unattributed. More importantly he has viewed my theorising and my involvement in academic life with a degree of humour, scepticism, and at times good natured contempt. This book is dedicated to him as an acknowledgement of his friendship.

1

Politics and National Development

BETWEEN 1760 and 1850 the world was radically transformed. The old world was challenged by industrialisation, nationalism and mass democratic politics and often shattered by the consequences. The impact of socio-economic change, unleashed by the industrial revolution, reverberated throughout the nineteenth century. Nowhere was this more apparent or more celebrated than in Britain. By 1850 Britain was the strongest power in the world, wielding unprecedented influence on a global scale through its industrial strength, its military prowess and its technological superiority. However industrialisation destabilised economies elsewhere, making them vulnerable to competition and integrating them for the first time into a world economic system. The cost of industrialisation for most of these economies had been high; economic change undermined traditional markets and production, often condemning the populations to extreme poverty as a consequence. In contrast, though the benefits of industrialisation were distributed unequally in Britain itself, the new age of expansion was generally believed to confer benefits on the society. There was a sense that an age of progress had dawned which carried with it the possibility of further growth and opportunity.[1]

This view rested uneasily on one part of the British state; that of Ireland. Outside the Belfast region, where industrialisation took hold, the industrial revolution had disastrous consequences for the Irish economy. Ireland did not share in the benefits which Britain received from industrialisation, but in large part experienced these changes in negative terms.[2] Capitalist industrialisation undermined a large pre-industrial sector and contributed to Irish poverty. Moreover as the dependence on agriculture increased, so did the dependence of a large proportion of the society on the potato for survival. Furthermore, Mokyr has estimated that Ireland had a lower level of commercialisation in the economy than most other areas of Europe; some 50 per cent of transactions between farmers and labourers being in the form of barter.[3] Much of the Irish economy was thus ill prepared for the ravages of industrialisation and, with the exception of North East Ulster, the response was essentially defensive and negative. The impact of industrialisation coincided with political and strategic decisions which fully integrated the island into the British state. Once the Union was complete, Ireland had become an integral part of the British state, a factor which may have disguised the differences between the agrarian south and the remainder of the United Kingdom. Despite changes during the nineteenth century, Ireland remained the poorest region of the state, apparently condemned to a future of narrow agricultural specialisation, high levels of emigration and the under utilisation of economic resources.

Ireland's pattern of economic development is an example of the regional impact of industrialisation during the nineteenth century. The effect of industrialisation was uneven in that some areas industrialised while others did not. Ireland's experience is not entirely different from that of other European regions which did not share in industrial expansion.[4] Where Ireland did differ was in the extent to which, despite participation in the British state and politics, it remained distinct from other regions within the United Kingdom. Uneven economic development elsewhere did not create the conditions for separatism or a distinct national identity, and as such the Irish case was unusual:

> In general, peaceful and symbiotic relations between industrialising regions and those that remained agrarian were the rule not the exception. The wedge between the two nations was not driven by Ireland's lack of an industrial sector, and not even by its poverty. The real problem was that Ireland was considered by Britain an alien and even hostile country.[5]

This is what laid the basis for mutual suspicion and incomprehension during the period of the Union. The differences between Britain and Ireland were so sharp that they underwrote Ireland's distinctiveness and led to nationalist demands for political sovereignty to institutionalise that distinctiveness through self-government. Separatism was justified by Irish nationalists on political, ethical and economic grounds. Shortly before the 1916 Rebellion, Patrick Pearse gave expression to the basic claim of Irish nationalism:

> National independence involves sovereignty. National sovereignty is twofold in its nature; it is both internal and external. It implies the sovereignty of the nation over all its parts; and it implies the sovereignty of the nation as against all other nations.

Though Pearse recognised that nationalism was essentially spiritual, he also maintained that 'nationhood includes physical freedom'.[6] By this time such views were widespread throughout Europe. In the Irish case Pearse was making a claim for self-government and the resources to carry out policies without any external interference.

Ireland had never been fully integrated into the British state during the nineteenth century. At a formal level a high degree of integration did take place, but this did not reflect the social reality or the wishes of much of Ireland. During the first half of the century a nationalist movement emerged which expressed a coherent set of values in opposition to the claims of the British state. Although Daniel O'Connell's main objective was not achieved, he had established a mass nationalist movement which represented an avenue of distinct development from that available to other citizens of the United Kingdom. Following the famine the nationalist movement consolidated and could, in the decades before 1914, effectively challenge the main pillars of the British state in Ireland. By 1914 only Ulster stood apart from the assertion of sovereignty reflected in Pearse's writings.[7]

Irish nationalism was not just a political phenomenon, it also carried socio-economic implications. Emigration, under-employment, and a lack of industrial development led nationalists to believe that the institutional link with Britain was the cause of Ireland's difficulties. Nationalists concluded that political independence was necessary before economic growth could be generated in Ireland. There is some validity in this assertion; political independence may not have guaranteed economic development, but it would have widened the choices available to an Irish administration. The success of Belgium, Denmark and

Sweden, also in comparatively weak positions, attests to the possibilities available to an independent state. It is unlikely that Ireland was the object of a conscious policy designed to undermine its economy and way of life, as many nationalists believed. Ireland's economic problems were different from those of an industrial state in the course of transforming the world. Policy makers frequently ignored the requirements of a small and alien agricultural region within the state, giving priority to the needs of the capitalist and industrial working class. Benign neglect rather than conscious malevolence would characterise the marginalisation of Irish concerns within the policy process. Free trade proved advantageous to North East Ulster which had an industrial capacity, but its benefits were never clear cut in the southern provinces. In these circumstances the nationalist argument carries considerable conviction, even if not for the reasons usually cited by them. George O'Brien, a leading nationalist economic historian, captured the essence of this case when he suggested that alternative outcomes had been possible:

> It is surely impossible to resist the conclusion that there is some connection between the legislative independence and the economic prosperity of Ireland: so that Ireland can never be a rich and prosperous country until her independence is restored.[8]

The economic argument was not the main objection to British rule, it simply reinforced other trends. The denial of national sovereignty proved to be an altogether more potent source of political mobilisation. While it is difficult to locate a coherent sense of Irish national consciousness in 1800, by 1914 not only was this consciousness present, it provided a powerful source of political legitimacy for nationalist elites and one that distanced Irish nationalism from the British state. In addition, the values which underwrote Irish nationalism were at variance with those dominant in industrial Britain. In Ireland nationalism, religion, and the land formed the most influential aspects of the political culture, while in Britain, class, industrialisation and secularism proved far more potent.[9] On this basis nationalist Ireland was able to resist integration into the British state, in contrast to the experience of Scotland, Wales or Northern Ireland.[10]

The relationship between Ireland and the rest of the United Kingdom was remarkably tenuous by the end of the nineteenth century, nor were the benefits from this relationship clear cut. The main beneficiaries were Ulster and the cattle exporters in the south. The former was fully integrated into the international economic system and had little or no connection with or impact on the rest of Ireland. The southern cattle economy was dependent on British markets, but the benefits from this were limited and did not contribute to overcoming the underdeveloped nature of the southern economy. It is very questionable if '... Ireland was in many respects a highly developed country by the end of the [nineteenth] century'.[11] In a comparative context such a conclusion can only be justified if the island is taken as a single economic unit. The experience of Ireland during the nineteenth century indicates that two distinct economies existed and that these supported two very different social and political structures. Greater analytical clarity is generated if the two areas are treated separately. Northern Ireland remained part of the British economy, while the agrarian south developed a distinct character which set it apart from the rest of the state. If Ireland is treated in this way then it is necessary to locate distinct developmental dynamics within each region.[12] This is most forcibly expressed by nationalist Ireland through its political demands for self-determination, but it also has a strong economic dimension. The cattle economy benefited greatly from the link with Britain, but even this sector was never representative of the economy as a whole. Dairy farming in the south, the marginal farmer in the west and large sectors of the urban economy either did not participate in the export economy or were threatened by international competition. National development, if not self-sufficiency, could become a realistic political objective by the twentieth century because most sectors of the economy were either dependent on the local market or undergoing competition from imports. In a sense the Irish agrarian economy was becoming 'nationalised' to the extent that the main focus of economic activity was internal rather than external. Moreover, change was increasingly perceived with suspicion and defensive, usually political, strategies adopted to offset its impact. A contrast might again be drawn with Sweden and Denmark both of whom responded actively to changing circumstances prior to 1914; one industrialised while the other restructured its agrarian economy on competitive and commercial grounds.[13]

The economic disparities between Britain and Ireland were

such as to generate and sustain the belief among Irish nationalists that British policy was consistently underdeveloping Ireland. It was confidently predicted by nationalist politicians that sovereignty would bring about a qualitative improvement in the economy. In retrospect one of the most alarming features of Irish economic development during the twentieth century has been the consistent failure of the independent state to provide for the welfare of its citizens.[14] Political independence may thus be a necessary condition for economic development, but it is not a sufficient condition. An independent state may provide an institutional environment for growth but cannot guarantee this. The Irish experience during the nineteenth and twentieth centuries demonstrates that even under quite favourable conditions growth will not necessarily follow. The type of sustained growth experienced by Britain and the United States during the nineteenth century and that experienced by Germany, Japan and Sweden since 1945 may be the exception rather than the rule. If this is the case then Ireland's difficulties may be more explicable. Despite this it is also necessary to explain why Irish growth was not sustained while that of some other small European states such as Austria, Finland and Switzerland, also predominantly agricultural for much of the twentieth century, has been far more impressive.[15]

Irish nationalists shared with other nationalist elites the simple belief that political independence would assure economic growth. When the experience of independence did not confirm this belief, there has been a tendency to argue that despite formal independence the metropolitan power continues to maintain indirect and therefore more insidious control over the economy. Neo-colonialism and its off-shoot dependency theory stress the external obstacles to economic growth and embrace what is an essentially pessimistic view of development. For these and related views the autonomy of the state is severely limited and, while the national elites are not helpless, it is usually concluded that economic dependency will be the main characteristic of economic relationships between developed and less developed states.[16] In his recent study of the Irish economy, Raymond Crotty has concluded that Ireland, in common with most of the world, remains 'undeveloped'; a result of 'colonisation by metropolitan capitalist powers'. At best political independence is a passive variable as the blockages to development are primarily external.[17] Yet despite this there has been considerable economic and industrial development, both in the newly independent states and in Latin America, since 1945. Various strategies have been adopted, with varying degrees of success; but each has in common the existence of an independent state apparatus with a programme for development.[18] A good *prima facie* case can be made that even the limited development that has occurred can be attributed to the existence of an independent state.

What is not as easily explained is why these independent states have not been as successful as existing industrial states. Neo-liberals take an essentially optimistic view of the possibility of economic development, while economic nationalists embrace a pessimistic view. However, both share a belief in the primacy of economics as the determining factor in growth and development. Liberals believe that the unfettered market will create optimal benefits for all participants, while economic nationalists consider the market to be the mechanism by which dependency is maintained. Both of these views share a form of economic determinism which, though with different points of emphasis, reduces the importance of the nation state as an economic actor and ignores the possibilities available to national elites. A possibilist approach involves taking seriously the view that political action operates as a variable independent of but influencing economic change. Rather than accepting the primacy of economics, it places politics as the primary focus for success or failure in development. Change cannot be brought about simply by an act of political will, but if a society is prepared to accept the costs involved in certain strategies, state assisted industrial expansion for example, then the choices available to it expand accordingly.[19]

There are also objective obstacles to development. These may be external, but are more likely to be internal. Nationalism has provided newly independent states with a powerful ideology to counter the residual elements of colonial influence and mobilise support for development. Development is never inevitable, even when the conditions appear favourable; but the possibility of re-ordering external economic relations and generating internal economic change necessitates identifying the sources of slow growth or lack of development within the national economy rather than as a consequence of continuing external interference or influence. The market is effectively neutral between economies, though its impact is not always benign. Moreover, not all states share in growth to the same degree, nor are the benefits from growth distributed equally. Disequilibrium remains the main characteristic of economic change, but to accept this is not to agree with those who assert that 'real' development is impossible. What it does mean is that if economic development is defined in terms of a high level of industrialisation with systematic and deep forward and backward linkages, then few states have ever achieved this.[20]

Without easy access to capital, technology, raw materials and food there is always an element of dependency, a dependency compounded by lack of military resources. The size of a state will also have consequences for development. The level of autonomy available to Brazil or India makes it more probable that such states will be in a strong position to design their own strategies for development, whereas small states adjacent to large ones will find it more difficult. For others the possibility of development is very remote: 'For some small countries with few resources, and split into quite separate ethnic groups autonomous development is hardly possible'.[21] A range of factors can influence the outcome; the size of a state, its proximity to a large and hostile neighbour, lack of resources, or divisions within the state itself. The terms of trade between two states can create dependency, particularly when one state relies on the export of a single commodity or crop. Multi-national investment can also have an adverse impact on the internal ordering of an economy, as can the linkages between sections of the national economy and external companies or states.

Despite this, decision-making remains in the hands of national elites who can determine the conditions under which economic activity takes place. A considerable amount will depend on the extent to which an elite is development-minded. Traditional patterns of economic activity will prevail if the state is not development minded. Alternatively if development is or becomes a policy objective, not only will new strategies be elaborated but traditional economic behaviour will be challenged. Even if the elite is not development minded this does not mean that their policies are determined by external influences. It is important to distinguish beween the constraints faced by a state and the control exercised over a state. In the formal colonial context, control was exercised by the metropolitan power over the colony. In the contemporary period the United States exercises control over certain Central American states, while the Soviet Union does so in Eastern Europe. In these circumstances the limits to autonomous development are narrow; to ignore them can involve military intervention. Control is not a normal feature of the post-colonial world, but constraints are. A constraint does not involve direct control over decision-making in an independent state. Policy is formulated in an autonomous fashion, but implementation may not be successful because of existing constraints. These constraints may be internal or external. If external they can be removed or reduced by negotiation or adaptation. If internal they usually take the form of social blockages which in terms of economic policy can become 'limits to growth'. Thus the behaviour of individuals, institutions or political parties within a society is probably the main obstacle to growth in many societies. It is often probable that external constraints, such as trade links, will be used by conservatives within the society to obstruct innovative policies. Even here the primary focus of analysis is on the social groups, their composition, and possible influence rather than on the external relationship.[22]

Control and constraint are part of a continuum; for some states control will be the dominant feature while for others it will be constraint. In general the exercise of national sovereignty during the twentieth century has limited the degree to which major powers have been able to exercise control over other states. Most independent states face constraints. The Irish case can be compared to two sets of independent states: those such as Denmark, Finland or Austria which have achieved considerable growth and sustained high standards of living; and another group, including Greece, Brazil and Argentina, sometimes characterised as the semi-periphery.[23] Ireland does not compare easily with the former but appears to have more in common with the latter. The concept of the semi-periphery is used to distinguish a group of states which have a history of parliamentary politics, some economic and industrial development, and a long period of political independence from many of those states which have achieved independence since 1945. Ireland does not fit easily into either group; its lack of sustained industrial development, its nationalism and populist and clientist politics overlap with the main features of the semi-peripheral states, while its per capita income, literacy and educational levels, and a history of political stability bring it closer to northern European industrial states.

Ireland may thus be a hybrid; a state with a strong civil society and effective parliamentary institutions, but a socio-economic system which remains underdeveloped. The lack of economic development could be attributed to British rule during the nineteenth century, but the challenge of independence in 1922 raised serious questions concerning the ability of an Irish government to formulate policy and more importantly to implement this in a society which has strong conservative features.[24]

Little of this was evident to the mainstream of Irish nationalism prior to independence. Yet most of the features were already in place by the end of the nineteenth century. When the time came for power to be transferred from Britain to Ireland, Irish society had become a proprietorial democracy with a strong commitment to self-sufficiency and stability. The socio-economic structure of agrarian Ireland reinforced this, as did the tendency for surplus population to emigrate. The political culture which had evolved by 1914 also reflected these phenomena and while all varieties of nationalism remained committed to separatism, the social implications for an independent Ireland were not radical. The 1916 rebellion has to be seen as a frustrated response to unfulfilled expectations, rather than an expression of radicalism. The period 1916-1922 can be construed in radical terms only if violence is equated with radicalism; the legacy of 1916 in socio-economic terms did not break with the certainties of an essentially conservative and stable society. That a social revolution did not take place between 1916 and 1922 reflects in large part the 'politics of a contented people'; made possible by the proprietorial nature of the society, its relative affluence and middle class dominance. At many levels continuity rather than change is the main characteristic of the decade after 1914.[25] The transfer of power from one ruling elite to another remained the only objective of Irish nationalism by 1914, not an inherently revolutionary objective even if the institutional arrangements for such a transfer remained open to doubt.

2

Independence and the Obstacles to Economic Development in the Free State 1922–27

> The Sinn Féin myth, which has been a decisive influence on public thinking and policy for more than two generations, has assumed that Irish political independence implied economic independence. The shadow of this unfounded dogma which identified political independence with economic self- sufficiency still remains.[1]

THIS view expressed by Paddy Lynch, one of the few independent economic thinkers that Ireland has produced since the 1950s, captures the essential characteristics of the revolutionary elite which sought for and acquired political power between 1916 and 1922. The new movement drew on an intellectual tradition which attributed Ireland's economic ills to Britain. By the 1920s, there was a widespread view that political independence was closely linked to the possibility of economic development.[2] Although nationalists drew on this critical literature, the nature of Irish economic development was not thought out in any systematic fashion. It was assumed that once political sovereignty had been achieved, the obstacles to growth would be removed. The Sinn Féin constitution, adopted in October 1917, reflected these assumptions. Secession was the primary aim, while economic objectives were general and symbolic in focus. The 1918 election manifesto advocated the protection of Irish industry and other economic changes. The main objective, however, remained the maintenance of a united front against Britain; consequently little thought appears to have been given to economic policy.[3] The Democratic Programme of the First Dáil, although initially drafted by Tom Johnson of the Labour Party, did not deepen the nationalist economic analysis. In the final version, its primary focus was on the duty of the nation and the responsibilities of its citizens. In outline, the Democratic Programme offered a form of nationalist collectivism, one in which economic forces would be subordinated to the requirements of the nation. In context, the Democratic Programme was not particularly significant; Dáil Éireann spent very little time considering the document.[4]

It is, perhaps, mistaken to lay too much emphasis on either economic or social policy at this juncture. The primacy of politics remained the central consideration: where economic matters intervened they tended to be concerned with political control over policy instruments, rather than the use that could be made of them. Prior to 1922, there is little evidence of coherent policy formation. In 1920, Ernest Blythe had proposed the establishment of a National Economic Council which would function as a forum for discussion on economic affairs between government, business, and labour. In the following year he proposed that the Belfast boycott be transformed into a general campaign to secure the Irish market for Irish producers.[5] Neither of these initiatives were realised in the context of a war, but they do draw attention to the continuing importance of protectionist assumptions. Despite this, there is no evidence that serious consideration had been given to the economics of independence. This can be attributed to war time pressures, but also to the belief among Sinn Féin elites that a clear statement of economic or social policy would disrupt the united front then facing Britain.

The complexities of economic policy became clearer once negotiations with Britain began after the Truce. Michael Collins insisted that British policy had effectively prevented Irish economic growth. He consequently sought compensation for the economic effects of the Act of Union, over taxation, and consequent damages for loss of population.[6] This view represented a consensus among nationalists at the time, and led to an insistence that Irish political autonomy would only be acceptable if fiscal and economic autonomy were also realised. The publication in 1921 of Britain's proposals for resolving the Irish crisis proved unsatisfactory to the Irish. Lloyd George was prepared to grant only minimum concessions. The status quo was insisted on in the crucial areas of taxation and fiscal matters. If this had been accepted, then Irish economic sovereignty would have been very limited.[7]

Robert Barton, the Irish Minister of Economics, set up the

Economic Relations Committee to advise the government on the implications of the British proposals.[8] George O'Brien, one of its members, noted that certain distinctions had to be drawn by the Committee:

> As I understand the desire of the Minister at the moment is not so much to have a case made in favour of protection as to have a case made in favour of obtaining the right to impose protection if necessary. The former question, namely, whether protection should or should not be imposed is one which would have to be decided by an Irish government in being; whereas the latter question will be vital in the negotiations with the British Government.

He goes on to warn that Britain would oppose any weakening of the free trade system. The minimum which Ireland could hope to achieve would be the right to impose certain duties and tariffs. Without this concession, O'Brien believed that any future economic policy initiated by an Irish government would be severely restricted. He maintained that a number of arguments could be used against British objections. Ireland's experience of colonialism had, he suggested, had a negative effect on the Irish economy. Furthermore, Britain had, in the past, used protection against Ireland and for its own interests. O'Brien also cited evidence from other parts of Europe where, in contrast to more recent British experience, protection had been the norm. In effect, O'Brien was adopting the 'infant industry' model to justify a break with the free trade system.[9]

O'Brien's view was strongly supported by two of Ireland's leading economists, E.J. Riordan and T.A. Smiddy:

> So vital do we consider Ireland's power to have unfettered control of her own fiscal policy that in our opinion no compromise whatever can be made on this primary principle of national freedom.

A more radical case was made by the staff of the Economics Department of Dáil Éireann. According to this view, Ireland had been actively exploited by Britain. Developing an early version of 'unequal exchange', it was argued that Britain's industrial dominance had forced Ireland to concentrate on a narrow range of agricultural output. Because of the differential price involved, Ireland had experienced considerable loss, estimated at £3.75

million per annum. An independent policy was the only method of overcoming the vagaries of this relationship.[10]

During the subsequent negotiations with Britain, the Irish delegation received the fiscal concessions which O'Brien, Riordan, and Smiddy had demanded. The Irish Free State received the right to determine its future tariff regime. A sizeable proportion of nationalist opinion believed that the terms of the Treaty were favourable to Ireland and laid the basis for independent development.[11]

Political independence is usually accompanied by a general euphoria about the possibility of economic and social development. Ireland was no exception in 1922; although here as elsewhere such expectations were to be often disappointed. A transfer of political power, in and of itself, will not induce people to adopt patterns of behaviour in conflict with those which have evolved over a number of generations. Political factors also contributed to the disappointment experienced; the Civil War, the challenge to law and order, and the need to build a stronger institutional framework for the new state prevented policy makers from turning immediately to serious consideration of economic and social matters. When, after the defeat of the anti Treaty Republican forces, the new state began to stabilise continuity rather than change was the main feature of economic and social policy. Free trade between the two states was maintained and the patterns of agricultural output and production remained unaffected by the changes; a common labour market remained in place; while a common currency reinforced the monetary links between Britain and Ireland. These trends were viewed with considerable hostility by the Republican opposition in the Free State which accused the new government of neglecting Irish interests and acting as an instrument of British policy in Ireland.[12]

The difficulties facing the Cumann na nGaedheal government were immense and the conventional ideology did not always provide an adequate answer. The Irish Free State though independent was not the state that Irish nationalists had fought for and the civil war reflected the continuing divisions within the Republican movement. At the socio-economic level the new state was one of the least developed regions of Europe. If the island is taken as the frame of reference then its pre 1914 profile is one of a relatively advanced economy. However, partition demonstrated the difficulties of using this approach. The Free State had one of the smallest industrial workforces in Europe.[13] Not only was Ireland a distinctly agricultural economy by 1922, its social structure also differed from the United Kingdom and other advanced industrial economies. A partial analysis concludes that, unlike Britain where the proletariat was the dominant force, in Ireland the propertied classes remained extremely strong. Crotty has estimated that some 30 per cent of the labour force were propertied or professional. A higher figure can be obtained if a distinction is made between one group comprising employers, the self employed, and relatives assisting and another group comprising employees and the unemployed. At the 1926 census the former stood at 49.2 per cent, while the latter stood at 50.3 per cent. Even this figure tends to disguise the extent of the propertied classes' influence over the society.[14] The lack of development in the economy and the preponderance of the propertied classes dictated caution rather than innovation during the opening years of the new state.

But other factors were also at play. Many of those who had accepted the nationalist criticism of free trade prior to independence altered their opinions subsequently. O'Brien and Smiddy were closely identified with the continuation of free trade after the establishment of the new state. Cumann na nGaedheal's cautious economic strategy can be accounted for in a number of ways: 'Any radical departure on tariffs would have upset the British, worried the Irish banks and alienated the large farmers and businessmen.'[15] Political considerations were also important: the government was attempting to restore normality in the face of an intransigent minority challenge, and the government received important support from groups closely identified with free trade. The strength of these sectors within Irish society meant that any government would have to take serious account of their concerns. It was also recognised that any precipitate break with free trade would endanger agricultural exports, the main source of Ireland's wealth. However, it would be mistaken to conclude that Cumann na nGaedheal was dependent on graziers, or on those most closely identified with the export market, and therefore reflected their economic interests. In fact, the social and regional basis of Cumann na nGaedheal support was not that dissimilar from Sinn Féin or Fianna Fáil during the 1920s. While there can be little doubt that the government promoted the interest of commercial agriculture, this was done for pragmatic reasons and based on the advice available to it, rather than as a reflection of the dominant influence of the graziers over the government. This sector of Irish agriculture was strong in economic terms but this was not reflected politically. The continuation of the export trade after independence resulted from the belief that it was in the national interest to do so and that the alternatives did not justify a change of direction. This approach was confirmed by the Report of the Commission on Agriculture in 1923 which concluded that the available evidence sustained the commitment to traditional agricultural production.[16]

The government accepted the view of Eoin MacNeill that sound national finance was '... the structural edifice of national power and national liberty.'[17] This view was shared by W.T. Cosgrave, who curtly rejected suggestions by Dr P. Coffey of Maynooth for a monetary and credit system distinct from that of the United Kingdom. While dismissing Coffey as an amateur in such matters, Cosgrave added an important point of substance: 'I am not disposed to recommend the issue of currency unless I am perfectly satisfied that our rate of exchange is going to be normal ... we should avail of the advantages of English currency.'[18]

These concerns interlocked with and were reinforced by the influence of the major government institutions. For most of the 1920s, the Department of Finance exercised an effective hegemony over economic policy. It acquired a central role in the administration at an early stage. Cabinet regulations provided that all draft legislation should be submitted to Finance. This ensured '... an important line of defence in the armoury of the Department of Finance in its unending struggle to curtail the proposals for expenditure put forward by other Departments.'[19] The Secretary of the Department, Joseph Brennan, opposed protection, state intervention and industrialisation in the interests of fiscal probity and caution. The deflationary policies of the 1920s were designed to achieve Brennan's aim of maintaining parity between the British and Irish currencies, and balancing the budget. Within this framework, there was no place for an interventionist or expansionist policy.[20]

The Minister for Agriculture Patrick Hogan believed that agriculture would remain central to economic development for a considerable period. Unlike Finance, Hogan had a developmental strategy, one based on promoting the most efficient sections of Irish agriculture. This implied concentrating resources on agricultural exports, enhancing their competitiveness, and capturing new markets with additional output. Whereas Finance's response was essentially conservative, Hogan believed that agriculture could provide the mechanism for growth. He was sceptical of the ability of other sectors to provide growth, and consequently he accepted the existing institutional and economic arrangements as the best framework for development. Hogan's approach was essentially positive, based on the recognition that exports were essential to pay for Ireland's very high import ratio. Economic policy would, therefore, be agricultural policy:

> For almost a generation national development in Ireland must mean, to at least 60 per cent or 70 per cent, agricultural development. There may be two opinions on questions like free trade, protection and the development of industry, but there can be no two opinions that the basis of our economy, for our generation, will have to be agricultural. The government,therefore, must have as a government, an agricultural policy, and cannot afford to leave it to any one minister, even if he be an external minister.[21]

The centrality of agricultural exports underpinned Hogan's approach to economic policy throughout the 1920s. He complained in 1924 that farmers were not receiving adequate support:

> The fact is that the farmer, who is the main producer, is not getting a fair chance, and that the distributive and non-productive industries are getting more than their fair share of the profits. The problem resolves itself into bringing down the cost of living.

According to Hogan, a fundamental problem for agricultural output was the difference between the price paid to farmers and the retail price. He estimated that retail prices on a range of products were inflated above the farm price by 50 per cent to 120 per cent.[22] This, he maintained, was a disincentive for farmers. The state should, he urged, concentrate policy on, and subsidise, the progressive farmer. The state should supplement the efforts of the farmers to expand production, but:

> If the state is to be healthy there must be a movement both ways. In the long run this can only be brought about

PROPERTY OF
ST. MARY'S COLLEGE
STRAWBERRY HILL

> permanently by farmers taking charge of their own organisations for buying and selling, coupled with the increased efficiency which the grading of products, testing of cows, etc., will bring about. The problem, however, is immediate.[23]

The legislation introduced by Hogan during the 1920s sought to develop the institutional arrangements to encourage this; in many cases the response from the farming community to these innovations was less than enthusiastic. Republican sentiment also remained hostile to Hogan's pre-suppositions and to those of Finance and the government. Yet the opposition did not usually offer a realistic alternative. The pressure of economic circumstances, in conjunction with the major social forces, during the early 1920s, prevented any radical departure. The electoral system also provided obstacles to rapid change, as did the dominant influence of the Roman Catholic Church. Independence provided Irish governments with the institutions to generate economic development; for the first decade after independence the incentive to do so was not strong.[24]

The position of industry in the Free State did not allow it to exercise a decisive influence over economic decision making. Within Cumann na nGaedheal there were those, such as J.J. Walsh and Alfred O'Rahilly, who supported protection on principle. They were not the dominant source of influence on economic policy, however. The industrialists themselves were divided on policy. The larger and more successful companies favoured the continuation of free trade, while smaller, vulnerable companies lobbied for tariffs or duties. The new government established the Fiscal Inquiry Committee in June 1923. It was empowered to examine the working of the fiscal system, its impact on Irish industry and agriculture, and to recommend any changes which might be necessary for future development.[25] Cosgrave insisted that the purpose of the Committee was technocratic. Its approach should be disinterested and analytical, the government would retain the power to introduce policy. He, furthermore, rejected the view that corporate interests should be represented on the Committee on the grounds that their views would reflect vested interests and could not be considered impartial.[26]

The terms of reference and the approach adopted by the Committee reinforced the status quo. Conceptually, the

Committee attempted to evaluate the outcome for the economy as a whole if tariffs were introduced for industry. In its final report the Committee emphasised that:

> It does not feel at liberty to make proposals with regard to the existing fiscal system which, however desirable in themselves or likely under other circumstances to be unobjectionable, would involve any considerable decrease in the existing revenue receipts.[27]

The Committee also accepted a view urged by agricultural interests, that any change in the fiscal system should take into account the effect on agricultural exports. A case had been made for duties on barley and malt. It was maintained that under these circumstances it was likely that brewers and distillers, dependent on export markets, would relocate their companies outside the state.[28]

The Irish Flour Millers Association invoked the national interest in their claim for tariffs. The Irish market remained depressed, they maintained; there was fierce competition, and Irish producers controlled less than half that market. However, the Association's case was considered to be weak. The Association, under questioning, disclosed that when flour milling had been controlled during the 1914–18 War, the Irish product had proved to be inferior in quality to other flour. Resistance to this poor quality resulted in American flour capturing a substantial portion of the Irish market. The millers' case was further undermined by the evidence of the Irish Transport and General Workers Union, the main representative of the employees. The union laid most of the blame for the difficulties with the employers. The main obstacle to growth was not wages, as had been urged by the flour millers, but the small size and inefficiency of the enterprise, bad business organisation, and a lack of confidence in the workforce. The union recommended that the industry should be reorganised to meet the challenge of competition, but that the consumer should also be protected.[29]

Because of the importance of flour milling, the Fiscal Inquiry Committee examined this sector with considerable care. The industry employed 3,000 workers and was long established. In the past it had proved to be flexible, overcoming by modernisation the crisis of 1879–84. The Fiscal Inquiry Committee considered that most of the difficulties were internal or short-term. Despite evidence from the flour millers, the Committee was unable to discover profit levels within that industry. No 'rational' accounting system appeared to exist, and notions of profitability appear to have been largely subjective. Most of the problems were considered to be self-induced and could be resolved by careful restructuring, marketing, and advertising. The Committee noted that the ITGWU was prepared to actively support such an approach if certain safeguards were guaranteed.[30]

The strongest objection to tariffs came from large, exporting, and long-established industries. W.& R. Jacobs maintained that the increase in costs following a tariff would force them to remove their company from the state. The tobacco industry claimed that following the imposition of a tariff in April 1923, their export trade had disappeared and they were now threatened by the establishment of a factory in the Free State by the Imperial Tobacco Company. The foreign company was more efficient and paid higher wages, consequently the witnesses for the Irish tobacco industry urged that restrictions should be placed on this competition.[31] The boot and shoe, tanning, confectionery and wholesale clothing industries, among others, attempted to secure substantial tariffs for their industries. The main reason offered was external competition and foreign control of the Irish market. In some cases, the competitive position of the Irish companies was disastrous. Agricultural machinery could be imported from America at a cheaper rate than any Irish product. In addition, rolling stock for railways could be imported which was £300 per unit cheaper than that produced in Dublin.[32]

The evidence available to the Fiscal Inquiry Committee leads to the conclusion that most Irish industry was relatively marginal to economic activity. In terms of volume, the anti-protectionist companies were predominant. The evidence from the companies favouring protection was frequently unconvincing, and often confusing and unsubstantiated. These interests found it difficult to sustain their case when evidence was demanded. Implicit in their approach was a belief that political independence should be used as an instrument to protect Irish industry from external competition. Many confirmed that in order to capture and retain the home market, protection would have to be high and permanent. It might also be inferred from the evidence that the majority of those favouring protection were too weak to reorganise their companies without state assistance.[33]

The Fiscal Inquiry Committee has traditionally had a bad press, particularly from economic nationalists. However, on the evidence before it, it is difficult to see what other conclusions could have been drawn. Its analysis was careful and exhaustive: it held over forty sessions between July and September 1923. Its conclusions were based on the evidence and on an acceptance that agriculture would remain the mainstay of economic growth. This view was reinforced by the evidence of the export industries, and fears that the cost of living would increase, that employment would be uncertain, and that monopolies would emerge. The Committee also evaluated in this context, the impact of the boycott of imports in 1920. The consequences of this boycott were, the Committee concluded, wholly negative.[34] Nor was it prepared to accept the classical 'infant industry' argument, which was considered inapplicable, noting that few Irish industries were of recent origin. The report characterised most of the industries demanding protection as debilitated and added that '... they cannot claim the indulgence which is, perhaps rightly, extended to extreme youth.'[35]

This evidence led the Committee to recommend that there should be no change in the general fiscal framework.[36] The reluctance to recommend a more radical approach appears consistent with the evidence available to the Committee. Despite this most members of the Committee were predisposed to the free trade position. George O'Brien was to recall a little later:

> The bias of the Committee was heavily in favour of free trade. Professor Bastable set the tone of the discussion. Nobody was better able to expose the fallacies of a protectionist argument. He was a survivor of the great days of Victorian liberalism when free trade was regarded by British economists as a religion rather than a policy. His reputation as a writer of the standard book on international law was very great.

This free trade 'bias' clearly influenced the Committee, but it is impossible to believe that independent thinkers such as O'Brien and Timothy Smiddy were simply swayed by Bastable's expression of free trade dogma. A more plausible explanation is that both O'Brien and Smiddy were convinced intellectually by the evidence before them, and as O'Brien was to argue later, it was this which led them to take 'A realistic line on Irish economic policy.'[37]

Notwithstanding these considerations there were a number of weaknesses in the Committee's conclusions. It presupposed that pre-war normality and stability in the international economy would return and that this justified continuity.[38] Such a view reflected Irish opinion at the time, a view probably influenced by existing British assumptions. The 'abnormal' conditions would, it was believed, soon disappear and Irish industry would be faced with obstacles to growth which, because of its location, would remain central to economic decision-making. The Committee, therefore, suggested that industry should concentrate on relieving the negative impact of small-scale production, transport, and energy costs, rather than attempt to reorganise the entire institutional setting. A related weakness concerned the rather narrow focus which the Committee adopted when assessing the merits of protection. It largely concentrated on the consequences for agriculture without offering an alternative policy for manufacturing industry. While accepting the case for agriculture, O'Brien recognised that the narrow focus of the Committee might have been mistaken:

> But in regard to manufacturers, some concessions might perhaps have been prudently made to sentiment. . . . There was a widespread desire, not only among the businessmen who would have duly profited, but among the public generally for some attempt to revive Irish industry. If the Committee had indicated the directions in which such an attempt could be most safely and least expensively made, its reports would probably have received more respect and would have led to positive action.[39]

Such positive action was forthcoming from only one agency within the Free State. The Department of Industry and Commerce was, from its origin, a committed advocate of an active government policy for industry. E.J. Riordan, whose book *Modern Irish Trade and Industry*, published in 1920, had been positively received, became an officer in the Department. Riordan was strongly protectionist and it was on his initiative that the Fiscal Inquiry Committee was established. A fellow departmental official with similiar views, T.J. Barrington acted as secretary to the Committee. Riordan may have believed that Barrington could influence the direction of the Committee's inquiries towards protection. If so he was to be mistaken as Barrington and the Committee clashed on the issue and he appears to have been excluded from the proceedings.[40]

The Minister for Industry and Commerce, Joseph McGrath, prepared a lengthy analysis for the cabinet on the final report. Unlike his officials he accepted the main thrust of the report and rejected some of the criticisms made of it:

> It would appear as if many believers in protection regard the mere mention of the word as establishing their whole case, the onus then resting on their opponents to disprove the case if they can. But the matter is not so simple as that. What is the essence of protection? It is an artificial device whereby certain activities are stimulated and fostered at the cost of preventing the general community from buying goods where they are offered at the lowest price. I am far from saying that any community is naturally so wise or virtuous that it can be left to its full development by the mere play of its natural inclination.
>
> But it must be recognised that advocates of protection necessarily have the onus of proof on themselves and that the onus is not adequately discharged by reference to the practice or policy of other countries whose conditions are essentially dissimilar and whose present state is not the best advertisement of their policy.

He also warned that prices would rise and cited other traditional objections to tariffs.[41]

Yet McGrath was not a principled advocate of free trade; he appears to have accepted some of the ideas formulated by his officials. He recognised that Ireland did not have a strong industrial base, the cause of which he was prepared to attribute to free trade. He maintained further, that unemployment would not be overcome by growth in the agricultural sector. McGrath also gave expression to Griffith's view that a balance between agriculture and industrial development was required. He urged his fellow cabinet members to recognise that:

> Ireland is one of the few countries not itself industrial, in which the immense productive plants created by the War have been able to find a market unimpaired by any serious

> fiscal barriers or by any general inability to buy. Our industries and manufacturers have survived the last four years to find that their home market is flooded by competition able to use those years to improve and develop their business and to obtain a start which the native manufacturer, unaided, has little hope of catching up. The position is so abnormal as to require remedies of an abnormal kind.[42]

It is not surprising that McGrath would emphasise these difficulties. As Minister for Industry and Commerce he had a more detailed appreciation of the condition of industry than the Department of Finance. Moreover, Finance's advocacy of free trade was ideological, whereas Industry and Commerce's approach was more cautious and conditional. McGrath's position was balanced between the realities of the status quo, which he readily accepted, and the belief that it was necessary to promote industrial development. He recognised that such development was limited in the existing circumstances, but advocated that protection should be available under strict supervision. The criteria and conditions for a tariff would be narrow. An industry could expect to receive state support only if

> ... it is one which with reasonable application and intelligence we can develop economically, and that there is a real prospect of the initial cost which the rest of the community would have to bear being returned to it in full measure in the future.[43]

McGrath's memorandum was endorsed by the cabinet in January 1924. The ambiguity in it was not detected by his fellow ministers at this time. The officials of the Department of Finance, who were in complete agreement with the report, did however. J.J. McElligott produced a doctrinaire defence of the Committee's conclusions. Although he admitted that 'the time has passed when either free trade or protection can be looked upon as a panacea for the economic ills of any country ...', he continued his analysis by disregarding his own advice and reiterating the traditional position. McElligott rejected protection on both general and specific grounds, putting forward a conservative case for not changing the fiscal system. He maintained that free trade was the natural environment for economic activity in contrast to the artificiality of protection. He warned that protection, once introduced, was unlikely to be reversed:

> The reason being that protection tends to force trade and commerce into unnatural or uneconomic channels and the industry thereby created requires artificial conditions in which to prosper: the tender plant of a hothouse will die in the open air.

McElligott's remedy involved reducing costs generally, particularly that of labour.[44] This approach was essentially doctrinaire because it is unlikely that any circumstances existed where McElligott would have accepted the validity of protection. In this sense his belief system could neither be verified nor falsified, because he believed there was no counter-factual evidence available on the issue.

McGrath's concern at this time draws attention to the differences between Finance and Industry and Commerce. At the end of 1922 he alerted his colleagues to the increase in unemployment and recommended that the government promote schemes to alleviate it by a programme of reconstruction. An Employment Commission should be established and empowered to advise the government on the possibility of public works. The general proposals were accepted at a subsequent cabinet meeting, but the use of public funds was ruled out.[45] McGrath's successor, Patrick McGilligan, returned to the topic in 1924 insisting that a lack of confidence existed following the Civil War. The government could improve conditions by tackling unemployment. McGilligan recommended that a number of schemes should be immediately promoted, and that a long term approach to counter unemployment and depression was required. The government should, in the interim, use its influence and finance to expand employment opportunities.

The Minister's proposals were far-reaching in that he expressed concern about the general development of industry. In contrast to most of his cabinet colleagues, he recognised that the State would have to play an active role in the development of the Irish economy. This was necessitated because private capital was not available for developmental projects:

> Private undertakers cannot be expected to show more economic confidence than the government and the

> government's economic policy has been so cautious that, whether it rests on confidence or not, the considerations involved are too technical for the elements whose discontent, whether intentional or not, tend to disruption, to appreciate. The situation is one in which if confidence is to be inspired the government must take the leading part.[46]

Neither McGrath nor McGilligan were ideologically committed to either protection or state intervention. Both men sympathised, in general terms, with free trade. However, the institutional setting in which they functioned forced them to recognise the limitations of free trade.

The Department of Industry and Commerce was an explicitly developmental agency, the only one in the new state. As such, the Department was more interventionist and sympathetic to protection than other departments. In addition to Barrington and Riordan, Gordon Campbell – the first secretary of the Department – was an individual of independent mind and high intellectual calibre.[47] The Department's competence was extensive, and this led it to adopt a self consciously developmental approach to policy making:

> Under the British regime there was no administrative machinery dealing with industrial development and in consequence a completely new start had to be made. With the exception of the Census of Production there was no body of information available officially as to the extent and position of existing industries with the exception of agriculture. The first step, therefore, made by the Industries Branch was to make a survey of the existing industries and ascertain the reasons for the difficulties which they were in to consider ways and means of effecting remedies.
>
> To obtain firsthand and accurate information as to the actual position of the various industries in the country it was decided to set up Advisory Committees in each industry composed of persons chosen by all those engaged in a particular industry. Advisory Committees have been established and are functioning in about 40 industries with considerable success. In addition to furnishing information those Advisory Committees have been found to be most helpful to the industries themselves and have proved a useful liaison with the Department in connection with administrative

> matters and also enabled manufacturers to have complaints re government contracts, difficulties with customs and revenue regulations, markets abroad ... dealt with in a much more expeditious and satisfactory manner than would otherwise be possible.[48]

The institutional bias within the Department was towards intervention. This did not involve rejecting free trade: it is possible to have intervention and retain a predominantly free trade framework. The Department was also committed to forging close links with the business community in order to organise development. McGilligan had identified certain shortcomings in the behaviour of private business, while the Fiscal Inquiry Committee had drawn attention to certain infrastructural obstacles to growth. The first major initiative by the Department was a response to these problems. The Railway Act, 1924 amalgamated or absorbed twenty-six separate railway companies, thus forming the Great Southern Railway Company. This was an explicit attempt to coordinate infrastructural development in the national interest. The Department believed that the new legislation would '... inevitably result in the combined undertaking being stronger, more efficient, and more capable of enterprise than any of the component parts.'[49]

The concern of the Department went beyond infrastructural problems and attempted to devise institutional arrangements to promote industrial expansion. At a very early stage, the Department recognised that many industries were in need of protection if development was to take place. At the institutional if not at the ministerial level these representations were received sympathetically. The report of the Fiscal Inquiry Committee was a serious setback to the developmental plans of Industry and Commerce. However, this did not prevent the Department from pursuing its case. Following the Dáil debate on the report, Campbell circulated a memorandum at the request of his Minister. The memorandum sought to nudge the Executive Council beyond the conclusions of the report, and indeed beyond the previous statements of McGrath. The Department had begun to examine all imports with the object of recommending the imposition of tariffs on certain items. Although the statistical data available were considered inadequate, the Department was prepared to make a limited number of recommendations.

Three criteria were applied to the possible items which might receive protection. In the first place, the industry should be able to expand production substantially if given support. Secondly, the tariff should not be difficult or expensive to collect. Thirdly, the tariffs should not have a direct effect on the cost of living; if this were unavoidable, then it would be necessary to adjust duties elsewhere on essential items. The objective, therefore, was to stimulate the output of indigenous industry without affecting the overall cost of essential goods to the community. The stimulus for these suggestions arose from a fear that the employment situation would remain serious unless direct action was taken.

Campbell believed that the existing economic environment could not provide the necessary opportunities to expand employment:

> Agriculture offers no prospect of being able to absorb any substantial number of workers, the main hope of diminishing unemployment lies in a considerable expansion of private industry. The Minister does not anticipate expansion on any considerable scale in the near future unless special steps are taken to promote it and he is of opinion that the most practical step would be the adoption of some such tariffs as are indicated in the attached memorandum.[50]

McGrath's memorandum expanded on Campbell's note, and suggested that his Department was taking seriously its role as a developmental agency. The troubled state of Irish industry was causing considerable concern. The volume of manufacturing industry had fallen, output was down, while spending power was less than previously. More importantly, there were 33,000 registered unemployed while some towns, such as Cobh, were suffering tremendous dislocation. In this and other areas unemployment was increasing. This difficulty was compounded by the absence of employment in other parts of the state. The Minister warned that this situation warranted action, even if the government's concerns were only for security. He added that there was a 'danger to the wellbeing of the state if a progressive remedy be not speedily applied.'[51]

Self-preservation, however, was not the main consideration. McGrath challenged the view, maintained most determinedly by the Department of Finance, that an industry which had to import its raw materials was in some way unnatural and therefore unsuitable in Irish conditions. At an empirical level, the Minister argued that such a view could not be defended; he cited the cotton industry in Lancashire and Guinness's as examples of very successful industries which were dependent on imported raw materials. McGrath believed that protection would allow a number of industries to expand in the Free State, and to function in a satisfactory manner. The only real objection to such a policy, he maintained, was the fear of a consequent rise in the cost of living.

Adverse consequences could be avoided if the policy was contingent. Certain conditions to protect the consumer could be imposed by the government. If these were abused by an industry, the tariff could be withdrawn. McGrath believed also that competition from foreign companies would continue to exert a direct and downward pressure on the price level within the state. More indirectly, a protectionist policy would force foreign companies to locate in Ireland in order to retain markets which might otherwise be lost. This would have the effect of creating employment and improving the skill and quality of industrial workers in Ireland. It was also preferable, he added, that foreign companies should produce in Ireland rather than have these goods imported from an external source, whereby all the benefits from such production would be lost to Ireland. The chairman of the Imperial Tobacco Company had, shortly before, declared that the company had established a branch factory in Ireland because of the imposition of tariffs. If these had not been in place the company would have supplied Ireland from Britain.

The Minister recommended to his cabinet colleagues that a programme for expanded industrialisation was necessary. He warned that dependence on agriculture meant that all the eggs were in one basket '... the bottom of which is by no means secure.' He concluded with an optimistic appraisal of the consequences of policy:

> An extension of industry, such as is possible, if a satisfactory policy of protection is adopted, would inevitably increase the flow of our export trade and would thereby lead to an extension of direct shipping between this country and countries abroad. This, in turn, would not alone open up additional markets for Irish produce of various kinds -

> markets which are closed to Irish firms at present owing to lack of transit facilities and the resultant prohibitive freight charges if goods are sent via Great Britain – but would reduce considerably the cost of all foreign merchandise and raw materials which are purchased for consumption in An Saorstat.[52]

This memorandum was designed to retrieve some of the ground lost by Irish industrialists as a consequence of the negative conclusions of the Fiscal Inquiry Committee. The approach of Industry and Commerce was quite different to that of the Committee. The Department believed that Irish industry could only expand if tariffs were introduced. Unlike the inquiry, which concluded that Irish industry was inefficient and self-seeking, the Department stressed that the state of Irish industry was due to conditions outside its control. The Fiscal Inquiry Committee accepted the status quo for quite good reasons. However, Industry and Commerce approached the question from a different perspective: that of economic development, and arrived at quite different conclusions. A major reason for this concerned the inquiry's belief that there would be a return to the pre-1914 economic environment; such a view had an essentially static perspective. In contrast, Industry and Commerce promoted a dynamic policy, one which included intervention and direction by the state. The Department's perspective was therefore at variance with that of the Fiscal Inquiry Committee and the Department of Finance, but it was also solidly based on evidence from industrialists. In one case, a combine in the candle making industry, controlled by Shell, was preventing the expansion of an Irish-owned Cork firm. This company had been invited to join the combine, but its allotted production quota would have made it unprofitable. The outcome for the Irish company was serious as it was denied essential raw materials usually supplied by Shell.[53]

A more general difficulty identified was the unwillingness of foreign companies located in Ireland to expand production to supply the home market. In 1922, cement to the value of £223,000 (approximately £3 million today) was imported. This occurred despite the presence of cement works in Co. Wexford and Skerries, Co. Dublin. Because of the ease of importation, there was no pressure on the companies to expand. The difficulty in the soap and soap powder industry was somewhat different.

Output in Ireland was regulated by the 'Lever combine', despite which imports were on the increase. The industry in the Free State was capable of supplying the home market, as had been demonstrated when the Dáil had prohibited all imports for a period, but refused to do so. In addition, the combine had prohibited all exports of soap products from the state. Industry and Commerce believed that in the case of soap and cement, a 10 per cent *ad valorem* tariff was justified to rectify this imbalance.[54]

In the boot and shoe industry, the concerns were small and the range limited. A tariff of 10 per cent would induce foreign companies already supplying the market to establish branch factories here. In the textile and glass and bottle industries the main obstacle to expansion was foreign penetration of the market. Imports were large and the indigenous companies uncompetitive. To revive these sectors, a tariff of 20 per cent would be required, although in the case of footwear and textiles, the Department suggested that the revenue from the tariff would be considerable and this could be used to reduce duty on some other essential commodities. A tariff of 20 per cent was also recommended in the case of confectionery, bicycles, railway rolling stock, and furniture, while margarine merited 25 per cent.[55] From the evidence produced by the Department, it becomes clear that much of Irish industry was indeed uncompetitive, but not necessarily for reasons of inefficiency as suggested by the Fiscal Inquiry Committee. Irish industry, it might be urged, was inefficient because of the pressures of large-scale penetration of the market by well-organised external companies. The cost of entry to an industry for most companies was therefore prohibitive. Nor had a company an incubation period to develop skills and strategy. From the outset the indigenous company was met with large imports and concentrated economic power from established concerns. Left to the self-regulating mechanism of the market in a free trade environment, it was unlikely that Irish industry could generate such advantages which would allow the growth of an industrial sector.

This view was not shared by McElligott. He accepted the report of the Fiscal Inquiry Committee as the last word on the issue. Having had his view justified by the inquiry, he reacted critically to Industry and Commerce's attempt to circumvent the Committee's findings. He suggested that McGrath's objectives, to relieve unemployment and to raise revenue, were incompatible.

In this he was possibly correct and was able to direct attention at some of the naive assumptions contained in the memorandum. Any revenue that might be raised, he added, would be small, while tax relief would be illusory. On other areas he was on weaker ground. He criticised the memorandum because it contained no estimate of employment gains. In doing so, he made a good debating point, but ignored the evidence from Industry and Commerce that unemployment was rising and that tariffs would induce employment creation.

McElligott's most serious criticism rested on the effect on the cost of living. In doing so, he ignored the main thrust of Industry and Commerce, which claimed that it was possible to regulate the conditions when tariffs were granted. Consequently, McElligott maintained that it would be the working classes who would suffer from the imposition of tariffs and this class was least able to do so. This is abstractly correct, but ignored the existence of unemployment among the very class who would benefit in employment terms from the proposals. For the poor there would be both costs and benefits from the policy; McElligott emphasised the costs and ignored the benefits. The suspicion must remain that McElligott was promoting the interests of the wealthy and utilising the poor in his campaign. His instinctive conservatism was reinforced by a basically static analysis when he came to assess the impact of the proposals.

> The principal effect would be that home manufacturers of goods would increase their prices by an amount equal or nearly equal to the tariff. The home supply would increase only slowly, and home requirements would of necessity continue to be filled by imported goods which would almost certainly be raised in price to the consumer by the amount of the tariff.[56]

Such a danger was indeed present, but McElligott either ignored or was unprepared to accept the inducement effect of tariffs.

Political events now worked to the advantage of the conservatives. As a consequence of the so-called 'Army Mutiny', McGrath resigned as Minister on 7 March and was not to be succeeded by Patrick McGilligan until 4 April. Shortly after his Minister's resignation, Campbell wrote to McElligott advising that as a consequence circumstances had changed. It would, therefore, be inappropriate to submit the memorandum in its present form.

He added:

> I don't want memoranda [sic] put forward to raise a discussion, which is what Mr McGrath intended, to be treated as containing the final views of this ministry.

In a minute to the Secretary of the Executive Council on the same day, Campbell urged that:

> Statements as to the probable effect of tariffs on prices, may be taken as the considered opinions of the Ministry which they are not intended to represent. The Minister wished this question to be considered in its relation to unemployment and the effect on prices to be weighed with all counter balancing advantages to be secured by industrial development.[57]

These two minutes are open to ambiguous interpretations. It may be that Campbell wished to go further than his former Minister or that he was attempting to mend fences before a new Minister was appointed. Whatever misgivings Campbell had during the changeover, he successfully persuaded McGilligan to promote an industrial policy based on the imposition of tariffs. He also gained an influential and surprising ally in Patrick Hogan, who recorded in a letter to Ernest Blythe,the Minister for Finance, his acceptance of Campbell's view on tariffs. Hogan and Campbell met to discuss the possibility of imposing a tariff on a very restricted number of items in the forthcoming budget. Campbell, apparently reflecting his new Minister's view, urged that a more comprehensive policy should be formulated. He successfully convinced Hogan of the merits of this policy, and Hogan subsequently wrote to Blythe supporting this approach:

> Without having some definite policy, it is quite impossible to pick out three or four items and say we will protect these. An examination would find that there were three or four others equally entitled to protection. His proposal is, and I agree with it, that a Tariff Commission be set up to examine tariffs from the point of view of (1) promoting industries;(2) relieving unemployment; (3) obtaining revenue. They should examine not unimportant things like the Bottle industry or the Confectionery industry because they don't matter from either of these points of view, but rather they

> should examine the question of import duties on some of the things that really matter ...

Hogan approached Campbell's suggestion in a flexible fashion. He accepted the need for a comprehensive survey of industry. This would take three or four months, but once concluded the Department would have the statistical knowledge to demonstrate the effect of imposing a tariff, utilising the three criteria noted above. Once this had been achieved, the government could consider the question in detail and, taking into account all relevant factors, come to a conclusion on the issue:

> This is not exactly what the Fiscal Commission did. This Commission would start with the presumption that tariffs were to be imposed, and important tariffs, examine the question in detail, show the results in detail, and the Government could then make up its mind.[58]

These views did not convince McElligott, who recommended to Blythe that he oppose the setting up of a Tariff Commission. In contrast to Hogan, he maintained that the issue had been dealt with by the Fiscal Inquiry Commission, and that it was absurd to set up another Commission. He further argued that the policy should be for advocates of tariffs to promote them prior to the Budget.[59] McElligott's strategy at this stage involved neutralising the pressure to set up an alternative agency with the power to examine tariff proposals and report to the government. Clearly, he believed such an agency would be pro-tariff and possibly under the influence, if not the control, of Industry and Commerce. Such a body would draw attention to the issue, and if it reported positively on the tariff, its recommendation would be difficult to oppose. By insisting that tariffs be taken as part of a package in pre-Budget submissions, McElligott attempted to increase his department's power to adjudicate on the issue and possibly even veto claims from interested parties. This approach was successful in the short term, for a Tariff Commission was not set up.

Although not successful in promoting a Tariff Commission, Industry and Commerce retained considerable leverage in advising the government on which tariffs should be imposed. At a basic level, the cabinet had accepted the principle in 1924 that tariffs could be imposed in the Budget. This may have been an attempt by Blythe and McElligott to deflect those advocating tariffs. If so, they were not successful. One of the objectives of the Advisory Committees, established by Industry and Commerce, was to assess the attractiveness of tariffs and to promote them. In turn, if accepted by the Advisory Committee, the Minister for Industry and Commerce would then support specific and documented proposals in cabinet. Despite McElligott's success in blocking the Tariff Commission in 1924, Industry and Commerce proved adroit in manoeuvring without a statutory body, and was successful in persuading the government to grant tariff concessions at subsequent Budgets between 1924 and 1926. The Advisory Committees also provided a mechanism for communication through which Industry and Commerce could respond quickly to industrialists' complaints and demands on tariffs. In addition, the Department could assess more accurately the progress of industrial expansion and have access to information not readily available.[60]

Industry and Commerce continued to apply pressure on the government to appoint a formal Commission to investigate tariffs. As a consequence, the terms of reference for a Watching Committee on Tariffs were circulated in 1925. The proposed body was empowered:

> To consider at various stages the effects of protective tariffs in force in Saorstat Eireann and to report from time to time to the Executive Council thereon.

The Chairman of the Commission was to be the Director of Statistics; academics, civil servants, and members of corporate bodies were to make up the membership.[61] Such a development did not meet with McElligott's approval: he minuted his Minister that receipt of the terms of reference was the first indication that such a commission had been proposed. Surprisingly, Campbell was more cautious than one might expect. He believed that the Commission would be advantageous, but that its appointment should await the enactment of the Statistics Bill. He believed it took at least six months before the impact of a tariff on the economy and the industry would become known. Not all of this information was available to Industry and Commerce; consequently it would be premature to act until Industry and Commerce had adequate information to advise.[62]

This may have been a tactical error on Campbell's part. When a Tariff Commission Bill was introduced in October 1926, it differed dramatically from the 1924 and 1925 proposals. The Tariff Commission Bill was basically restrictive and neutral in its approach, whereas the earlier proposals had envisaged a bias towards protection. In addition, the Department of Industry and Commerce had been considered the most appropriate institution for determining tariffs in the early proposals. When the Bill was circulated it was envisaged that the Commission would be composed entirely of civil servants and effectively dominated by Finance.[63] Furthermore, it is probable that the imposition of tariffs would be far more difficult under the new conditions, and that Industry and Commerce would be effectively cut off from influence in this policy area. The change in content between June 1925 and April 1926 is striking and can probably be attributed to McElligott's opposition to the earlier proposals. It may be, though I have been unable to discover direct evidence of this, that in June 1925 McElligott concluded that a Tariff Commission was inevitable whether he wanted it or not. With this realisation, he organised a retrieval operation in order to reduce the damage that could be done; the best method of achieving this was to restrict the competence of the Commission and to bring it under the effective control of the Department of Finance.

The primary result of the Bill was to remove the power of initiative from Industry and Commerce. All subsequent applications had to be made to the Commission, which would then report to the Executive Council.[64] In reality, the Executive Council accepted all the recommendations of the Tariff Commission between 1927 and 1932. In effect, the composition of the Commission was therefore of crucial importance. The appointment of McElligott as chairman of the new agency reinforces the view that the influence of Industry and Commerce was being reduced. This is further confirmed by the method in which the Commission was empowered to function. Whereas the Advisory Committees entered into close contact with the producers seeking tariffs, this corporate relationship was to end:

> When considering any application referred to it ... the Commission shall hear every person who desires so to be heard and appears to the Commission to be substantially representative of persons, trades, or interests who might reasonably be expected to be affected by the granting or

> refusing ... of the concessions asked for in such an application. ...[65]

This approach broke the privileged access to Industry and Commerce which industrialists had hitherto been conceded. It meant that each application would be examined by a body not necessarily favourable to tariff policy. In contrast to previous procedures, those opposed to tariffs could now mount an effective opposition well in advance of each examination of the applications. This process was inevitably slow and cumbersome, given that a wide range of opinion was examined. The main responsibility to prove the efficacy of a tariff rested with the applicant. However, as had been shown by the Fiscal Inquiry Committee, the industrialists had not been able to make a convincing case for tariffs in 1923, and this had not substantially changed during the intervening period. The emergence of Industry and Commerce as the advocate of tariffs had changed the circumstances under which an industrialist could seek concessions. The Department was a powerful institution in its own right: it had the resources to promote policy, and it was evolving a strategy which pre-supposed some type of protection.

The Tariff Commission as it emerged blocked these developments. Essentially neutral in approach and technocratic in its functions, it tended to reinforce the status quo. The existence of an institution to determine tariffs effectively depoliticised the issue. The government could afford to ignore direct political pressure by maintaining that the Tariff Commission was the body to determine each case, and that it could not intervene in the process before that body had reported. This strategy was not entirely successful, as the revival of the tariff campaign by Fianna Fáil demonstrated, but for a period at least it deflected criticism of the government. The objective of the Act was to constrict the growing demand for tariffs. The Act sought to narrow the grounds on which a tariff could be imposed. When Thomas MacEoin moved an amendment in the Dáil which would make the terms of reference more flexible and more specifically protectionist, the government refused to support the change.[66]

The role of the Department of Finance was made explicit by McElligott in a brief he prepared for Blythe:

> It will be the duty of the Department of Finance to see that the time of the Tariff Commission is not wasted in

> examining a particular proposal unless there appears, *prima facie*, to be a case that is worthy of consideration.

The Tariff Commission, McElligott claimed, would be able to take 'a more comprehensive view and to devote more concentrated study to the question than would be possible under the present circumstances in any individual government department.' Additionally, civil servants can do this more adequately than others because they can '... examine questions of policy from the single point of view of the interest of the state in general.' The Tariff Commission in the form proposed was required because the government was still experimenting on tariffs; to date the results of this experiment were not obvious:

> The Saorstat is still at a very early stage in its development and undoubtedly one of the most effective weapons at its disposal for maintaining an existing industry against unfair competition and for fostering new ones in their nascent stage is the power to impose protective tariffs. The weapon is however, a somewhat dangerous one and unless it is used with care and discrimination it may ultimately do more harm than good. It is not considered that we have yet arrived at a point where we can definitely arrive at a conclusion as to the desirability generally of imposing tariffs or the reverse.

This appeared to leave open the question of whether a systematic tariff policy should be introduced. In fact, it prevented the development of such a policy by investing the Department of Finance with the power to channel the tariff question into a neutralising institution. It drew attention to the balance of power within the government and the civil service and reinforced the dominant position of the Department of Finance.[67]

The establishment of the Tariff Commission was a severe setback to Industry and Commerce's developmental strategy, but it did not end the attempt to generate an industrial economy. Even earlier, Campbell had set himself the task of developing the intellectual framework with which his Department could generate policy for the dynamic expansion of the Irish economy. In a letter to Professor J.G. Smith, a former member of the Fiscal Inquiry Committee, Campbell outlined what he had in mind.

> Some people realise that we inherit all the remarkable technical discoveries of the war, that we can supply some

> such essential ingredients of their application as cheap power, that we have no sure abundance of material resources and that our future progress depends on the genuinely skilled exploitation of such resources as we have. Fortunately, the war induced many discoveries as to how to make the most of relatively scant material and we are practically unencumbered with any large vested interest in antiquated methods. We therefore are in a favourable position to devise and adopt a native technique based on the most advanced modern application of intelligence and science to industry.

Campbell believed that this situation justified experimentation. However, efforts to achieve such an end were obstructed at that time by the absence of trained scientific personnel, practical intelligence, and a limited respect in the society for scientific thinking. He wanted Smith to identify suitable individuals to convene an enquiry into his proposals. A decision had to be taken soon, he maintained, as this was a 'unique opportunity if seized while ideas – political and economic – are in their present fluid state.' An enquiry along the lines outlined by Campbell would question the existing economic realities. It is, perhaps, not surprising that Smith refused to cooperate with him, informing him that he could not recommend the type of individual Campbell desired for the enquiry.[68]

Campbell believed that Irish complacency should be challenged and that the rhetorical commitment to industry should be tested. An environment for industrial development was available, he maintained; Ireland was underdeveloped in industrial terms. Campbell's assessment of the nature of the Irish economy was strikingly similar to analyses carried out a quarter of a century later by many of the newly independent states. A better balance was required between agriculture and industry. Agriculture was an uncertain economic activity, due to weather conditions and price fluctuations. Dependence on agriculture would have to be broken, because such economic structures though 'sure of the necessities of life are the most poorly endowed in respect of its refinement.' An agricultural economy, he continued, also produced workers, specialists, and graduates in sectors other than agriculture which it effectively exports, as the demand for their particular skills is severely limited. Campbell outlined what he thought were the general factors which obstructed the organisation and development of a strong industrial base. In the existing environment, Irish producers were faced with intense competition from external sources: sources which had the benefits of mass production. Nor could investment in luxury goods be substituted, due to the restricted nature of the Irish market. He further recognised that the export trade provided the best possibility for building and expanding large factories.

The difficulty was that the specialist skills required for organising production on a large scale were not available in Ireland, nor did Irish producers have a monopoly over a commodity or raw material which would enhance its competitive advantage. Campbell concluded that if Irish industrial development was to be export orientated, then it must attract foreign enterprise to bridge the gap between what was available and what was required. To do so, however, required special measures by the state. Furthermore, he placed the responsibility for meeting this challenge with the government:

> There is no visible prospect of industry arising unstimulated in the country, at least to the extent necessary to bring about a better balance in the economic situation. Stimulation there must be and it will inevitably take forms open to objection if measured solely by the criteria current in prosperous countries with large resources and established manufacturers.
>
> Unless assured that the government was prepared to pay a price for early industrial development there is no incentive to work out a basis for it in the certain knowledge that every such basis must, in the existing circumstances of the country, involve payment of a price whether in the form of a tariff, subsidy, bounty, special credit or other fiscal adjustment. The contiguity of Ireland to Great Britain should not obscure the fact that in all the smaller countries it has been, since the war, a recognised necessity for governments to take a greatly increased share of responsibility in measures for the direct promotion of industry.

Campbell recommended that a comprehensive policy be devised, which would promote industry, institute a regional policy, and rationalise economic resources to achieve policy objectives.[69]

When Campbell wrote this memorandum, the Tariff

Commission had just become operational. As noted above the Commission restricted the autonomy of Industry and Commerce in the area of industrial policy. Indeed, it is probable that if Campbell's suggestions had been accepted, then policy would have reverted to, at least, its pre-1926 institutional status. McGilligan welcomed the general thrust of the memorandum, but was unwilling to support its specific proposals which would have involved revising all aspects of economic policy.[70] By 1927, therefore, Industry and Commerce's influence had been seriously weakened. This did not prevent the Department from considering alternative strategies, but it did reduce its ability to have them considered seriously or implemented. Campbell believed that if industry was to play a role in economic development, contemporary assumptions would have to be questioned.

Nor did Campbell restrict his criticism to industrial policy, he also believed that the emphasis in agricultural policy was mistaken. Campbell urged that a radical departure should be encouraged if the full productive potential of agriculture was to be realised:

> There is an entirely opposite conception of protection for all agricultural produce that can be produced at home, either by tariffs or by restriction of imports leading to substitution of a home for an imported product, of guaranteed prices and subsidies, and of the development of industries allied to agriculture. In short, of intensive and largely arable agriculture with a view to reaching the maximum possible production of wealth. That conception involves the risks of any large experiment and the payment of a price even if successfully carried out. But it offers the prospect of a greater rural population, of a greater volume of wealth production and of greater internal stability.[71]

The neglect of industry by state policy was a related consideration for him. The manufacturing sector in Ireland was weak:

> Before it can obtain a desirable strength many special measures must be taken. If the consequent gains of industry are then largely to be diminished in order to keep agriculture going, industry will remain feeble and agriculture suffer indirectly in a proportionate measure.

> National development is a problem combined of the national temperament and economic factors.[72]

The legislative framework for the Trade Loans (Guarantee) Act, 1924 proved so restrictive that the Department believed it could make no useful contribution to the expansion of industry. The Department had identified a number of concerns which failed due to their inability to acquire working capital under the Act. Working capital had been expressly excluded from the Act as a consequence of Finance pressure. This difficulty was compounded by continuing hostility to the act by Finance, by the chambers of commerce, and by the joint stock banks who argued that there was no unmet demand for capital.[73]

The Irish banking system also obstructed development. Departmental officials estimated that Irish industry required at least £1 million for capital investment. This was not forthcoming from the banking system, which proved unwilling to promote an industrial banking service. There was also a need for long-term credit facilities for industries, which only a government-supported agency could provide. This could be achieved by the establishment of an industrial bank, the purpose of which would be:

> The mobilisation of the loose capital of the community and its application to those branches of trade and industry which are most in need of development from a national point of view. The industrial bank must, accordingly, be prepared to forego the possibility of an immediate profit in the interests of national development.[74]

This approach was strongly maintained by R.C. Ferguson when he gave evidence to the Banking Commission in June 1926. He criticised Irish financial institutions for their reluctance to provide credit for industry. The inadequacies of the Trade Loans (Guarantee) Act, he maintained, compounded the difficulties which industry faced. A more positive approach was required:

> When I am talking of the need of long-term credits, I am talking altogether of this bunch of industries where there has been little move towards development, and I am not talking of the other industries which for one reason or another were in a very depressed and bad condition. These people very rarely come near us. In the matter of employment I mentioned the new factories. The increased employment in the

> tariff industries suggests the same thing. There are some of these industries on these tariff lists in which there are clearly and definitely openings for the making of money at the moment and I have no doubt that there would be a great many factories established if capital were easily available for people who were quite good business people and of quite good reputation.[75]

Industry and Commerce's critique was even more fundamental than this. In his evidence to the Banking Commission, T.J. Barrington questioned the intellectual basis for macro-economic and monetary policy. Quoting contemporary works by Hawtrey and Keynes, he challenged the commitment to deflation. Barrington maintained that a policy of reflation was more suitable to Ireland's conditions, and argued that current government policies would lead to further unemployment. He also urged that the monetary link with Britain should not be continued as the interests of the two countries were not compatible.[76] This approach complemented Campbell's view, who had previously advocated the establishment of a Central Bank to oversee monetary policy. He was later to criticise the 1927 Currency Bill on the grounds that it reinforced the status quo and did nothing to enhance monetary independence.[77]

The reports of the Banking Commission rejected Industry and Commerce's submissions. The Commission recommended the maintenance of monetary links with Britain, a deflationary macro-economic policy, and the promotion of agriculture. Campbell noted that without the evidence from his Department, even these issues would not have been adequately treated. The report, he concluded, displayed 'a failure of vision and energy'. Barrington complained of the treatment which his evidence received, adding

> That the time is approaching when the stand taken by the authorities of this Department will receive a full measure of appreciation from the Irish people. At present the people know too little about the subject to be able to express any valuable opinion upon it. You will, however, note that the Banking Commission have treated the Department's evidence in no light-hearted spirit and every word of their comment upon it constitutes at least a justification for the evidence itself. So far as I am personally concerned this

comment, far from weakening my faith in the views put forward by this Department, serves only to strengthen and confirm it.[78]

In sharp contrast to the general policy consensus on free trade represented most vigorously by Finance, Industry and Commerce argued for a policy organised around the principle of state intervention. Officials recognised that little could be changed without state involvement. This led them in turn to design policies to facilitate state intervention. Despite the availability of an alternative perspective Industry and Commerce did not manage to change the general direction of policy. Yet some successes can be noted; a number of tariffs were in place, and the Department continued to acquire experience and information about industry. More spectacularly, the Shannon Electrification Scheme confirmed Industry and Commerce's view that developmental projects such as this should play a leading role in economic expansion. Its success was enhanced because the political and institutional variables converged in support of the scheme. Moreover, opposition from Finance officials was effectively overridden once the politicians had accepted it as an objective.[79]

The role of the Department in the electrification scheme was crucial and draws attention to the real obstacles to development in an economy devoid of industrial experience or skills. Because the expertise was not readily available in Ireland, Campbell had to coordinate most aspects of the scheme, leaving him little time for other tasks in the Department.[80] Further obstacles arose when the question of control of the concern was discussed. At first the Department believed that a private concern should operate it under conditions set down by the government.[81] This approach was to prove unsuccessful. The Department invited foreign companies to submit proposals for operating the new utility. The Irish approach was dealt with brusquely by these companies. United States companies, in particular, were unwilling to meet Industry and Commerce's conditions in the belief that Ireland could not successfully operate such a large undertaking. In effect, these companies wished to treat Ireland in a similar fashion to that of their sister companies in Central America. In this they were to be mistaken: Industry and Commerce now resolved that the state should take complete control of the utility and develop an institutional framework suitable to it. The outcome was to be the Electricity Supply Board, which became in 1927 the first state sponsored body to be organised as a public corporation. The attraction of this approach was that it facilitated state control without the obligations of nationalisation. Ready access to state credit would be an added advantage. The concern would be ultimately controlled by the Dáil, but would be a business proposition. Its staff would not be civil servants, and normal business procedures relating to employment conditions and promotion would be maintained. Authority to operate the utility would be delegated to the officers and staff, although:

> Final control may be secured by a provision that the members of the Authority (or Board of Control) are appointed only for short periods, and that their dismissal or reappointment depends on the results they show.[82]

The discussion within Industry and Commerce on the ESB draws attention to the opportunities and obstacles which existed. The scheme itself had been questioned by Finance, certain business and agricultural interests, and to some extent by foreign capital. However, as a prestige scheme, Industry and Commerce was in a good position to mobilise support for it. Further, the Department skilfully evaded the attempt by foreign interests to control the utility by devising an effective organisational scheme which fell short of nationalisation. This not only enhanced the Department's authority in industrial matters, but also demonstrated what could be achieved if the political will to develop was present.

However, by 1927 this political will was usually absent, and while the Department believed it had discovered the blockages to Irish economic development, these were not acknowledged by most other institutions or policy makers in the new state. As a consequence the Department had not acquired institutional instruments to remove these blockages. Economic policy remained passive in the belief that the operation of the international economy and the growth of agricultural production would stimulate economic development. But this policy also reflected an aversion to risk taking, particularly among the affluent. Continuity enhanced the attractiveness of wealth creation for this section, without creating a method to channel finance to other sectors of the economy. Although there had been a change in political power in 1922, there had been little socio-economic change.

For many, particularly the well-off, political independence was an end in itself. This section was comfortable: continuity in economic policy reinforced the stability which they demanded. For those without property, the promise of independence had not been fully realised. However, an independent Irish government had to consider the wellbeing of the nation as a whole. The Cumann na nGaedheal government successfully promoted its policies up to 1927, insisting that these were the best available. Under such circumstances, Industry and Commerce could influence but not transform policy. The experience of the first five years of independence would appear to justify the belief that Ireland's status had changed from colonialism to neo-colonialism. However, it depends at which level the analysis is framed at. The foreign policy of the new state was extremely successful; while the political system had been integrated within a democratic structure by 1927. These are not inconsiderable achievements and compare very well with the experience of other newly independent states.

It is at the socio-economic level that the Cumann na nGaedheal government appears least successful. Industry and Commerce was unable to mobilise opinion around a commitment to industrialisation. One reason for this is that by 1927 the status quo on most economic issues had been reiterated. The dominance of Finance, the reports of the Commission on Agriculture, the Fiscal Inquiry Committee, and the Banking Commission provided a formidable anti protectionist consensus. This was further aided by the reluctance of the farming community to embrace protection, in the belief that it would be detrimental to its interests. In a sense the policies followed approximated very closely to what a majority wanted at the time; there is little evidence in 1927 of widespread sympathy for protection. Under these circumstances, a departure from the stability recently achieved would be viewed with suspicion; and this accounts in large measure for the success of conservative measures up to this time.

3

Fianna Fáil and the Challenge to the Free Trade Economy 1927–32

BY 1927 economic stability had taken firm root in Ireland. Despite the formulation of an ambitious developmental programme by the Department of Industry and Commerce, policy remained defined by the interests of the exporting sector of agriculture. National wellbeing continued to be equated with the wellbeing of agriculture, and industrial, banking and welfare policy were subordinated to its requirements. Government policy presupposed that the staple industry would remain central to economic growth, and that its expansion would lead to other beneficial outcomes.[1] This presupposed, further, that international trade would continue to be of benefit to all participants. In Ireland the export staple remained dominant, but there were few spin-offs from it. It is also doubtful if in every case the international trading system is necessarily of equal benefit to any individual country. Certainly, if benefit is defined in terms of national welfare, Ireland experienced considerable losses during the 1920s as a consquence of depopulation due to emigration, unemployment, and under-employment. The Irish staple did not have the characteristics attributed to it elsewhere: of stimulating the emergence of indigenous industry and generating government support of these industries.[2]

Gordon Campbell had written in 1927 that 'National development is a problem combined of the national temperament and economic factors.'[3] As Campbell recognised, neither of these criteria appeared to facilitate development at the end of the 1920s. The absence of industry in the new state and the traditional specialisation in agriculture for an adjacent market prevented Industry and Commerce from initiating a comprehensive development strategy. More importantly, perhaps, Irish agriculture performed quite well throughout the 1920s; especially the export sector. Understandingly, this led policy makers to adopt an extremely cautious approach to the question of national development; particularly if new policies should endanger the benefits from this sector. While understandable, this approach contained a number of mistaken assumptions. Policy makers outside Industry and Commerce assumed that development would occur spontaneously, with linkages deepening as a consequence of growth in agriculture. Yet, between 1922 and 1932 there is little evidence to suggest that this occurred, or that the surplus from exports was invested in such a way as to generate development. Nor did the impressive rise in national income over the same period contribute to expansion, in particular to industrial expansion.

The Irish experience between 1922 and 1932 indicates how difficult it is, even under fairly good conditions, for a country to mobilise its resources to achieve developmental objectives. The existing economic structure continues to influence the overall direction of policy and the choices available. As Albert Hirschman has noted: '... the same staple its characteristics and mode of production, may unexpectedly lend strength to two totally different social arrangements and political regimes.' The consequence of this indeterminism leads Hirschman to maintain:

> Not that a staple will determine the socio-political environment in any unique and exhaustive way, but that each time it will imprint certain patterns of its own on whatever environment happens to be around and that it is possible and worthwhile to study the imprinting process. A related point is that there are different degrees of affinity or compatibility between specific economic activities, on the one hand, and varieties of socio-political environment on the other. [4]

This imprinting process can have different effects on different environments. The staple in post-famine Ireland imprinted certain characteristics which prevented alternative economic development. By the time the Free State was established, the Irish socio-political environment had not only acquired characteristics imprinted by the nature of the staple, but had internalised them. As such, it provided an important blockage to any attempt to generate alternative forms of economic activity. The absence of an industrial class committed to economic expansion was another contributory factor. Ireland had a strong middle class but not an industrial bourgeoisie. More decisively, most sectors of the Irish economy did not become committed to industrialisation. A majority during the 1920s remained committed to the traditional and familiar framework. Even if there had been individual innovators promoting industrialisation, their initiatives would have encountered major difficulties unless the culture of industrialisation permeated large sections of the community. This culture was absent, partly because of the existing economic activity, but also because the culture of the staple was profoundly anti-modern and consequently anti-industrial.[5]

The export economy in Ireland can be characterised as a precapitalist social formation embedded in an international capitalist economy dominated by Britain.[6] In this, commercial agriculture did not radically differ from the experience of the America slave south, which provided cotton, or from coffee production in Brazil.[7] In each case production of a staple product was stimulated by the growth of a world market with an explicit division of labour. Comparative advantage in cattle, coffee, or cotton, gave considerable benefits to each country through their participation. The outcome for each was different: the slave economy disintegrated; the coffee economy in Brazil generated linkages which contributed to industrial growth; a stable economy with little growth emerged in Ireland. In each case, pre-capitalist elites played an important role in developing the staples. Only where a strong state and a bourgeois class – albeit a weak one – committed to industrialisation emerged, as in Brazil, can we see the process going beyond the staple. In the case of the American South, the abolition of slavery did not remove the obstacles to industrial growth; this was only to occur in the mid twentieth century and under radically different circumstances to those prevailing between 1865 and 1920.[8] To confirm Hirschman's point, the relationship between the staple and the socio-political process can lead to quite different outcomes.

The outcome in Ireland was determined by a number of specific features. Unlike Britain, the United States, or Sweden, Ireland did not acquire an economically active stratum committed to exploring industrial investment. Most Irish industrial concerns were small, uncompetitive, and clearly not the focus for industrial investment. The nature and weakness of the Irish industrial bourgeoisie may explain their reluctance to invest, but there was also no expansion detectable in the agricultural economy. Not only did Irish farmers not provide a stimulus for industrial expansion, there is evidence that agriculture itself had been under-capitalised for most of the twentieth century. Capital was available, but there is little evidence that it was invested in productive activity.[9]

Comparative analysis of both large and small economic units has emphasised that the introduction of an industrial system, whether capitalist or socialist, into a pre-industrial economy requires the emergence of a cultural framework which can facilitate the transition from one social formation to another. This can lead to a society adopting new patterns of action, new values and beliefs, in addition to creating new or adapting old institutions. This industrialisation cannot simply be equated with the introduction of machinery; it involves more fundamentally a change in the relationship betweeen the individual and economic activity. This culture was particularly strong in Britain and the United States.[10] It is also apparent, though expressed somewhat differently, in Japan and Sweden during the first half of the twentieth century.

In Ireland the transition from agriculture to industry did not occur spontaneously. In the Irish case the possibility of industry seemed to depend on either capital accumulated in agriculture being diverted to industrial purposes, or agriculture itself developing linkages to the manufacturing sector by investment in agri-business, particularly processing. These were the most likely avenues of progress, but neither occurred. Economic behaviour in Ireland after 1922, and for possibly fifty years prior to this, was characterised by a distrust of change and an unwillingness to confront it.[11] Solow has suggested that Irish producers, rather than respond to economic change by adapting to a new economic environment, sought to insulate themselves from these pressures. The 1881 Land Act has been described as 'a wholesale income maintenance programme'; while the same author concluded that '... the Irish sacrificed economic progress on the altar of Irish nationalism ...' In contrast Denmark, faced with a very similar threat, responded by meeting the challenge of market change and reorientating its productive capacity. These changes also stimulated the growth of an industrial sector and further strengthened the commercial agricultural sector.[12]

This is not to suggest that Ireland could have made exactly the same choices as Denmark. It is to suggest that the collective decision of the Irish tenants to adopt a political strategy, which involved either rent reduction or tenant purchase at reduced rates, altered the culture within which economic decisions were taken. Following the emasculation of Irish landlordism, further market pressure was removed from the new proprietors. In the first place repayments were lower than the previous rent; secondly, the market for land became static; thirdly, security of tenure and compensation for improvements had been secured. This led to what Crotty has described as the 'long-term equilibrium' of Irish agriculture and the Irish economy.[13] This had a number of consequences for economic growth. Irish farmers received a considerable increase in income; this surplus was not generally reinvested in the farm or elsewhere. It is doubtful if, as Crotty maintains, investment opportunities were limited. The Agricultural Credit Company was of the opinion that at least £100 million would be required to improve Irish farming. Rather than invest, Irish farmers improved family consumption, provided dowries, and saved on deposit.[14]

During the First World War Irish farming received a substantial bonus from its monopoly position in the British market; yet the surplus generated appears to have been consumed rather than invested. By 1922 there was little pressure on a farmer to either invest in his farm or to seek investment opportunities elsewhere. Moreover, because the control over land was secured, the individual farmer tended to be insulated from competition for land, which had not been the case prior to the 1880s.[15] It is also possible that ownership of property was not based on strict economic criteria. Even if the sale of land was a rational economic proposition, this course of action was rarely followed. There was insufficient knowledge concerning the market for land; partly because so little of it changed hands, and partly because culturally the continued ownership of land, often for non-economic reasons, became an objective in itself. Each of these developments enhanced personal security, but also diminished the willingness of individuals to expand production, to reinvest, or to look elsewhere for investment.

As a consequence the main source of investment funds in the new state was remarkably stable and indeed suspicious of change. This stability was reinforced by independent governments, when

PROPERTY OF
ST. MARY'S COLLEGE
STRAWBERRY HILL

they continued to subsidise farming rates. Such a policy was not only inegalitarian, in that it transferred resources from the non-propertied to the propertied, but it also was of greatest benefit to the largest farmers.[16] At a more general level, Meenan has argued that Irish culture has not been conducive to economic growth. He suggests that the main assumptions about economic life have frequently been based on political axioms rather than economic reality. Most of these assumptions, he believes, were wrong even when the state was established.[17]

The difficulties for Ireland were perhaps more serious than this. Assumptions can change, given enough pressure. There was no economic constituency seriously promoting industrial expansion during the 1920s. Industry and Commerce promoted industrialisation from an institutional viewpoint, but received little support from other agencies or interests. Change at this stage would have challenged the basic stability of the society and most sectors of the economy had little interest in doing so. Industry was not stimulated by private initiative during the 1920s, because all the main sources of potential investment were at the very least ambivalent, if not actually hostile, to it. The economy remained pre-industrial and proprietorial in its structure. In 1926, the economy was essentially agricultural; manufacturing industry accounted for a low level of GNP, and employed a small proportion of the labour force. Industry was, in effect, an enclave centred on Dublin, with its linkages outside Ireland rather than within the economy. This was reinforced by the relatively high level of personal ownership of the means of production. Some 50 per cent of the labour force can be included within the proprietorial strata in 1926. Only in Leinster did employees outnumber proprietors. Even here, however, there was no strong industrial base. Occupational status was concentrated on agriculture and low-skill employment. There was also a high proportion of artisans and craftsmen, while, as one would expect to find in Dublin, there was an expanding tertiary sector.[18]

The pre-industrial and proprietorial nature of the Irish economy also had major social consequences. Although industrialisation was not impossible during the 1920s, these elements of the social structure did not contribute to it. The economic culture, based as it was on pre-industrial values, was not capitalistic, but instead underwrote other forms of economic behaviour. This is not to maintain that a pre-industrial property owning democracy will in all cases obstruct the evolution of national capitalism. In theory, at least, accumulation at this level will lead, in time, to investment which will contribute to industrialisation. In the case of Ireland this did not occur, and it might be suggested that the specific character of Irish society in the 1920s prevented the development of this process. The evidence from France, from Eastern Europe, and from Ireland sustains the view that such societies, however wealthy they may be, either do not have the incentive to generate industrial growth or are unwilling to do so. It is therefore doubtful if industrialisation will occur without external stimulation.[19] The existing structures, whether economic, institutional, or political, can impede change, because they were designed for a social system unsympathetic to such change.

There were also differences within the economy itself. The structure of Irish agriculture has traditionally been described in terms of export led commercial farming in the east of the country, and small marginal farms in the west. Although it is probably incorrect to describe western farmers as uncommercial, they were certainly not capitalist in the sense that they were committed to accumulation, reinvestment, and expansion. Moreover, Hannan has suggested that the market was not the main focus of economic activity for this section of Irish agriculture. The family and its requirements were central to decision making. He notes that the 'peasant economic unit' tends to be self-sufficient; a considerable proportion of production is consumed by the members of the economic unit. A major consequence is that there is a low level of interaction between the farm and the market. Accordingly: '...the aim of production is not "profit" maximisation but family welfare ...' For such an economic sub system the intervention of the market, particularly when it is disruptive, is something to be resisted. This sector remained large until the 1950s: in 1931 58 per cent of all agricultural holdings were less than thirty acres in size.[20] To say that a sector was not capitalist or integrated into the market economy does not imply that the individuals constituting that sector were either irrational or stupid. What it does mean is that the use of a 'rational calculus' by them was determined by factors which only partially, if at all, took the market into consideration. In the case of Ireland and France, marginal proprietors were in a position to exercise political influence to contain disruptive pressures on their economic environment. In Ireland the experience of the Land League and the myth of the small farmer reinforced the political and social importance of this sector. The security of the sector was assured throughout the 1920s and 1930s. Its main aim was stability: in this it was remarkably successful. Given these circumstances, it would be naive to expect active capitalist entrepreneurship from this source.

What is more surprising is the absence of 'push' from the commercial sectors of Irish agriculture. This area enjoyed the highest income in the state, it was located close to expanding markets, and some industrial skills were available. Despite this, and the availability of capital, industry did not spontaneously emerge. There are a number of reasons for this. Stability was valued as much by commercial farmers as marginal ones, if for different reasons. The stability they sought was continued access to the United Kingdom market, and the enhancement of their income. Market change during the 1920s continued to be viewed negatively, as it had been in the 1880s. The state was pressurised to ensure that income did not decline. De-rating, for example, may have led to a reduction in agricultural output. This implies that farmers, even commercial farmers who were the main beneficiaries of this scheme, had a subjective appreciation of income: output was therefore increased or decreased to meet this level. In Ireland, possibly more so than elsewhere, the search for stability had a stronger influence on economic behaviour than market change or investment incentives.[21]

Although commercial, Irish agriculture did not internalise the dynamic values usually associated with capitalism. Accumulation was not for further reinvestment, but frequently for non-economic ends. Non-economic values, such as religious participation, may have had a stronger influence on behaviour than those associated with the capitalist ethic.[22] Most decisively, the Irish economy as a whole remained pre-capitalist throughout the 1920s. The values conducive to capitalist industrialisation, the only form which would have occurred in the Free State, were restricted to Industry and Commerce, and isolated industrialists such as J.J. Walsh. If the market stimulates capitalist behaviour then the linkages between Irish commercial agriculture and the international trading system did not have this effect. This linkage in any case was reasonably weak. It is true that external demand had promoted agricultural adjustment during the nineteenth century, leading by the twentieth century to the dominance of the export sector. Much of Irish wealth was centred here and in its urban hinterland. Once internal supply met external demand the economy essentially stabilised. The Irish economy benefited from this integration but, unlike Brazil, was unable to generate further economic linkages in order to promote industry. Without the intervention of other factors, the changes necessary for such a transition would not be forthcoming and indeed probably resisted. Nor is it possible to detect any cultural changes during this period which would underwrite such developments.

It is important to distinguish Ireland from other small economies whose economic development has been based on export led growth. Export led growth has been part of a conscious decision, based on the assumption that the economy must adjust to market change and locate market niches where it has, or can develop, a comparative advantage. Sweden and Denmark pursued such a strategy during the first decades of the twentieth century. The export of cattle was Ireland's comparative advantage, but it was not a policy consciously undertaken. The mechanism for change was external; it was not generated internally. The economy was only tenuously linked to the international economy, and was to continue until the 1960s to be linked at a very low level of integration. Both sectors of Irish agriculture can be characterised as non-capitalist and pre-industrial, one of which was more closely integrated into the market economy. As a result, there is an asymmetry between the existing social formations in Ireland and those located within the European industrial economy. Political independence closed off the possibility of change imposed by the British state, and produced institutions more amenable to pressure from internal social forces.[23]

If this characterisation is accepted, then the inability of Industry and Commerce to generate industrial development is explicable. It also explains the behaviour of the Department of Finance, which represented not only 'treasury orthodoxy', but also reflected in large part the conservative culture embedded in the status quo. The banking system also reflected these certainties. The banks were never a source of industrial finance, but operated as clearing houses for the profits of the farmers. A banking system is rarely independent: if left to itself it tends to reflect the interest of the dominant social groups. The banks and the Department of Finance supported the basic objectives of the farming sectors which were to maintain a sound currency and facilitate the transfer of capital to the United Kingdom. The fiscal and monetary link with Britain was the avenue through which Irish farming could be connected to its external markets, its prices stabilised, and its profits secured.

The main obstacle to industrialisation was not economic, nor was it lack of capital. The blockage was mainly social. The Irish experience demonstrates that while economic growth is realisable, economic development may be far more difficult to achieve. Growth is essentially quantitative, and in these terms the economy grew during the 1920s. However, development has other implications. The Department of Industry and Commerce believed that economic growth without industrialisation would not lead to development. Economic development is more extensive than growth; it includes qualitative factors such as welfare, income distribution, and social mobility.[24] It also draws attention to the inadequacy of models of growth related to the preconditions for growth or take-off. Ireland appeared stuck in a particular socio-economic formation and not to have the internal capacity for change. During the 1920s there was no movement towards economic management or planning. New values emphasising competition, productivity, accumulation or technological advance did not gain wide acceptance. Patrick Hogan's attempts to change the environment in which agricultural production took place were resisted, and were only partly successful. The blockage in the economy could only be removed if new variables were introduced. Until 1932 the state, which was the most likely source of change, and most of its agencies approached economic policy in a passive fashion. Consequently, the interests of traditional groups were advanced against those of the industrialisers.[25]

These circumstances are not uncommon among less-developed states. New states which are heavily dependent on a narrow range of exports for wealth are reluctant to change economic direction because of possible adverse consequences. The staple industry also creates interest groups within the society whose fortunes are linked to an external economy, and therefore can operate as a 'commercial fifth column' in their opposition to national economic policy. Advocates of neo-colonialism and dependency theory would equate the existence of a class within a society dependent on the staple export with the continuing dominance of their political influence within the new state. The presence of an urban and rural comprador bourgeoisie, whose economic links are with the former metropolitan state, is usually taken as proof that they are dominant. This further presupposes that the national bourgeoisie cannot command sufficient resources to offset the challenge from the comprador bourgeoisie and that the state apparatus cannot be used to develop the economy as a whole. Whatever merit such an approach may have, it does not adequately explain the complexities of industrialisation in the less developed states. A more adequate explanation will discover whether an independent state is experiencing constraints (which are alterable) or interference (which presupposes external control). Measuring each of these variables will differ from state to state; but a state which has acquired considerable legislative, fiscal, and economic autonomy cannot be said to suffer from interference. The possibility to change course and to alter the terms of the constraint will depend on the nature of the state and the political will of the society. Development can be achieved by a strong state removing the internal blockages to growth and re-negotiating its external economic relationships. It is possible to identify two types of post independence states; the minimal state which is essentially passive, and the maximal state which is developmentally minded. By 1927 the Irish state can be characterised as minimalist.[26]

The Irish situation thus resembles a number of cases in Southern Europe, as well as Latin America, where it is possible to identify independent states which are faced with obstacles to growth, because important social groups are able to veto changes in the economic structure. If the blockages to industrialisation are internal, then the response appears to be located at the social and political level. One of the paradoxes of Irish development during the 1920s is that while the Free state acquired political, economic, and social stability by 1927, the conditions also emerged for a challenge to that status quo. Until 1926 the main challenge to the state remained extra-parliamentary and military; subsequently with the formation of Fianna Fáil a constitutional republican opposition emerged. Fianna Fáil reluctantly recognised the legitimacy of the state in 1927 by accepting their seats in the Dail. By doing so the party sought to change the direction of policy by using democratic means. Once Fianna Fáil accorded this legitimacy to the state it could no longer dismiss every government action as of no significance. In criticising the government from within the system it became part of that system. This led in turn to the formulation of alternative policies, in part to confront the government, in part to attract electoral support, and in part due to pressures to refine republican principles within a state not entirely acceptable to them.[27]

Fianna Fáil was not merely a continuation of the Sinn Féin party it had left. Although it contained strong elements of continuity with the past, it also attempted to define itself as a radical party on socio-economic policy as well as political sovereignty. Both wings of Sinn Féin had been conservative on socio-economic policy in 1922; the main division between them rested on the acceptance or otherwise of the Treaty. Nor did this change prior to the formation of Fianna Fáil in 1926. Fianna Fáil adopted policies which were radical on both socio-economic and on political grounds. In particular, Fianna Fáil stressed the need to use the state apparatus to achieve national aims. The new party was in a strong position to challenge the government's authority. It drew its electoral support from a wide social spectrum and claimed at an early stage to be the representative party of the nation.[28] Its policy framework united the various strands of the party behind a cohesive leadership: by 1927, in contrast, Cumann na nGaedheal appeared weak. Despite the government's achievements, Fianna Fáil proved to be the first credible opposition it had to face. The Labour Party had played an important oppositional role between 1923 and 1927, but its largely unrepresentative social and electoral composition and its inability to penetrate urban centres prevented it from expanding.[29]

The Labour Party, nevertheless, provided important support for Fianna Fáil. As early as 1924 the Irish Labour Party and Trade Union Congress adopted a tariff policy, albeit by a narrow majority. By 1927 on this and other issues, the party was remarkably close to Fianna Fáil.[30] To compound the government's difficulties, there were differences within Cumann na nGaedheal on economic policy. An important minority led by J.J. Walsh, who had been Minister for Posts and Telegraphs between 1923 and 1927, advocated an aggressive tariff policy. Following conflict with Kevin O'Higgins on the issue in 1927, and the failure to promote tariffs as part of an electoral strategy, Walsh refused to stand in subsequent elections. Others, such as Alfred O'Rahilly, one of the leading intellectuals of independent Ireland, who had supported the government on the Treaty now moved towards the more active social and economic policies of Fianna Fáil. Once Fianna Fáil accepted the Free state, its brand of nationalism proved attractive to a widening range of the electorate.[31]

These changes led to an electoral realignment, primarily along a left-right axis. The conservative, commercial, and large farming voters moved towards Cumann na nGaedheal, while the working class, republican, and small farming vote gravitated towards Fianna Fáil. In contrast to Cumann na nGaedheal, Fianna Fáil contained a significant elite committed to industrialisation. This group committed the party to a developmental strategy, the logic of which involved a considerable degree of state intervention and industrialisation. Sean Lemass, in particular, while perceiving the obstacles, appreciated the need for an industrial programme. His strategy implied a break with the stable elements in the economic system which had dominated throughout the 1920s. Lemass was one of the few republican leaders committed to socio-economic change. As early as 1924 he was successfully mobilising working-class support for his candidacy, and was in the process of fashioning a social democratic component for the republican movement. Lemass supplemented this with an appeal to positive nationalism, an appeal which involved a comprehensive socio-economic platform.[32] Lemass's dissatisfaction with Sinn Féin prior to 1926 was based on his recognition that republicanism in isolation from an active socio-economic policy would condemn itself to political marginalisation. This was a return to Connolly's view that the national question was the social question and more importantly that despite political independence there remained an 'unfinished' element to the bourgeois revolution.

It is very questionable if Fianna Fáil could have achieved significant political success between 1926 and 1932 if it had not adopted an active socio-economic policy. The party's June 1927 vote corresponded closely to that achieved by Sinn Féin in 1923. As the 1923 election was fought on the question of sovereignty, it is probably the case that much of the June 1927 vote was a carry over from the traditional Sinn Féin constituency. This constituency has been characterised as 'essentially a party of the "rural lower middle class", of smaller farmers, shopkeepers and "traders" vulnerable to economic depression'.[33] The Fianna Fáil vote in June 1927 was weakest where the 1923 Sinn Féin vote had been weak; in urban areas, among the commercial bourgeoisie, and in the east of the country. In June 1927 Fianna Fáil could only capture a quarter of the national vote; nor could it capture more than a third of the vote in the western areas. Indeed, Cumann na nGaedheal were as strong, if not stronger, than Fianna Fáil in the west at the June 1927 election. Thus the danger for the new party was that it would remain a marginal party, reflecting the interests of a peripheral economic area and of a declining electorate. Cumann na nGaedheal had won the debate on sovereignty, foreign policy, and the state; unless Fianna Fáil countered this with a comprehensive alternative strategy its future remained uncertain.

Table 3.1 Election Results in Urban Constituencies 1927–33

	1927 (June)	1927 (Sept)	1932	1933
Dublin				
Fianna Fáil	23.2	28.6	24.1	43.4
Labour Party *	10.2	11.7	8.0	4.8
Cumann na nGaedheal	31.4	47.8	38.9	40.4
Cork City				
Fianna Fáil	15.0	31.5	35.9	39.1
Labour Party *	23.7	13.7	20.0	20.0
Cumann na nGaedheal	28.4	46.3	44.1	37.2
Limerick				
Fianna Fáil	30.4	34.7	46.5	52.6
Labour Party	13.9	15.3	7.4	8.8
Cumann na nGaedheal	26.8	38.0	32.3	28.9
Galway				
Fianna Fáil	33.6	44.0	55.0	62.4
Labour Party	4.6	5.0	3.9	4.2
Cumann na nGaedheal	35.0	46.8	39.6	33.3
Waterford				
Fianna Fáil	18.5	37.9	44.9	50.3
Labour Party	6.7	—	9.0	2.1
Cumann na nGaedheal	15.1	17.4	46.1	34.1

**Includes Independent Labour.*

Source: Vincent Browne, ed. *The Magill Book of Irish Politics* (Dublin 1981).

The change can be traced in the speeches of de Valera during 1926 and 1927. Once the break with Sinn Féin had occurred there is an increasing emphasis on economic and social policy. Whereas references to these issues occur in earlier speeches, they tend to be rhetorical and with little substance. Thereafter, without losing sight of his main objective, a more vigorous expression of national sovereignty, de Valera gives expression to the main socio-economic policies of Fianna Fáil.[34] The central place of these issues marks a new departure for the republicans and reflects the influence of Lemass and the industrialising wing of the party. Lemass, in particular, had recognised that Fianna Fáil could not hope to win political power without attracting support from the urban areas and the east of the country. He could point to Fianna Fáil's success in the Dublin area in June 1927, when its vote increased substantially over that of 1923, the only area where this occurred in 1927. The electoral history of Fianna Fáil between 1927 and 1933 as outlined in Table 3.1. is one of enhanced presence in urban areas.

Fianna Fáil after 1927 can no longer be considered a party of the periphery; it is now both a party of the periphery and a party of the urban working class and to an extent the lower middle class. The most rapid expansion of the Fianna Fáil vote in September 1927 and thereafter occurs in working class areas, an outcome even more stark at local government elections.[35] This development created a new cleavage in Irish politics which supplemented the divisions over sovereignty. In effect a left-right cleavage emerged with a worker-small farmer alliance represented by Fianna Fáil and the Labour Party facing a bourgeois coalition dominated by Cumann na nGaedheal.

Fianna Fáil's success in the September 1927 election, its new socio-economic programme, and its willingness to accept the parliamentary system ensured that protectionism became a major issue. The future of the Irish economy could and was now debated in political terms and not, as had been the case up to 1927, mainly within the institutions of the state. Ironically, Fianna Fáil reintroduced the issue of protection just as it had been neutralised at the institutional level by the establishment of the Tariff Commission. Lemass became the main advocate of economic nationalism and the party's spokesman in the Dail on most economic and social issues.

He was fortunate that he could utilise the symbols of

sovereignty to give legitimacy to these economic objectives.[36] The revival of the protectionist agitation after 1927 was further justified by the ineffectiveness of the government's economic policies in fulfilling the promise of independence. The 1923 election had effectively been a referendum on the Treaty and the Civil War. After June 1927, welfare, economic growth, and social policy tended to dominate the considerations of the electorate. The elections of September 1927 and 1932 confirmed both this and Fianna Fáil's success in attracting votes on a programme of economic nationalism and enhancing political sovereignty. Fianna Fáil insisted that a change in economic policy was necessary if Ireland was to benefit from independence. The challenge to the government was successful by 1932, but until then Fianna Fáil remained in opposition. The institutions of the state remained in the hands of Cumann na nGaedheal and policy continued to be determined by considerations completely at variance with those maintained by Fianna Fáil.

The politicisation of economic policy further weakened Industry and Commerce's influence over government policy. The Tariff Commission also placed the Department in an invidious position: it was the main institution within the government advocating tariffs, yet, partially because of this, it proved difficult to influence the course of tariff policy through the new agency. It would be mistaken, however, to conclude that tariffs and protectionism disappeared entirely from the policy agenda. Industry and Commerce continued to maintain the efficacy of tariffs. The tariffs imposed between 1922 and 1926 remained in place throughout, and continued to be administered. The Department was able to draw valuable lessons from its administration of the existing tariffs: their existence provided a framework through which officials could learn how to use policy instruments and influence policy in so far as this remained possible. Most importantly, the department could demonstrate that protection and intervention could sustain benefits for the state. Prior to 1932, at this institutional level, if not always at ministerial level, the Department had already become committed to an ambitious developmental strategy: far more ambitious than policy prior to 1932 would allow. The weakness of Industry and Commerce might be attributable to the apparent success of the Irish economy up to 1931. Stability had returned by 1924 following the post-war dislocation, and thereafter the economy continued to expand. As a consequence, any government would have had misgivings about changing the course of macroeconomic policy. The success of the economy is frequently measured in terms of the successful export drive. By 1929 the volume of exports reached a level not to be surpassed until the 1960s, while the value of exports stood at 77 per cent of the value of imports: a ratio not repeated again during the 1930s. Most of these exports were agricultural, yet industry also appeared to have performed quite well. It might be concluded that even in a free trade environment, economic policy led to more beneficial effects than its critics would concede.

On the surface these claims are impressive; however, they did not entirely meet the objections raised by protectionists. It is true that certain agrarian sectors performed well, as demonstrated in the export figures, but such a conclusion cannot be drawn for policy in a wider context. The increase in industrial employment during the 1920s has to be set against an overall decline in population, a drift from the land, and continued emigration. Moreover, in urban centres, there appears to have been considerable under-employment. From a nationalist viewpoint the policies followed could not be considered entirely successful, given that substantial human resources remained unused or were diverted to productive use outside the state. Associated with this is the question whether, in fact, the increase in employment can be attributed to free trade, or at least that free trade did not prevent such increases.

In 1926 there were 192,515 employed in concerns enumerated by the Census of Industrial Production; by 1931 this had increased by a further 8,073. Of these over 7,000 were accounted for by four broad areas as outlined in Table 3.2. Most of these increases can be attributed to government action: (iii) and (iv), involving as they do direct government intervention, cannot be considered industrial jobs in any strict sense. The increase under (ii) was a direct consequence of protection.

The export industries fared badly in employment terms throughout the 1920s. These sectors were the most active advocates of continued free trade. Their output grew, but this was at the cost of less employment. Brewing and distilling experienced an overall decline between 1926 and 1931, while bread, flour, confectionery and biscuits experienced a decline between 1926 and 1929 and a slight rise up to 1931. In the export sector only bacon curing experienced a significant increase in employment terms, from 1,823 to 2,078 by 1931. The most substantial decrease in employment occurred in the motor vehicle sector. Between 1926 and 1929 this had increased from 1,447 to 4,355 but by 1931 had declined to 1,996. The main cause of this was the closure of the tractor section of the Ford Motor Company in Cork. This closure demonstrated to protectionists how fragile and unreliable the free trade arrangements could be in maintaining employment, particularly when a multi-national company was involved. Protection would not have maintained these jobs in Cork as the tractor section was committed to exports. In any event economic nationalists considered control to be the critical issue.

Table 3.2 Employment Increases in Certain Sectors

Sector	1926	1931	Increase
i Building & Construction	9,852	12,530	2,678
ii Clothing (wholsale factories)	4,001	5,846	1,845
iii Electricity	1,319	2,276	957
iv Local Authorities/ Government Departments	17,518	19,213	1,695
Totals	32,690	39,865	7,175

Source: *Census of Industrial Production, 1926 and 1931.*

The traditional industrial sector, therefore, made little contribution to employment by the end of the 1920s. Within this sector overall employment remained static, although net per capita output increased. The most significant increases in employment were either in public utilities, construction, or protected industries. Indeed it is possible to suggest that all these sectors have a measure of protection and/or monopoly, and can be treated accordingly. Increased employment is noticeable in a number of industrial sectors such as boots and shoes, furniture, and clothing, all of which had received some protection between

1924 and 1926. If the export industries are excluded from the CIP figures there is a net increase of 5,000 in employment, although in comparison with the export industries, net per capita output fell between 1926 and 1931.[37]

The expansion of employment in the protected sectors was accompanied by foreign economic penetration of the national economy. By 1931, at least £70 million had been invested by foreign sources in the Free state. This figure should be compared to the estimated £195 million invested by Irish nationals outside the state.[38] Both these developments were criticised by Fianna Fáil. Lemass complained that this penetration of the Irish economy did not bring advantages and investment outside the state depleted Irish resources:

> those who control industry can exercise a considerable influence on the determination of National Policy. If such persons are foreigners, to any large extent, their only interest in the country is the profit that they can make out of it and they will undoubtedly render it difficult to adopt measures designed to protect national interest when these interests are in conflict with their own.

Lemass was not prepared to advocate interference with established concerns in Ireland, such as Guinness or Fords, but he warned that branch industry could not make a major contribution to development in the economy, and in particular these industries would not generate an export trade.[39]

The Department of Industry and Commerce shared some of these concerns. In contrast to Lemass, however, the process of penetration was interpreted as a reflection of the relative success of the industrial policy initiated by the Department. In October 1928 the Intelligence Branch prepared a thirty page analysis of the 'Laws Governing the Rights & Liabilities of Foreign Companies in Various Countries'. This report was circulated by T.J. Barrington who added his own view in an accompanying minute. He began by describing the environment in which foreign investment takes place, noting that the problem, though not a new one, was more pressing for the less developed countries. As Ireland clearly fell into this category, there was considerable evidence that not only had penetration occurred but in certain sectors, particularly those that had been granted tariffs, foreign concerns frequently dominated the sectors. A case in point was the tobacco and cigarette industry: the domestic market had reached saturation point, but the industry was under the control of foreign companies. Seventy-four per cent of those employed in this sector were concentrated in foreign-owned companies. In the case of soap manufacturing the imposition of duties had led at first to penetration, then to the virtual monopolization of the sector by Lever Brothers. Given Lever's size, the Department doubted that any competition would be forthcoming from within the state. The situation was rather different in the jam making and sugar confectionery sector. The structure of this industry was complex, with over sixty firms competing for the limited Irish market. However, most of these concerns were small and output was concentrated in a few large companies. Thus, Crosse & Blackwell and Clarnico-Murray between them employed 50 per cent of the workforce.

Barrington added that penetration was not a general phenomenon; in the readymade clothing industry there was little evidence of it occurring. Nor, he noted, did it appear to make much difference to the progress of a protected industry whether there had been penetration or not:

> From the foregoing facts it will be seen that the experience of protection which the Saorstat has had ... and it is now fairly extensive ... affords no proof of any guiding principle in the tendency towards economic penetration by outside firms ... in a situation of this kind generalisation would obviously be futile. The circumstances which attract the outside firm seem in part to be peculiar to the management policy of the firm itself and the conditions that obtain in the industry in the parent country, and in part to the attractivensss of the external market which it wishes to invade; the extent of its present export trade to that market and the threat to that trade ...

Barrington added that he believed equilibrium had been reached in terms of penetration. However, he suggested that if there were further changes in the fiscal structure there would be an increase in penetration.

From the evidence cited, it is clear that economic penetration was closely related to the extent of protection offered to companies located in the Free state. This penetration could have negative consequences: Williams & Woods received protection in

1924, at a time when the company was in severe difficulty. The tariff saved the company, permitted a doubling of its capital value, and secured an increase in employment from 477 to 844 over three years. Yet Williams & Woods was subsequently absorbed by Crosse & Blackwell:

> By selling the concern the owners turned into cash for their own pocket the concession which they, in common with other firms in the industry, were given by the state on national grounds.

The Department recognised that as long as a common capital market and free trade existed between the United Kingdom and Ireland, there would be a strong tendency for larger United Kingdom companies to enter a protected Irish market through amalgamation with or acquisition of existing Irish firms with the consequences enumerated above. There was evidence to suggest that a pattern along these lines had emerged since 1924, and that Williams & Woods was not an isolated example. To prevent such abuse of fiscal policy, departmental officials recommended that any transfer of ownership should first receive approval from the Minister, and that he should be empowered to prohibit such transactions, or to permit them only after the added value had been surrendered to the state.

The other form of economic penetration which caused concern was the establishment of new firms by foreign companies. In the circumstances of the 1920s there was nothing to prevent this occurring. Drawing on the research of the Department into the activities of other countries, Barrington advised that if a licensing system was introduced to control such investment it should not be used in a discriminatory fashion against foreign firms. Noting that there was an important international dimension to the question, Barrington maintained that regulation should recognise this and not be applied solely on nationalistic grounds. In addition, if government policy was aimed at attracting foreign investment, then a method of licensing should not be framed in such a way as to give the impression that the licence would be temporary and revokable at the whim of a minister. Any such concession, Barrington realistically concluded, should be permanent and recognised as such; otherwise, no-one would be prepared to invest capital in a country where that investment did not have minimum security.

Notwithstanding these difficulties, the Department was in the main favourably disposed towards foreign investment. It recognised that there were problems associated with a policy of industrialisation promoted by foreign capital:

> It must, of course, be recognised that the industrial development of the country by outside firms represents a more satisfactory condition of things than no industrial development at all, but that nevertheless industrial development by domestic firms is the ideal to strive for.

The impact of foreign companies on an economy was, therefore, neither completely positive nor negative, as the ideologists of free trade or protectionism would assert. An outside firm could introduce improved methods, new factories, increased wages, contribute to taxation, in addition to actually supplying goods internally which would, under other circumstances, be imported. The danger of such investment was that the control of the company would be external and that the concern would remain an enclave with foreign staff controlling its organisation.

On balance, given the weakness of Irish industry, Barrington believed that foreign companies made a positive contribution to the economy. The relative weakness of Irish companies, particularly those which owed their origin to tariffs, introduced a note of caution to the analysis. Industry and Commerce recognised that in these circumstances a large number of small and inefficient firms had been established, and that cut-throat competition had been the norm. While this 'excessive growth' due to tariffs concerned the Department, Barrington felt that this could only be dealt with when the direction of industrial policy had been settled. The nature of Irish-based companies and the apparent unwillingness of foreign companies to export from Ireland led Barrington to a pragmatic if not a clearcut conclusion:

> The justification of any legislative measure must, of course, depend upon the extent of the evil or the disability it is designed to remove. I am not satisfied that the economic penetration which has followed on the wake of protection here has yet attained the dimension of a national evil. If, however, greater and still greater industrial expansion is aimed at along the lines already followed I fear there is a very real danger that the effective control in the new

> industrial enterprise thus started will pass to outside concerns.[40]

In 1928, however, these fears were premature. The importance of Barrington's observations for the Department and its orientation should not be ignored. It was the apparent success of tariff policy that created the difficulties which Barrington addressed. Unlike the Department of Finance or other government agencies, Industry and Commerce recognised that an active industrial policy had consequences which had not been fully understood when the tariffs were imposed.

Nor did the Department accept that price increases were an inevitable consequence of tariffs. The traditional economic and financial sectors in Ireland rejected an active industrial policy because they feared that an inflationary environment would result, which would de-stabilise their economic performance. This view was challenged throughout the late 1920s by Industry and Commerce. Ferguson noted that while no clear conclusion could be drawn, Irish industrialists were not responsible for price increases. He noted that a number of distinctions had to be made: in particular between those sectors where there was considerable competiton and areas where there was not. Where competition prevailed, prices settled at or around the British or Northern Ireland level. Furthermore, it was also necessary to distinguish between the wholesale and the retail price of a commodity. The factory price was usually competitive insofar as the Department could ascertain, but retailers often demanded what Ferguson considered to be an excessive profit. In addition, there was evidence that retailers:

> Frequently treated home produced goods unfairly as compared with imported goods. When an effort is made by a Saorstat manufacturer to compete with imported goods the retailer is in a position to destroy the home manufacturer's chances of success.

The small firm could not, he concluded, control retail prices and therefore the retailer could impose conditions or prices as he saw fit. Only a very large company such as Mahony of Blarney could achieve an integrated pricing policy which the retailer would have to accept.[41]

It was also questionable whether, in fact, tariffs in the Free state led to higher prices. The assumption of opponents was that the duty imposed would be absorbed in extra profit by the manufacturers: that the consumer paid the difference between the pre-tariff import and the protected product. In the Irish case, and probably due to the proximity of Britain, the outcome was not as clearcut. Where competiton existed, prices tended to be stable. Yet, even when the internal market was effectively protected, general price increases did not necessarily occur. The margarine manufacturers had been granted a tariff but had guaranteed to sell their products at the prevailing British price. This guarantee was regularly checked by the Department. In addition, the depression was pushing down prices for the consumer, as British producers often sold cheaper in the Free state than in Britain.

The partial nature of protection up to 1932 allowed Departmental officials to limit the criticism against tariffs. They could also demonstrate that tariffs had contributed to employment and reduced the level of imports in certain sectors. Indeed there was also a strong positive correlation between the expansion of industrial employment and the existence of tariffs in a particular sector of the economy. It was this optimistic assessment which led McGilligan to review government policy during 1930. The Minister requested his staff to provide him with extensive information concerning tariffs. The data provided was to be collected on the assumption that Industry and Commerce had acquired the sole authority to impose tariffs. Specific information was required on the most suitable imports to be taxed. McGilligan also requested information on alternative methods which could achieve the same objectives as tariffs; he specifically mentioned the use of monopoly, subsidies, and bounties on exports. To supplement this, he also required a list of all tariff applications to the Department and the outcome of the application. Finally the Minister asked for a list of potential goods which could receive a tariff, and the minimum tariff required to protect them.[42]

Within twenty-four hours a substantial memorandum had been produced outlining the salient features of the case. This case was put vigorously and demonstrates how far the protectionist view had been accepted within the Department. Ferguson included in his list any commodity which the Department believed could be produced in the Free state, but without commiting the Department to supporting a tariff in any individual case. Tariffs already in place were having positive effects on Irish production levels. Steel girders to the value of £100,000 were being produced, most of which was protected. However, he added, it would require a more effective tariff policy to ensure that various items could be produced internally. The Department believed that the items listed in Table 3.3 could be produced without difficulty if protection was extended. It was maintained that only the restrictive nature of the tariff regime prevented the immediate production of all of these items within the state.[43]

Table 3.3 Value of Selected Imports in 1929

Sanitary Ware	£427,088
Brass, Copper, Lead and Tin	£627,609
Corrugated Iron	£336,761
Steel Girders, Joints, Steel Structural Works	£284,083
Water and Gas Pipes	£357,601
Wire Manufactures	£234,899
Various Classes of paper	£560,050
Total	£2,828,091

Source*: McGilligan Papers: P35/153. Industry & Commerce, 16 July 1930.*

The evidence confirmed Ferguson's belief that tariffs could play a decisive role in augmenting, if not leading, economic growth. Between 1922 and 1926, according to estimates supplied by the Statistics Branch of Industry and Commerce, the tariffs permitted under the Finance Acts of 1922 to 1926, had led directly to an increase in employment in the protected industries of at least 10,275. Table 3.4 details the increase in employment after the imposition of these tariffs. Moreover, once a tariff was in place, there was a gradual expansion in the number of new factories established as a consequence. During 1929 and 1930, at least forty new factories had come into operation in the Free state.[44]

Table 3.4 Employment in Protected Industry as a Result of Tariff Policy 1922–27

Year of Tariff		Item	Employment: Year of Tariff	Employment 1927	Change
1922		Tobacco	500 (est)	1,868	1,368
1924	1.	Bootmaking	359	1,019	660
	2.	Glass Making	25	146	121
	3.	Soap and Candles	263	360	97
	4.	Motor Bodies	249	222	27
	5.	Confectionery (including Jam)	3,878	5,436	1,558
1925	1.	Wholesale Clothing	845	2,018	1,173
	2.	Shirtmaking	801	1,712	902
	3.	Hosiery	988	1,377	389
	4.	Hats and Caps	89	196	107
	5.	Umbrellas	48	43	–5
	6.	Tiemaking	101	136	35
	7.	Blanket making	229	514	285
	8.	Furniture	482	1,036	554
	9.	Metallic Bedsteads	24	76	52
	10.	Brushmaking	195	304	109
	11.	Handcraft Tailoring	N/A	N/A	400
	12.	Corset Making	N/A	85	85

Source: McGilligan Papers: P35/153.

The imposition of tariffs could have a hidden impact on the economy in addition to their direct effect on employment and the erection of factories. Without them, it is possible that imports would have increased. In the boot and shoe industry, imports to the thirty-two counties in 1921 were valued at £4 million. In 1924 some 337,000 dozen pairs of boots and shoes valued at £1,907,652 were imported into the Free state. In that year the government imposed a 15 per cent *ad valorem* duty; by 1926 the volume of imports had actually increased to 350,957 pairs. However, in the interim, nine new factories had been established. It is arguable that the market for shoes was an expanding one. Moreover, the cost of boots and shoes actually fell by 13 per cent between 1924 and 1927. Over the same period net output in this industry expanded and employment grew. There were certain difficulties within the industry; machinery was considered to be elaborate and expensive, expansion was curtailed by a shortage of skilled workers; it also proved difficult to reduce the volume of the remaining imports. The duty imposed in 1924 secured a foothold for Irish industry, but not a monopoly. This industry was rather uncharacteristic in that all the factories established were relatively large, whereas in most other protected sectors the factories were small.[45]

Tariffs were considered the most appropriate method of stimulating small-scale industries. Such tariffs would, it was maintained, lead to increased home production of each commodity. Although Industry and Commerce does not, at this stage, appear to have considered a full tariff regime possible; it did suggest that there was considerable scope for further intervention. In addition to the items detailed in Table 3.3 the Department believed that further savings could be achieved by tariffs on cement, rubber tyres, and electrical apparatus. Yet, even this list is incomplete in that there were other items which could be protected with benefit to the economy, although probably not as easily as those mentioned above. Table 3.5 details these items which the Department considered 'would produce results in employment almost immediately without incurring any very obvious economic loss in consequence.'

Table 3.5 Value of Imported Items which could be Protected

1.	Railway Vehicles and Parts	£17,142
2.	Water and Gas Iron Pipes	£357,601
3.	Stoves, Grates and Ranges	£188,872
4.	Steel Structural Works	£284,083
5.	Agricultural Machinery	£254,103
6.	Bicycles	£341,879
7.	Galvanised & Corrugated Iron	£336,761
8.	Linen Manufactures	£135,311
9.	Hollow Ware	£155,091
10.	Gas Meters	£20,148
11.	Manufacture of Brass, Copper etc.	£627,609
12.	Ropes, Cord and Twine	£152,423
13.	Superphosphates & Compound Fertilisers	£277,348
14.	Certain Classes of Cotton & Union Goods	£1,839,208
15.	Wooden Boxes and Parts	£189,221
16.	Jute Boxes	£20,041
17.	Stationery	£504,793
18.	Refined Oils	£419,067
19.	Paints	£259,752
20.	Blacking and Polishes	£65,971
21.	Starch & Destrine	£30,576
22.	Monumental & Architectural Works	£19,007
	Total	£6,496,007

Source: McGilligan Papers, P35/153.

In theory, at least, the possibility of a protected industrial expansion was strong. In practice, it was not as clear-cut. As discussed above with the boot and shoe industry, there remained serious obstacles to the advance of a tariff regime within what was otherwise a free trade environment. Some expansion could be expected, but without substantial increases in duty or the prohibition of imports, it was unlikely that there would be widespread development. In reviewing the situation, Ferguson recognised the difficulties and suggested a policy approach which anticipates the more comprehensive protectionist policies of the 1930s:

> In the case of establishing an absolutely new industry in the country I am of opinion that it is, generally speaking, better to proceed by way of giving an inducement to some company, home or foreign, by special arrangement taking even the form of a virtual monopoly. The imposition of a tariff of sufficient magnitude might in itself, of course, bring about the establishment of a new industry, but it would be an unbusinesslike proceeding to put on a tariff in the dark without having previously had negotiations with certain firms or groups resulting in an understanding that some firms would undertake the production of a certain class of goods if it were granted certain terms ...

Without a comprehensive tariff policy Irish industry, even prior to the crisis of the 1930s, was in a weak position. Not only was industry dependent on imported raw materials, but the prevailing free trade conditions and low level of duty, where it did exist, meant that there was considerable import penetration. Outside of agriculture and related sectors, Irish industry still appears uncompetitive by the end of the 1920s.

This evidence reinforced Campbell's view that the Tariff Commission, as then constituted, presented the main obstacle to any developmental strategy. He noted that the Commission had recently refused to grant a tariff on wheaten products. Over £2 million worth of this commodity was imported each year, yet under the prevailing circumstances it could not be considered a taxable import. The inference that can be drawn is that Industry and Commerce was constrained in its policy making operation by the Commission. McGilligan was more sensitive than his secretary to the political pressures within the government. Although willing to seek adjustments in the operation of the Tariff Commission, he appeared loath to advocate a vigorous tariff policy. He reminded Campbell that even:

> Under existing legislation, it is not for us to express any official opinion on 'taxable' or 'non-taxable' imports. Even if the Tariff Commission Act were not in force we would be slow to express an opinion without contacting various interests likely to be affected either directly or indirectly.[46]

Despite this, McGilligan moved quickly once the government decided to amend the Tariff Commission Act. He urged the Department of Finance to transfer its effective control over the Commission to Industry and Commerce. McGilligan wanted a nominee of his department to be chairman, and that the Commission should report to him rather than to the Department of Finance as hitherto:

> I think this is essential if we view the work of the Tariff Commission as being of special value on the development of industry [sic] and not merely as machinery for the raising of extra money.

Such a view was rejected by Finance. The Minister endorsed McElligott's view that no concession should be made to McGilligan. It would involve a fundamental change, he added, as applications would then be made to Industry and Commerce. This was obviously something that McElligott wished to prevent, for he believed that Industry and Commerce as well as Agriculture' ... are in a sense partisan' in the matter. He subsequently noted that Finance officials were 'the proper people to hold the scales between Agriculture and Industry and Commerce'.[47]

A new tariff commission was appointed on 15 November 1930. As one of the new members was T.A. Smiddy, previously chairman of the Fiscal Inquiry Committee, it can be concluded that Industry and Commerce made little headway in its attempts to transform the arrangement. The legislation confirmed this. An early draft of the amendment empowered any Minister to refer an application to the Commission. This was later altered to empower the Executive Council as a collective body to do so. Again this reduced the autonomy of Industry and Commerce in initiating changes in the tariff regime.[48] The decision to amend the Tariff Commission Act and make it permanent indicates the balance of power between Industry and Commerce and Finance. Although Finance remained dominant, there were limits to this dominance. John Leydon, a Finance official, was selected to chair the new Commission. This decision was subsequently reversed, probably due to pressure from McGilligan. The decision to propose Leydon appears to have been an overt attempt on the part of Finance to ensure that tariff policy would not be changed. Subsequently, Leydon was appointed secretary to Industry and Commerce; but at this time there was no indication that he dissented in any way from the current orthodoxy of his superiors. Like them, he distrusted state intervention and on a number of occasions declared strong opposition to policies based on such assumptions.[49]

The failure to confirm Leydon's appointment did not have an appreciable effect on the Tariff Commission. Its approach was as cautious after 1930 as it had been during the previous three years. The original Act and the amendment continued to constrain its activities. It is difficult to agree with Fanning that 'this ... seems to suggest an attempt to give teeth to the Commission while at the same time lessening the control of the Department of Finance over its operations.' The reports published between 1930 and 1932 indicate that, whatever about personnel, the Tariff Commission remained imbued with the caution evident under McElligott.[50]

The external constraints imposed on Industry and Commerce prevented them from realising an active industrial policy. The Department was unable to acquire the political or institutional leverage to promote it. In addition, the officials did not have the active or full support of their Minister. One possible reason for this is that McGilligan had two ministerial portfolios: that of External Affairs in addition to Industry and Commerce. Both departments were important; yet the concerns of each were divergent. Given the nature of each department, anyone with responsibility for both would experience considerable pressure in carrying out his duties. There is no direct evidence that this division of tasks resulted in neglect of either department. However, McGilligan's main concern was increasingly with foreign policy and inevitably Industry and Commerce became less central to his concerns after 1927.[51]

This was, however, only a contributory factor. McGilligan was an individual of considerable ability and if he had chosen to actively pursue the strategy which his staff recommended, it is probable that the outcome would have been somewhat different. McGilligan differed from his department on the merits of an active industrial policy. He was more cautious in his approach and accepted the primary importance of agriculture in the economy, and all that that entailed for policy. If industrial expansion could take place without damaging agricultural output and exports, then McGilligan was prepared to support departmental initiatives. In all other cases he maintained the status quo. In doing so, the Minister effectively tied the hands of his staff by accepting the presuppositions of the majority of his government colleagues. McGilligan in effect reinforced the pre-industrial socio-economic structure by marginalising the impact of Industry and Commerce which, for most of the 1920s, remained the only self-conscious centre for industrialisation.

This situation allowed the Department of Finance to exercise great control over the direction of government expenditure. Without a clear cut commitment to development, the Minister for Industry and Commerce could not with consistency demand resources to expand the economy. The government's fiscal policy restricted Industry and Commerce's manoeuvrability. This is not to claim that an expansionary fiscal policy was the only alternative, but that the existing policy was locked into a set of presuppositions which prevented an innovative policy. Thus, because policy was concentrated on relieving the burden on agriculture, fiscal policy was based on an assumption that taxation of farmers should not be increased; indeed that local taxation and wages were already too high, and that new impositions could not be countenanced.[52] The crux for policy in the 1920s was this unwillingness to tax more heavily. Total taxation per head of population in Ireland was one of the lowest among European democracies.[53] Irish officials believed that the relationship between taxation and expenditure put demands on fiscal policy which did not allow for further expansion. The consequence for a Minister in charge of a spending department was to restrict his willingness to incur increased expenditure. When, as was the case with McGilligan, the Minister also accepted the ideological argument for the policy, this inhibited the formulation of alternative policies within his Department.

Prior to September 1927 a case could be made that government policy was essentially cautious rather than conservative. However, by the end of the decade an inertia in policy making can be detected; conservative (if not reactionary) assumptions had come to the fore. Any policy which appeared to depart from the ideological certainties of the government was vigorously opposed. Political considerations meshed with economic ones after Fianna Fáil entered the Dail. There is a detectable hardening of opinion within the government on tariffs once the opposition instituted an active campaign for protection. McGilligan supported Hogan's view that a tariff should not be imposed on agricultural imports, a policy which ran counter to Campbell's earlier recommendation. When the Tariff Commission undertook to consider such a tariff, Hogan urged McGilligan to support the rejection of it. He argued that the Tariff Commission should remain the institution for determining tariffs. Hogan maintained that the Commission should undertake to consider whether an industry seeking a tariff would be a business proposition and, particularly in the case of wheat, what impact a tariff would have on the farming community. The Minister for Agriculture, making an essentially political point, rejected what he considered to be:

> The patriotic point of view ... that the Tariff Commission should be a body for recommending tariffs. They incurred the odium of the patriots and the vested interests when they don't, but these two classes are not the country thank God ... I think it is absolutely essential to establish definitely that agriculture cannot be directly assisted by tariffs of any kind and I believe we ought to expect from the Tariff Commission considerable help in doing this...[54]

More specifically Hogan believed the time was appropriate to reverse the trend towards protectionism, a trend he insisted which had little public support. He added that he believed the government was now persuading the country that tariffs on agriculture could not help that industry. However, in what may have been a sop to Industry and Commerce, he added '... when that is definitely established it will make the industrial tariffs situation easier ... I think it will make our position easier.'[55] McGilligan was sympathetic to Hogan's approach. He recognised that agriculture remained the most important export and that interference with it could have disastrous effects on the economy itself and particularly on Irish farming. Hogan and McGilligan differed from Finance in their approach. Finance had principled objections to tariffs of any kind. Hogan and McGilligan believed a distinction should be made between tariffs on agriculture and those on industry. This approach was considerably more flexible, but it accepted the overall dominance of agriculture and consequently a limited place for even industrial tariffs.

McGilligan also questioned the heart of Fianna Fáil's economic nationalism; the belief that the domestic market could be expanded to absorb all home production as well as significant increases. He estimated that in the event of exports ceasing, a population of 7 million would be required to absorb them. This turned a traditional economic nationalist argument around. Fianna Fáil usually argued that Ireland had the potential to provide for 8 million, albeit frugally. McGilligan suggested that, at the present level of production, that population would be required now rather than later. He also shared the orthodox economic view that there were indirect benefits from international trade. Ireland, for example, was importing £2 million of American bacon but exporting nearly £3 million of Irish bacon. Fianna Fáil wanted to exclude the American imports, absorb Irish production, and export the residual. McGilligan maintained that it was not as simple as that. The consumer in Ireland would probably pay more, as the only way of enforcing the policy was to institute a complete monopoly in the industry. Moreover, it was unlikely, he believed, that the British would accept that Ireland would in future supply only a small percentage of its requirements. Britain would turn to Canadian bacon for their full requirements. Thus, McGilligan rejected the protectionist claims of Fianna Fáil, but added that tariffs were already in place in a number of sectors and working adequately. In contrast to Fianna Fáil, McGilligan suggested an alternative approach:

> It is not a choice between producing for export and alternatively for home consumption, but rather a choice between producing for a possible profit or producing for a certain loss.

The Minister believed that protection on a large scale would be disastrous for the Irish economy, leading to significant losses, particularly in agriculture.[56]

For the governing party, agriculture was working well and there was no need to change policy. Further tariffs would offset the benefits which Ireland received from international trade and access to Britain. McGilligan furthermore rejected the view that tariffs provided a solution to unemployment, asserting that such a reliance had not been successful elsewhere and would not be in Ireland. The only responsible policy was one where each application for a tariff was examined carefully. He added:

> The public is shrewd enough to know that if tariffs were a single obvious cure for unemployment any government seeking its votes ... would adopt that cure.[57]

While McGilligan's view may have approximated closely to the reality of the economic environment, it ignored the political pressures for change. Both Hogan and McGilligan were incorrect in believing that the reasoned deliberations of the Tariff Commission or its rejection of a tariff on wheat would in any way kill the general agitation for protection. Trade unions, some farmers, and sections of the business community all expressed support for tariffs.

These developments worked to Fianna Fáil's advantage by the end of the 1920s. The party's strategy was based on a commitment to completely restructure economic and fiscal policy in the context of a protectionist framework. Self sufficiency would be the norm, while monetary policy would be nationalised.[58] Fianna Fáil believed its economic policies challenged the neo-colonial structures imposed on Ireland by the British. Economic policy was consequently based on the assumption that self-sufficiency had considerable merit. In contrast to the claims of Cumann na nGaedheal, Fianna Fáil believed that its policies would be positive-sum rather than zero-sum. Frank Gallagher, a leading Fianna Fáil publicist, insisted in his history of the party that all sections of Irish society would gain from these policies.[59] Sean Lemass was less sanguine about the positive-sum nature of the party's policy. He recognised, even when in opposition, that difficult decisions would have to be taken if emigration was to be stemmed and unemployment reduced. A policy that did not contribute to this objective was, from Fianna Fáil's viewpoint, worse than useless; 'everything else, even cheap living or accepted notions about efficiency, must be sacrificed to that end.'[60]

For the most part Fianna Fáil emphasised the positive attraction of its policies. By entering the Dail it presented the government for the first time with a challenge to its economic policy. Lemass led the party's criticism of the government, demanding a change in the direction of policy. In July and October 1928 de Valera urged the government to appoint a committee to examine unemployment and the general economic situation. Cosgrave eventually accepted that an economic committee should be established for these reasons. The main consequence of this decision was that the question of protection was not only opened up again, but was placed firmly on the parliamentary agenda. It also put the government on the defensive for the first time on economic matters. The terms of reference were wide ranging, rather vague, attempting to balance the need for employment creation against the fear of inflation and inefficiency.[61] It is unclear what the government hoped to achieve by this. The committee itself was immediately divided between protectionists and anti-protectionists. Given its composition and the mutually exclusive points of view, agreement would have been difficult.

The first and second interim report of the committee demonstrated the entrenched positions. In each case majority and minority reports were issued which reflected the ideological divisions between government and opposition. Fianna Fáil confidently predicted that protection would induce growth and create employment, while the government offered a scathing criticism of what it considered to be unrealistic policies. McGilligan, in particular, considered Fianna Fáil suggestions both dangerous and irresponsible.[62] The collapse of the economic committee in early 1929 was perhaps inevitable. It demonstrated, not only the differences between government and opposition, but the challenge Cumann na nGaedheal faced. Once the Treaty settlement had been accepted *de facto* by Fianna Fáil, the debate centred on the nature of Irish sovereignty and on economic policy. The government had no real answer to Fianna Fáil on the economic issue. The party utilised nationalist symbolism to give direction to an economic strategy which, though coherent, may not have been entirely rational or logical. As Fianna Fáil's attraction was based in large part on nationalism, Lemass utilised its emotional power to challenge the orthodox nationalist free trade position. He viewed the idea of a European Customs Union with suspicion, believing that such a movement was simply a vehicle for the international bankers and industrialists:

> There appears to be a definite movement in influential quarters in support of the idea of an international economic policy, overriding and replacing the various, and generally conflicting, national policies now in operation.

He admitted the theoretical attractiveness of the free trade thesis, but insisted that the underlying assumptions were flawed. By ignoring national differences, advocates of European Union and interdependence evaded the interface between economics and politics which were integrated into and were an aspect of national culture. Because the nation is more than a collection of economic actors, the criterion of policy could not be the cost of living index or the inflation rate.[63]

Lemass's primary assumption was that individuals constitute themselves first as part of a national grouping and only on this basis can economic policy be evaluated. If this is so, then economic policy must be nationalistic, in that the primary concern must be for the citizens of the nation rather than a vague commitment to international fellow feeling. Moreover, this approach could be justified by the uneven impact of wealth creation in the British Isles: mainland Britain had benefited from free trade; Ireland had not. Lemass's economic nationalism is given coherent expression through a twentieth-century version of mercantilist ideas based on the political sovereignty of the nation. In this situation economic and political sovereignty are primary necessities: only when these have been acquired can the state adequately provide for its members. Self-sufficiency, not free trade, therefore, should be the objective of policy-making. Once the perspective shifted in this way, Lemass was in a strong position to challenge not only the 'rational calculus' of McGilligan, but the more general assumptions of the government, which placed its faith on the competitive advantages for the cattle trade within the framework of international trade. Having questioned the internationalist assumption of free trade and found it wanting, Lemass questioned the practical experience of the Irish economy since 1922. Citing evidence from the government itself, he was able to demonstrate that an increased output in agriculture did not in itself lead to increased employment.

An economic nationalist policy required a radical reorganisation of the economy to offset the impact of international exigencies which resulted in market failure. To achieve Fianna

Fáil's policy objectives, Lemass argued that all but the most necessary imports (usually raw materials) should be excluded and the home market preserved for Irish producers. This was the first step in a strategy to create employment. The second involved shifting the emphasis within agriculture away from cattle to tillage. Tillage could maintain a far greater number on the land than pasture; therefore the community would gain from this new emphasis. Lemass presupposed that output would increase by a factor of three and that beef and milk production would parallel the increase in tillage. The third arm of the strategy was to be state-induced industrialisation. Industry would, Lemass affirmed, be the main focus of policy. Yet, unlike his party leader, he recognised the difficulties facing the strategy. Ireland had no natural or competitive advantage in the industrial sphere. It would, therefore, be foolish to participate in a free trade environment, for only traditional agriculture proved successful. However, Lemass believed that there was substantial capacity within the nation state to absorb increased production. Such a strategy would be supplemented by a central bank, an active capital market, and the attraction of Irish capital invested abroad back to Ireland. Furthermore, there is an appeal to national identity to secure the foundations of the strategy:

> The need for patriotism did not disappear with the handing over of Dublin Castle. In our efforts to bring prosperity to the country we will find that the spirit of Irish Nationality – the determination of our people to survive as a separate nation – will be our greatest test and our surest guarantee of success.[64]

The onset of the great depression did not at once make Fianna Fáil policy more attractive. It did, however, increase the pressure on the government from all sources. Yet, at first, Ireland seemed to be largely unaffected by the collapse of the international trading system. As late as 1931 the worst effects of the depression had not been felt in the Free state. Despite this, Fianna Fáil continued to challenge the government. This challenge was enhanced when the economy eventually began to suffer from the recession in late 1931. It was further reinforced by the economic and fiscal crisis which hit the United Kingdom during 1931.[65] Fianna Fáil provided an analysis of the crisis which rejected what it believed to be the complacency of the government. Following the collapse of the MacDonald government in Britain, which was one consequence of the financial crisis, Lemass maintained that continued close trading and financial links with Britain would have serious repercussions:

> There would be no security for Irish producers, or no certainty of continued prosperity here until the country was made self-supporting to a degree much greater than at present. This could only be done by the protection of industries.[66]

Lemass accompanied this appeal for economic sovereignty with remedial action for those sections of Irish society most affected by recession. At a meeting at Wynn's Hotel, Dublin, Lemass demanded that the unemployed should be absorbed by state works. Protection, an independent currency, and a state housing policy, could, he argued, absorb a significant element of the unemployed.[67] At the Fianna Fáil Ard Fheis in October 1931, the delegates supported the establishment of a Wheat Control Board and advocated protection for all sectors of agriculture. The aim of Fianna Fáil's policy, de Valera declared, was to make the country as self-sufficient as possible. This was not only good in itself, but should be sought to maintain an essentially Irish character:

> The countries which today are suffering most from the prevailing depression are those most dependent on foreign trade. Ireland, thanks to her soil and climate, is able to produce all the necessities of life for her own people. It is our intention to enable home producers to take advantage of that position by giving them security in the home market.[68]

Such a view did not go unchallenged among the government's supporters or in the conservative press. McGilligan turned to this issue shortly before leaving office. He derisively rejected the entire Fianna Fáil prescription:

> I regard the Wheat Scheme as bad husbandry and worse economics. The beet scheme is a ... joke. The maize meal admixture scheme is strangling the livestock products industry in this country. Livestock and livestock products are the *only* hope of Saorstat agriculture. No tariff that will increase the cost of raw materials of the agricultural industry should be tolerated. *All* quotas are bad; quotas must logically

> and inevitably lead to state socialism in industries to which they are applied as a protection. Most tariffs are bad, but tariffs on raw materials of our export industries are bad and mad.

McGilligan continued to believe that Ireland's economic policy should be based on a cattle economy dependent on the British market. Within this context, tariffs could only be defended as a defensive measure against dumping, subsidies, or cheap labour. The political and economic consequences of Fianna Fáil's expansionary policies would be disastrous. These developments, he added, '... must end in somebody having to undertake retrenchment to the point of driving people to revolution.'

This pessimistic conclusion tended to ignore the inadequacies of the government's own policies and particularly its 'wager on the strong'. Believing that the export based farm sector could create wealth, the government also assumed that as an industry it could create jobs and stem emigration. Despite government claims to the contrary, this proved not to be the case. Ireland experienced statistical economic growth during the 1920s but not economic development. Moreover, despite the undoubted success of the government in establishing the state and maintaining order, the economic and social policies of the government were not such as to excite enthusiastic support among a significant section of the electorate. McGilligan recognised the problem but approached it from an economic rather than from a political point of view. He questioned the government's land policy which divided large estates and distributed small plots to the rural proletariat or marginal landowner:

> The Land Commission Policy of creating £10 valuation holdings for tenants without any adequate examination and largely for men who have no capital and no stock is creating a rural proletariat which will become the plaything of revolutionary agitators in due time.

Such a view, based as it was on rational economic calculation, was undoubtedly correct, given the premises from which McGilligan began. However, they were not the premises of Fianna Fáil or of an increasing body of the electorate. This point may have been recognised by McGilligan himself, for he concluded his analysis with an italised sentence: *We Should Either Face the Issues or Get Out and Let Fianna Fáil Alone.*[69]

Fianna Fáil's electoral victory in 1932 was a significant rebuttal of the Cumann na nGaedheal government. It reflected the growing attractiveness of Fianna Fáil's economic and social policies, but more importantly a rejection of those promoted by the government. Despite the tariffs that had been imposed, industry had not become an important element in economic growth. Although the attempt in 1927 to restrict tariffs had been successful, the government failed to persuade the public at large that protectionist policies were mistaken. Electoral support for Fianna Fáil reinforced the conservative attitudes within the government. This allowed Fianna Fáil to promote an ambitious social and economic programme. Industry and Commerce remained on the defensive up to 1932 and proved unable to influence the overall direction of policy. The dominance of agriculture and the commitment to the export trade remained the major obstacle to any radical change. Change could only occur when the political structure was modified: this Fianna Fáil was to do after 1932.

4

The Drive to Industrialise: Fianna Fáil and Protectionism 1932–39

Many economic and political certainties were challenged by the depression. Free trade and democracy frequently lost their attraction for many faced with the consequences of unprecedented economic change. For some, in particular Britain, the move from free trade was reluctant and externally imposed. For others the great depression was a source of opportunity; a time when political outsiders challenged the certainties of the 1920s and established a new set of political norms. The Nazi takeover in Germany is probably the best known example of this; but the American New Deal and the Swedish Social Democratic government policy both attest to concerted attempts to restructure national economies to meet the challenge of unemployment.[1] In each of these cases policy was reformulated in an effort to revive the economy.

The Cumann na nGaedheal government reacted slowly and reluctantly to these pressures. The government remained ideologically committed to free trade, but recognised the need for defensive action. Fianna Fáil displayed no such reluctance: the events of 1931 and 1932 confirmed them in the belief that free trade was not suitable for Ireland. Even prior to this, the party had maintained the need for protection and self-sufficiency. Economic decline allowed them to press their political advantage. In 1932 Fianna Fáil was elected to power on a programme which, *inter alia* committed them to transforming the Irish socio-economic environment. Sean Lemass expressed the party's commitment to this process well before coming to power.

> Every Nation is, naturally, desirious of maintaining and increasing its population and of providing a reasonable

> average standard of living for its people. Experience has taught us that these ends can be best achieved when a Nation is politically and economically free, that is to say, when control of the factors affecting the internal life of the Nation is exercised within its boundaries and, primarily, in its interests. Each Nation, therefore, strives towards economic self-sufficiency.[2]

He maintained that protection of existing Irish industry, and the promotion of industrial expansion were the only realistic methods of achieving this goal.

Fianna Fáil's economic strategy owed a considerable debt to List and other nineteenth century economic nationalists. It is also an early example of the policies pursued by many of the less developed states in Latin America and elsewhere.[3] For economic nationalists the attraction of mercantilism as a system is its emphasis on the central role of the nation, and the importance of politics in effecting change. Fianna Fáil's charge against Cumann na nGaedheal was that their economic policies, however well intentioned, allowed economic policy to be formulated outside the state. Fianna Fáil's strategy called for the 'nationalisation' of economic policy. This necessitated breaking trading links with Britain, and integrating economic policy firmly within the state apparatus. Policy formulation would heretofore be determined internally: the state would not just administer the existing system, it would define the context within which all economic activity would take place.

This involved re-ordering the relationship between state and society. Whereas under Cumann na nGaedheal the state had been passive and minimalist, under Fianna Fáil it became dynamic and interventionist. Fianna Fáil also penetrated the state apparatus and moulded the institutions to reflect its concerns and objectives.[4] This pre-supposed continued electoral success throughout the 1930s. If Fianna Fáil had been replaced in office during the 1930s, there would have been a considerable redirection of policy. The party required a sustained period in office to secure its ascendancy. The 1933 election laid the basis for Fianna Fáil's electoral hegemony. As a 'critical election', it allowed the party time to impose a new policy agenda on the electorate. The subsequent return to government in 1937 and 1938, led to the neutralisation and eventual assimilation of the opposition, in policy terms at least.[5] At the electoral level, within the state apparatus and in social terms, Fianna Fáil had redefined the broad institutional framework by 1939. Not all its objectives were achieved. However, a majority of Irish citizens accepted Fianna Fáil's political and economic strategy; even the opposition had to accommodate itself to this reality. Moreover, in political terms, the party had created an electoral coalition not unlike the 'New Deal' coalition in the United states. This was essentially non-propertied and based on re-distributional principles. The internal workings of this coalition were complex, but without it Fianna Fáil could not have retained the levers of power to adjust the direction of policy.[6]

When Lemass was appointed Minister for Industry and Commerce, his party was not yet secure in power. If this power was still tenuous, it did not obstruct him in his commitment to change the direction of policy. He came to office armed with a coherent ideology and a specific set of policies. On one interpretation, Lemass subsequently enacted most of these policies. Indeed, there is a close correlation between the legislative output between 1932 and 1938, and the various statements of policy attributed to Lemass and Fianna Fáil between 1926 and 1932.[7] An alternative view accepts that Lemass was ideologically motivated when in opposition, but '... once in office, was to begin to have doubts about the wisdom of his policy and by the end of his long political life had completely reversed his views.'[8] If this refers to the 1930s, it is mistaken. There is no evidence that Lemass had any doubts about the policy as such. Where doubts arose, these were concerned with policy implementation. He believed that the revival and protection of industry would eliminate unemployment. He calculated that the economy would have to produce £13.5 million worth of goods each year to create 50,000 new jobs. The first step would be to substitute Irish production for imports which could be replaced easily. Lemass estimated further that £17 million worth of imports could be immediately substituted. However, the mechanism for achieving this end was more suspect:

> The limits of a possible industrial revival coincide with the country's capacity to consume the goods produced. This capacity would increase with the volume of employment available. If we find, therefore, that within the limits of the market available at home we can provide employment for a

> greater number than the number of those now seeking work then we can reasonably hope for a continuous development for a long time to come.[9]

Import substitution was clearly designed as an initial stimulus for the economy. The consequent increase in employment would stimulate demand, which in turn would initiate a further cycle. Under-consumption was isolated as the main constraint on internal development: with an insulated market and positive policy instruments, this constraint could be overcome. Lemass did not reject this general view of economic reality prior to the Second World War. He was, however, forced to modify his optimism in the face of economic circumstances. Despite this, neither Lemass nor Fianna Fáil questioned the policy assumptions worked out prior to 1932, nor would they, at this stage, accept that autonomous, nationalist economic development could involve greater costs than development within an international trading system. Prior to 1939, policy was framed in an either/or context: either the policies of the 1920s or those being followed during the 1930s. No consideration was given to the possibility of industrial development within an international system, which might bring benefits to the Irish economy.[10]

Lemass had an immediate impact on his new Department, effectively removing the constraints under which it had suffered. The Minister's commitment to industrial expansion provided a basis for reorganising the Department to achieve these objectives. For the first time since 1922, Industry and Commerce had the resources to carry out what many officials had believed should be its task.[11] In Lemass, the Department had a Minister who actively supported an interventionist perspective and who, more importantly, believed it was necessary to use that power to achieve economic and social objectives.[12] The shift in policy and its vigorous expression by Lemass constrained the traditional influence of the Department of Finance on economic policy. This did not mean that Finance's influence had been completely overcome, only that it was no longer the dominant department. Lemass politicised economic and social policy, and removed it from the technocratic considerations which had been uppermost prior to 1932. The economic war and the changes in agricultural policy further weakened Finance and enhanced Industry and Commerce.[13]

Once Lemass acquired institutional control, he undertook a series of initiatives. The Trade Loans (Guarantee) Acts were interpreted more flexibly, their use widened, and eventually amended to suit the new circumstances. A scheme to make finance available for industry was circulated to the Economic Committee of the Cabinet. By November 1932 Lemass recommended that a Board for External Trade be established to control all aspects of foreign trade, including agricultural exports. The radical nature of this proposal was not lost on the Cabinet, which declined to support it. It draws attention to Lemass's commitment to radical alternatives, but also to the institutional and political obstacles which remained.[14] Lemass recognised that a passive approach to trade policy would leave Ireland no better off than had been the case during the 1920s.

By the middle of November, Lemass concluded that the economic pressures on the government were becoming intolerable. Unemployment had increased,the balance of payments were worsening,and there was a serious crisis in agriculture. Consequently:

> It is, to say the least, doubtful if we are in a position to maintain the 'economic war'. It is equally doubtful if the termination of the 'economic war' will alone greatly improve our position. We have reached the point where a collapse in our economic system is in sight.

These conditions forced him to adopt a more cautious assessment of Ireland's economic potential than he had taken prior to 1932. Whereas previously he had believed that a self-sufficient economy would, given certain stimuli, generate self-sustained growth, he now advised that industry could not absorb the unemployed. He recognised that industrial expansion would be slow, dependent as it was on decisions taken by private individuals. An export market for industrial goods would be urgently required if unemployment was to be eliminated. In the absence of a substantial increase in consumption, an export market would have to be secured. Lemass further recognised that an immediate increase in consumption was unlikely, and recommended that a treaty should be negotiated with Britain. Prior to this the emergency import duties should be abolished, industrial and agricultural production and exports should be closely controlled, while a public works programme should be undertaken. A central facet of the proposals involved breaking the monetary link with Britain and weakening Finance's control over public expenditure.[15]

Although not all the proposals were consistent with one another, their cumulative effect promoted a significant increase in state control of the economy. As the Minister most concerned with economic affairs, Lemass quickly recognised that the certainties of opposition could not easily be transformed into policy. Yet, he was unwilling to give up the basic commitment to self-sufficiency. He argued that Ireland would be faced with difficult conditions, whether there was a conflict with Britain or not. For Lemass, at least, the economic war did not affect the general policy mechanism, nor did it undermine his commitment to protection. In this sense, the conflict with Britain was a side issue which diverted attention from economic development.[16] Self-sufficiency remained the goal; these proposals were a response to a specific set of circumstances which weakened the environment for its achievement. The main thrust of the proposals were rejected at a Cabinet meeting in December 1932, a Cabinet frightened by the consequences of the proposals themselves and, in some cases, persuaded by their departmental officials to oppose them.[17]

These proposals may have been pre-emptive in character. It is possible that Lemass appreciated the difficulties and opposition and, given the opportunity, took the initiative. He does not produce another systematic memorandum until 1945, but throughout the intervening period, and thereafter, his concerns remained close to those enumerated above. Deflected from this approach, he concentrated on inducing an increase in consumption and employment to facilitate internal development. His proposals to relieve unemployment in 1932, which led to the Unemployment Assistance Bill in 1933, were based on the belief that under-consumption was a major obstacle to growth. Although the legislation enacted was less radical and generous than originally proposed, it complied with Lemass's view that a minimum income should be available for the genuinely unemployed. This raised the real basic income of a minority of the urban labour force and small farmers. It also meant that more money was circulating among those with a propensity to consume, rather than save. This should, in theory, boost consumption of Irish goods in a closed economy. Additionally the employment which subsequently became available in the new industries, and as a result of the building programme, further enhanced this approach.[18]

Notwithstanding Lemass's failure to redirect policy in a radical way at this early stage, many of his policy initiatives were successful. His major successes were in the detailed reorganisation of the economy. His impact was almost immediate, and policy implementation occurred with impressive speed: initiatives which had been under consideration by the Department prior to 1932 were quickly implemented. There had been sustained opposition to proposals to impose tariffs on wheat and flour. In 1929, the economic committee of the Cabinet had broken up acrimoniously on the issue, while the Tariff Commission rejected all submissions in this area. Even before they came to power, market forces were making the Fianna Fáil case for them. McGilligan feared that Irish and British millers were colluding to ensure dominance of the Irish market. Moreover, the British millers Ranks were poised to gain control of the Irish market. Despite Lemass urging a radical change in policy McGilligan was not prepared to act precipitately.[19]

One of the early acts of the Fianna Fáil administration was to initiate discussions on the wheat industry. Fianna Fáil had promised to control the industry in the interests of the Irish people. They were following a precedent established by Germany, France, and Italy, each of whom had imposed or raised import duty on wheat. The main consideration in both the Irish and the Italian cases appears to have been self-sufficiency rather than efficiency.[20] Following the circulation of proposals to reorganise the industry, Industry and Commerce held a meeting with J.V. Rank to discuss the future of that company in Ireland. The Cabinet subsequently agreed that if no Irish group was prepared to buy out Ranks then they would be allowed to continue but not to expand their operations. The government also decided to reserve the right to acquire Rank's interests in the state at a future date. The intention of the government was, then, to prevent further investment by foreign companies, control existing industry, and promote Irish firms in their place.[21]

The reorganisation of the mills was the second stage of Lemass's strategy. Control over milling rested with the Minister who was empowered to issue licences to those engaged in production. No mill could operate without a licence, while foreign-owned companies would be subject to certain conditions. To facilitate the expansion of the industry, import duties were imposed on flour and bread. Subsidies would also be provided for Irish millers, whose output would be strictly regulated. Fines would be imposed if quotas were breached. In a full year, it was estimated that £40,000 would be paid in subsidies.[22] Without this direct intervention, it is unlikely that the Irish milling industry could have survived. Only by instituting a legislative framework for the industry was Lemass able to secure his objectives. The Bakers Union complained that Irish wheat was more difficult to use than the imported variety. Clearly, if left to the market, Irish wheat would not have been used. The regulation of the industry had other consequences. Wage rates increased after 1932. It was also estimated that some 25 per cent of the existing firms would go out of business if output was not regulated. This indicated that there was considerable over-production, a point which Lemass had frequently rejected in the past.[23]

Political change was clearly decisive in the case of flour milling; this was also the case with the cement industry. The circumstances differed however. In the case of flour the industry was already established; government action was used to protect it. The manufacture of cement was not well established in the Free state, and consequently it had to be promoted as part of a developmental strategy. Lemass would not have dissented from the departmental memorandum on cement circulated in 1931.

> In recent years there have been few countries of any industrial importance which have not developed the home manufacture of cement to such a point that the greater part of the requirements of the domestic market has been met from domestic sources. The raw materials of cement are found in abundance in almost every country ... and its production yields opportunities for considerable employment. The result has been to create a universal effort to secure national self-sufficiency in its manufacture.[24]

The main difficulty facing Ireland was the technical nature of the process. Lack of experience and a shortage of capital had prevented the growth of the industry. McGilligan had been prepared to offer monopoly control of the market to a company establishing production in the state.[25] The Department eventually accepted a proposal from a Belgian company, but Cabinet reluctance to proceed and strong Finance opposition neutralised any advance prior to 1932.[26]

It was again the change of circumstances which allowed Industry and Commerce to act. In a secret memorandum for the Cabinet, Lemass outlined the Department's proposals and the conditions which would be imposed. No Irish scheme proved acceptable and it was assumed that a foreign company would be granted an effective monopoly. In the event, Industry and Commerce could not proceed as quickly as had been hoped, as the Attorney General advised that comprehensive legislation would be required in advance. The Cement Act 1933 was framed to give the Minister effective control over the importation of cement. The Act was to be used as an instrument to regulate the circumstances for all cement production in Ireland. In addition to this, the profits of the company would be controlled. Leydon believed that anything above an average of 10 per cent per annum would be considered excessive. Satisfactory arrangements were not agreed until 1936, when a licence to manufacture cement was issued.[27] The contrast between McGilligan and Lemass is clear: McGilligan had been in a weak institutional position to promote legislation; Lemass had a clear set of policies, and although flexible in application, he was not prepared to compromise on essentials.

There were, of course, certain limits on the policy of inviting individual companies to fulfill developmental projects which Irish industrialists were unable to promote. Lemass's strength included his political control over the economy. Access to that economy by outsiders was dependent on his good will. There were also certain weaknesses. The government could not simply demand that a company comply with its conditions, if these were perceived as onerous by that company. There was a trade-off between Industry and Commerce and the incoming company. A certain degree of compromise proved necessary, with the final outcome involving gains to both, but perhaps not the victory of one side or the other. The Dunlop Company had little interest in establishing a rubber plant in Ireland and prior to 1932 it had supplied the country from Britain. The control exercised over imports by Lemass restricted this approach. The Department applied further pressure by circulating four major rubber producers, including Dunlop, inviting proposals to locate in Ireland. Given the existing international economic conditions, each of the companies had an interest in gaining control of the Irish market, even though it still was quite small. The Department's preference was for Dunlop to establish the company. However, it was only when Industry and Commerce threatened to give the monopoly of the tyre market to another company that Dunlop agreed to set up an Irish subsidiary with a specific Irish identity and capital. The terms on price, quality, and output were agreed between Industry and Commerce and the company; in addition the Department agreed to use its control mechanism to exclude competition. Industry and Commerce was less successful on the question of a location for the plant. A western location or Waterford had been desired by the Department, but Dunlop insisted on and eventually located in Cork. The government's decision was finally based on the consideration that a large company with 600-700 employees would be located in Ireland, and that it would provide most of the requirements for the Irish market.[28]

In each of these cases, specific responses were designed within a policy framework, the objective of which was to develop an indigenous industrial base. Each industry had its peculiarities, and therefore it proved necessary to adopt specific structures for each. In the case of cement and rubber, Industry and Commerce had to promote the industries, creating the institutional conditions for their foundation. The 'infant-industry' model may be utilised here. For wheat, a somewhat different situation brought about government intervention. This industry was threatened with 'exit' by consumers if competition continued, but the industry induced 'voice' to demand government support. The response of industry conformed with Fianna Fáil policy, and therefore the possibility of exit was restricted by the removal of choice.[29]

The most dramatic feature of economic policy during the 1930s involved the active use of state agencies to carry out Fianna Fáil policy. Lemass quickly imprinted his economic nationalist ethos on the Department and on other agencies with which he was in contact. In promoting industries such as cement and rubber, he was following what he considered to be a strategy of national industrialisation. In the case of insurance, he provided the conditions for the reorganisation of the sector along national lines. Industry and Commerce utilised the armoury of state socialism to generate conditions for the expansion of capitalist industry. In doing so, they were self-consciously expanding the areas where state intervention was permissible. This movement from passive to active involvement reflects the belief that only through active pressure could changes in the economic structure be brought about. The fate of the Tariff Commission illustrates the change of emphasis. When Fianna Fáil entered government, the Commission was still functioning, and there were a number of applications pending. The Commission continued to submit its reports to the government, but policy changes increasingly questioned the effectiveness or continued viability of that body. Administrative decisions under the new legislation were frequently used to obviate the need to deal with Tariff Commission reports. By 1934 the Commission had lost its *raison d'être*, and no further referrals were made. In 1938 the Department of Finance recommended the abolition of the Commission, in part because it had no applications and in part because the Prices Commission, as constituted in that year, took over its basic functions. In contrast to the Tariff Commission, the Prices Commission was set up with specific functions within an institutional environment with a bias in favour of tariffs. In his evidence to the Banking Commission, John Leydon emphasised that the Department explicitly rejected the cautious and consultative approach of the Tariff Commission.[30]

The institutional bias in favour of protection becomes clear from the behaviour of Industry and Commerce. Given the legislative power to promote industry actively, it proceeded to develop strong, if limited, corporate links with the new Irish industrialists. Although Irish industrialists did not acquire a veto over policy, they did receive significant rights of access and consultation.[31] In real terms, it marked a radical change in policy. After 1932 the state was no longer passive in its approach to industrial policy. The state, through Industry and Commerce, played a decisive role in the implementation of industrial policy. A protectionist bias was supplemented by a corporate bias on the part of the Department.

The objectives of industrial policy were determined by the government, and legislation was framed to direct the native industrialists, not always successfully, in a specific direction. This directive role for the state operated at a number of levels. At the level of the national economy, it provided a defensive framework in legislative form to protect the Irish market from competition.

Within the economy, it provided for the control of most companies by Irish nationals.[32] This legislation removed the obstacles to industrial growth, and provided opportunities for investment. They could not guarantee that investment and expansion would occur. This depended on individual decisions taken by potential entrepreneurs. This, essentially micro-economic, level of activity is notoriously difficult to influence by macro-economic policy. In particular, a process that might be of benefit to one sector or industry could be a disincentive to another. The unpredictability of behaviour is crucial to this outcome.

In May 1932 the government approved the establishment of an Industrial Development Branch within Industry and Commerce. This branch was to deal exclusively with the establishment of new industry, the expansion of existing concerns, and the administration of the Trade Loans (Guarantee) Acts.[33] The latter Act was amended in 1933 to make the loans more accessible to small companies. The Act had hitherto been administered very stringently; the amendment, for example, removed the obligation of the applicant to be a limited liability company before seeking a loan. The amended Act was designed to offset disadvantages inherent in the Irish industrial system which prevented growth and investment. There was, according to the Department, a body of potential investors who though willing to invest, were unable to gain access to the banking or other parts of the financial system. The Act now broadened the criteria available for applications, recognising that the size of a new company, its location, and social consideratins often restricted the availibility of private capital to them.[34] These considerations were supplemented by guaranteeing loans for working capital, whereas formerly the guarantee was only given for plant and machinery. The Department believed that the availability of a guarantee for working capital would secure the continued operation of a large number of concerns which would otherwise face liquidation. The changes in 1933 stimulated an increased volume of applications. Between 1924 and 1934, there were forty-eight applications; thirty of these were placed between 1932 and 1934. The main consideration of the Act was employment creation and protection, but in its 1933 form it also provided relatively easy access to capital for those marginal producers who could not offer security to the banks. The Act circumvented the normal criteria for loans applied by the financial institutions, and supplemented the resources available to the individual to permit him to operate.[35]

Within the new economic framework, there remained considerable obstacles to promoting development. The traditional financial institutions did not cooperate with the government to facilitate the expansion of industrial credit. The interests of finance and industry were at variance throughout the protectionist period. The course of development would, it was believed, induce certain structural strains, particularly inflationary pressures, to which the financial sector objected. This is not to claim that expansion of the money supply or accelerating public expenditure is per se justifiable, but that industrialisers have traditionally maintained that these costs were, in the short run, justifiable.[36] Lemass believed that certain costs had to be absorbed if industrial advance was to occur, otherwise little would be achieved.[37] This view is also reflected in the Department's policy towards the availability of credit for industrialists. It accepted that there was considerable risk involved in making soft loans available, but believed that industrial, rather than financial, considerations should prevail. To promote development, therefore, the financial institutions had to be redirected. If this proved impossible, as was the case, then the state had to intervene directly.

Lemass proposed in November 1932 that the government should establish a state bank and an Industrial Credit Organisation.[38] The proposal to provide state-aided industrial credit was accepted by the Cabinet. The original stimulus for this came from the Chairman of the Agricultural Credit Corporation who, in a memorandum to Industry and Commerce, pointed out that industrial credit was not readily available, and as a consequence, new industrial projects were not undertaken in the state. This credit could only, Colbert maintained, be provided outside the banking system, because the banks were not willing to do so. A state agency would be required to carry on the work, and it should have a monopoly if its objectives were to be achieved efficiently. Colbert noted that there were certain difficulties specific to Ireland. Appeals to the public by prospectus were inadvisable because the Irish industrial unit was small and the amount of capital required was also small. Issues had to compete with those in Britain, while the Dublin Stock Exchange did not provide the basis for industrial capital.[39]

Colbert suggested that the functions of the Agricultural Credit Corporation be expanded to include the provision of industrial credit. Despite objections from McElligott, the Cabinet appointed a committee to examine the question.[40] The Cabinet accepted the committee's recommendation that an Industrial Credit Company be established. The company was to be state-supported, and would underwrite the ordinary and preference shares of industrial companies. The Cabinet rejected Lemass's proposal that the new body should also finance industry itself where necessary. This decision restricted the scope of the legislation, and may have prevented a more flexible approach to the financing of large-scale industrial development.[41]

The creation of the ICC and the expansion of the trade loans had both a direct and indirect impact on industry. Decisions by industrialists were affected directly because credit was more readily available. More indirectly, the modifications of the fiscal system indicated that there was a governmental bias in favour of industrial investment. In 1932, £6,000 was raised for industrial and general investment through public issue; by 1935 over £3.5 million had been raised in this fashion. Moreover, private institutions and individuals repatriated over £5 million previously held in external assets. It is unlikely that all this was reinvested in new industrial projects. Given the income tax relief for investment in nationally-owned public companies, and the high yield on industrial issues, it is possible to conclude that a considerable proportion of this capital did enter the new industries. Another feature of this process involved Irish nationals acquiring control of foreign companies. Industry and Commerce estimated that nearly £2 million of Irish capital was exported as a consequence of these acquisitions.[42] This point can be reinforced in another way. Over 1,000 new companies were registered as joint stock companies under the meaning of the Companies Acts between 1932 and 1938. The majority of these were private rather than public companies. The extent of investment in private companies is not easily ascertainable. John Leydon, in his evidence before the Banking Commission, believed that there had been a considerable amount of investment in private concerns, but was unable to quantify it. The Department also sought to maintain and expand a thriving capital market in Dublin; though its success, it was admitted, was due to the specific involvement of the Department.[43]

The Joint Stock Banks had claimed in evidence to the Banking Commission and elsewhere, that there was no shortage of capital in the Free state. This was true, but it was the nature and direction of that capital that was in question. Without incentives from the government, little of it would have found its way into industry. Although the ACC and the ICC operated along commercial lines, they also had to engage in investment of a social nature. The criteria, though narrowly defined, emphasised the need to invest in agriculture or industry. One of the obstacles to investment was the reluctance of farmers to invest either in their farms or elsewhere. The ACC believed that money was frequently retained by the farmers for non-economic activity. The ICC defined its role carefully, and in this they appear to reflect the views of Industry and Commerce:

> We are not prepared to underwrite any industrial project which is either not a sound financial proposition for the investor or is such a proposition as requires the assistance of an exceptional tariff on the consumer. If it is not economic from that point of view, we reject it.[44]

The ICC also played a crucial role in ensuring that a prospective company flotation would be successful. In underwriting a company, the ICC virtually guaranteed its success. Leading industrialists, in particular FIM leader J.J. Walsh, criticised the company for refusing to support the floatation of certain companies, which were subsequently successfully floated privately. The ICC rejected this criticism. What was involved appears to have been the level of interference by the ICC in the propositions. In the case of Clondalkin Paper Mills, the ICC had received two proposals to establish a paper factory. It recommended that the proposals should be amalgamated and a joint approach made. This proved unsatisfactory to both sets of promoters, who then withdrew their applications. In the event, one of the promoters successfully floated the Clondalkin Paper Mills. This draws attention to the limits of the government's micro-economic strategy: in the case of the ICC and the trade loans, a macro-economic policy was designed to be applied at the factory or individual level. The discretionary nature of the legislation meant that certain criteria had to be fulfilled. In the case of Clondalkin, certain conditions were imposed when the ICC declared 'if you want a paper industry here that is the way we think it should be done'. There is a further implication to be drawn from this and similar cases; a number of concerns were successfully floated without support by the ICC. This implies that the presence of the ICC, even without recourse to it, permitted others to attract capital for their enterprises.[45] It furthermore implies that many investors now believed that there was adequate security for industrial investment, security previously not available. This indirect effect is not quantifiable at the micro-economic level, but in any assessment it must have an important place.

Up to 1938 industrial policy was structured in such a way as to curtail imports which could be substituted in the state. This was successful, particularly as the economic war allowed the government to give its industrial policy a patriotic hue. Between 1932 and 1937 there was a close relationship between the granting of tariffs and the elimination of imports. Domestic consumption remained relatively stable for most commodities, but domestic production was considerably enhanced. The consequence of the tariff regime for wheat flour, probably the most controversial tariff, illustrates this point. In 1929 home production accounted for 57 per cent of total consumption, by 1935 this had increased to 97 per cent, and as a consequence between 1931 and 1936, thirty-three new grain milling concerns were established. The main impact of protection by 1939 was to stimulate a considerable degree of import substitution which promoted self-sufficiency on a relatively large scale. By reducing imports, there was a transfer of wealth and profits to Ireland. The benefits were shared by the industrialists and the newly employed workers. Furthermore, although it is difficult to quantify, industrial expansion facilitated a learning experience within the factory system which would not have been otherwise possible.[46]

A number of different, but compatible, strategies were pursued. The simplest involved the imposition of duties on imports. This increased the price for a commodity and permitted Irish producers to compete. The first duties were imposed in August 1932 on British coal. This was a specific response to the economic war. Other duties reflected a determination to protect the home market.[47] At a more complex level, the Control of Manufactures Acts were utilised to control the presence of non-Irish companies in the Irish economy. Foreign firms had to comply with strict criteria before receiving permission to locate in the state. The obstacles were not insurmountable, as department officials recognised that foreign companies might be of benefit to the economy. Decisions were taken on an individual basis, having assessed the readiness of Irish nationals to provide the particular commodity. The restrictions were clear. In 1933, a Scottish company proposed to set up a company to manufacture 'instantor coupling', a product it had previously exported to the country. Their proposal was a clear attempt to avoid exclusion from the market. The Department refused to support the scheme, as a Cork company had been given guarantees by the Minister and was already producing a similar item. Although the Cork company believed there was room for only one such producer in the state, the Scottish company did locate in Dublin and claimed to be producing the product at prices which had prevailed prior to the imposition of duties. The inducement effect of the Acts can further be demonstrated by the decision of British United Shoe Machines (BUSM), which notified the Department in 1934 that they intended upgrading and expanding their depot in the state due to the changed circumstances.[48]

Frequently, the tariff level had to be quite high before Irish companies would expand into specific areas. In the case of knitting fabric made from artificial silk, the Department entered into negotiations with a British company to produce it. It was proposed to award the company an effective monopoly to ensure that an industry would be established. Irish companies in related industries complained about this approach, and guaranteed that if a tariff was imposed they would produce all that was required. Protection was, thus, an essential stimulus for the emergence of many industries.[49] The level of production considered 'adequate' was an essential factor in determining the future development of Irish industry. The 1938 trade agreement with Britain imposed certain conditions on the Irish government, and in particular obliged it to grant specific import concessions to British manufacturers. Following the agreement, a number of industrial sectors complained that the new tariff levels prevented their expansion. The construction steel manufacturers complained that there had been a reduction in the basic tariff from 75 per cent to 37.5 per cent, while the preferences for British manufacturers had been reduced from 50 per cent to 25 per cent. This margin was considered inadequate to sustain the profitability of the Irish industry. The limited market was another restriction. The Irish Aluminium Company, Nenagh, believed that the Irish market for its products had become saturated and further development could only occur if the company expanded its range of goods for the Irish market.[50]

The policy of Industry and Commerce throughout the 1930s was relatively permissive in relation to the new industrialists. A large degree of flexibility was allowed to the manufacturers in order that '... the main object of promoting employment and absorbing as many as possible of the unemployed into gainful occupations was, to a large extent, achieved.' The factors determining departmental considerations also facilitated a considerable degree of flexibility:

> It was only necessary to ensure that the home market was large enough to absorb the total production of the new factory and to decide if there was room for further expansion. The great majority of the new industries were based on supplying the home market and not on an export trade ... the Department did not approve a new industry if the existing productive capacity of the country was already sufficient to meet the requirements of the home market. In other words it was government policy to prevent, where practicable, an increase in productive capacity above home requirements to such an extent as would injure the legitimate interests of existing enterprises.[51]

These new industries were further secured by an unstated departmental policy to support all but the most inefficient in their operation; 'there would be very strong resistance to any policy of wiping out industries once they are firmly established.' In effect, both politics and national economic interest conspired to stabilise industrial expansion within the Irish market. The Department received complaints from time to time concerning the competitive advantage of one company over another. The successful penetration of the printing ink market by Punch & Co., Cork, led to complaints that this had been achieved unfairly and that as a consequence, employment in the existing firms would suffer.[52]

It is possible that the cultivation of a positive environment for industry will not have the consequences for which the government aimed. The institutional arrangements for the promotion of industry were radically changed between 1932 and

1936. Any investor would be aware of these changes, and could thus make a rational choice. Consequently, government intervention in industry and agriculture served as a stimulus to economic activity, which under other conditions might not have been undertaken.[53] Between 1931 and 1938, the number of firms included in the Census of Industrial Production increased from 3,209 to 4,296. There was, however, no guarantee that this industrial spurt would continue. The most rapid phase of expansion was between 1932 and 1936; thereafter the process decelerated. Between 1929 and 1938 there was a 41 per cent increase in the number of industrial concerns. The annual rate of expansion differed considerably: between 1929 and 1931 the rate was 2.5 per cent; between 1931 and 1936 the rate was 5.68 per cent; between 1936 and 1938 the rate was 2 per cent. In effect, by 1938 the first stimulus for industrialisation had worked through the economy, while the rate of expansion thereafter was slower than that of the pre-protectionist years, 1929–31. Despite protection, the number of new firms enumerated by the Census between 1936 and 1938 was only slightly higher than the two years immediately prior to these major policy changes. The growth of new firms is concentrated between 1932 and 1936.[54]

A willingness to impose protection provided the basic conditions for industrial expansion, but did not ensure the creation of a dynamic sector with self-sustained growth. Leydon believed as early as 1935 that though industry had expanded rapidly, a point would come – and he implied that this would occur shortly – when 'we will have established all the new industries which will have to be established. . . .' He noted, furthermore, that any new capital required thereafter, would be for replacements and in smaller quantities.[55] This sense of equilibrium is confirmed by the employment figures in those industries expressly awarded tariffs. In numerical terms, the peak had been reached by 1937; the 1938 recession was accompanied by a loss of some 2,000 in the labour force. By September 1939 these losses had been made up, and further expansion had occurred. By this date protected industry accounted for around 50 per cent of industrial employment. Approximately 51,000 new jobs had been created as a result of protection, although the apparel sector accounted for nearly 39 per cent of this increase. This does not suggest that further expansion was impossible, only that the first and easiest phase was probably over by this date.

Table 4.1 Employment in Specific Industries, pre-tariff compared with September 1939

Industry		Full time employment immediately prior to date of Tariff*	Employment at September 1939
1.	Food,Drink and Tobacco	10,070	17,665
2.	Textiles	3,495	7,791
3.	Apparel	2,038	21,820
4.	Leather	805	8,759
5.	Manufactures of Wood	261	1,119
6.	Metal Manufactures and Machinery	1,152	2,056
7.	Iron and Steel	2,398	4,813
8.	Assembly and Construction of Vehicles and Parts	375	3,251
9.	Chemicles, Fats, Oils and Fertilisers	1,719	3,083
10.	Paper and Printing	4,471	7,067
11.	Building Materials, Clay and Concrete Products	1,202	3,154
12.	Miscellaneous Industries	1,262	3,407
	Total	31,386	82,433

* Tariffs were imposed at various dates between 1924 and 1937.
Source: SPO Employment in Protected Industries, S.11219A.

Table 4.1 outlines employment at the date of imposition of the tariff and at September 1939. The rate of growth in employment tended to decelerate after 1937. The most substantial increase after that date occurs in the textile industry, and this is attributed by the Department to the establishment of two large companies: Salts in Tullamore and the Spinning Company, Ltd. at Blackpool in Cork. The continued expansion in building is attributable to the government's housing programme. It can be concluded from this that after 1937 industrial progress became more difficult. The fall-off in the number of new apprentices and learners after 1937 may be attributed to this slowdown. Industry was now absorbing the 1932 to 1936 intake, but without further expansion industry was unlikely to train any further new workers.[56]

From the vantage point of 1946, one of Lemass's admirers concluded that protectionism had been a success. This was a view echoed by many Fianna Fáil supporters. Others have been less sure. It is sometimes maintained that certain losses occurred: while these might have been inevitable, the benefits were not clearcut and in particular did not generate sustained growth after 1945. As early as 1943, James Meenan raised serious objections to Fianna Fáil's policies: objections he reiterated throughout his academic career.[57] To some extent, an evaluation of the 1930s has to be based on how much weight one gives to the costs or benefits of protection. It is unlikely that a commercial farmer would reflect favourably on the policies, while a businessman receiving protection or a Dublin worker might. Evaluation can be more objectively grounded on the benefits, or otherwise, that a policy contributes to the national economy. Patrick McGilligan believed that protection had not made a significant contribution to employment; indeed he suggested that the rate of employment increase had been higher between 1926 and 1931 than it had between 1931 and 1938.[58] As McGilligan does not make clear what his data are based on, it is difficult to form a firm conclusion. It has traditionally been assumed that employment rose quite quickly during the 1930s.

In a recent careful review of the literature, David Johnson has raised two objections to protectionist policy. The first concerns inflationary tendencies. That prices increased is without question; what is in question is whether price increases can be considered objectionable in themselves. There can be no principled objection to price increases if they conferred benefits on the society at large. In the case of a protected economy, such as Ireland at this time, these tendencies can effect a redistribution to the non-propertied classes. The 10 per cent price rise over free trade levels was the cost of more employment, welfare benefits, and new housing. Only a strict neo-classical economist could conclude that no benefits were forthcoming.[59]

A more serious objection is that much of the employment

increase was illusory: a result of changes in how the Census of Industrial Production was enumerated over the years. Following Fitzgerald's earlier study, Johnson suggests that 'the true rise between 1926 and 1936 was not 51,000 as the Census of Production would indicate but nearer 9,000.'[60] If accurate, this means that the industrial sector produced only an extra 900 jobs per annum. However, is this a statistical sleight of hand or is there substance to the claims made by Fianna Fáil and reflected in the Census? It may be conceded at the outset that Fitzgerald's point is important. The statistical skills at the disposal of Industry and Commerce were improving over time; consequently the Census was probably becoming more accurate and detailed. Even allowing for this discrepancy, there is evidence within the Department which upholds the general trends in the Census, if not the specific figures. As noted in Table 4.1, the Department concluded that some 51,000 jobs had been created by tariffs between 1922 and 1939. The most vigorous use of protection occurred after 1932, when nearly 2,000 items were protected in one form or another.[61] The Department estimated that some 10,000 new jobs had been created between 1922 and 1927, subsequent to the imposition of limited protection.

A more restricted analysis in 1931 concluded that the number employed in selected protected industries had more than doubled. If at least 10,000 new jobs were created between 1922 and 1931 in protected industry, the figure for 1932 to 1939 is remarkably close to that in the Census. It would appear that the Department drew a clear distinction between the total number of new firms coming into operation, and those whose origin they attributed to tariffs. It was estimated in 1931 that forty new firms could be designated in this way, while the Census gives a figure of 153.[62] Between 1931 and 1938, 1,088 extra establishments are included in the Census. If Fitzgerald and Johnson are correct, then the majority of these are not new but are simply included for the first time. The Census enumerator concedes that a number of small concerns (usually single proprietor with few if any employees) were not included in the 1926 Census. It is possible that some 70,000 individuals were excluded in this way. These very small concerns could have grown as a result of protection, and are only included in 1936 because their increased size allowed the Census to identify them. Undoubtedly, some were included in the 1936 Census, but the category where one might

PROPERTY OF
ST. MARY'S COLLEGE
STRAWBERRY HILL

expect to locate them, establishments with less than ten employees, expanded quite slowly between 1931 and 1936. There was approximately a 17 per cent expansion in the number of establishments in this category, while there was a 41 per cent increase in those employing ten to nineteen and 35 per cent increase in those employing twenty to forty-nine.[63] It is most likely that the Census was more accurately identifying the real number of concerns employing more than ten and, as one would expect, the largest volume of net output is concentrated in this sector.

It is possible to advance all these reservations while accepting the thrust of the criticism. Alternatively, the figure for the number of new establishments approximates very closely to one calculated from Industry and Commerce's statistical data. These data were collected in 1947 for the Department of the Taoiseach. They supplement the Census in that they list by county all industries established after 1932, adding the number employed and identifying firms employing twenty or more workers. Insofar as it has been possible to identify individual firms, most of them were established prior to 1939. The total number of firms identified is 1,091, and these employed approximately 40,000 workers. This figure is very close to the 1936 Census total. If the figure for 1922–31 is included, then the figure contained in Table 4.1 is reached. The reliability of the data might be questioned, but it can be urged that the collection of these data arose from a very specific requirement, and that the Department had made a practice of keeping specific details of industries and companies which received protection. Consequently, Industry and Commerce was in a strong position to reliably identify the extent of industrial expansion. It is probable that the Census figure slightly over-estimated the extent of expansion, but the real figure is considerably in excess of that suggested by Johnson. Furthermore, the data do not confirm the view that building and construction constituted 'a considerable proportion of this increase'. Of the firms included, building and construction accounted for 23 per cent of the total (254). This appears impressive until the level of employment is examined: these firms only account for 8.6 per cent of the total increase in employment. Moreover, the vast majority are small, some having only one or two employees.[64]

Despite the particular difficulties which Ireland faced during the 1930s, industrial expansion was impressive. Although clearly not comparable in scope to the Second Five Year Plan in the Soviet Union, as Johnson points out, the outcome was far more successful than is sometimes thought. Indeed, the real cost of industrialisation in Ireland was considerably less than that experienced in the Soviet Union.[65] It is important to stress that no attempt has been made here to assess who were attracted to the industrial factories: what has been stressed is that protection as an industrial strategy induced considerable growth in the Irish economy, which would not have occurred otherwise. The long-term economic effects of protection might be more doubtful, but this should not obscure the successes during the 1930s. Protection did not substantially reduce unemployment, but it did prevent it from rising higher. It also protected the Irish market for Irish producers, thus creating employment. Without a strict tariff regime, Ireland would have been overwhelmed with industrial imports, particularly from Britain. Additionally, while self-sufficiency was not achieved, the composition of imports changed. Increasingly, imports concentrated on commodities which Ireland could not produce: raw materials or semi manufactured goods for final processing. The first phase of protection is usually characterised by import substitution. Further phases are possible, but not inevitable, as Lemass discovered.

There were certain limits to the further development of simple import substitution. This limit may have been encountered by 1937. Nor is it surprising that this should be the case. Import substitution has certain limits: the extent of the home market. The Free state was not a poor country, but its population was small and its purchasing power limited. Fianna Fáil's welfare policy and increased employment probably allowed an initial expansion of the internal market. Without a dramatic rise in the real purchasing power of the agricultural sector, there were severe constraints on that market. Leydon believed that a time would come when all the industries that could be established would have been. Although he did not put a time limit on this, he assumed that the new industries would not make a contribution to the export trade in the near future. The Department does not seem to have given serious consideration to future developments at this time. There may have been some hope that exports could begin in the future, or that industries providing linkages to the new industries could be promoted.[66] There is some evidence that the imposition of protection, while accelerating production, reduced the volume of exports for existing exporting concerns. The Greenmount and Boyne Linen Company had exported 70 per cent of its output prior to 1932. Following the imposition of protection, it was able to expand its production, but by the end of the 1930s its exports constituted 25 per cent of its output.[67] In a captive market, the producer had little incentive to explore new markets or to introduce new methods of production which would enhance efficiency and competition.

In effect, the industrialists, in common with other producers in Irish society, wished to stabilise production at levels deemed appropriate for their economic security. The Department was influenced by this search for security. Although it always refused to give formal commitments to any concern that protection would be indefinite, the government proved to be reluctant to revise tariffs downwards, because of protests from industrialists. It was hoped to use tariffs to exert pressure on industrialists to comply with the Department's strategy. The reality was quite different. In theory, at least, tariffs provided a wall behind which Irish industry could prepare for competition once trading conditions were suitable. The logic of this position necessitated a change in policy once full capacity had been attained. Whatever the Minister might have believed, and it is probable that he thought this was the best course to follow, he was never able to do it prior to 1939.

The protectionist era has generally been received unsympathetically by economists, historians and politicians. Johnson has concluded that, despite some progress, overall economic performance in both parts of Ireland was poor: 'In the Free state, particularly in the stagnant 1930s, the government must receive part of the blame for this.'[68] Equally, Cullen compares the protectionist period unfavourably with the decade preceding it and that which followed.[69] Meenan's major study of the Irish economy since 1922 reviewed the protectionist era carefully and, while noting a number of achievements, his conclusions are also fairly negative.[70] Finally, Crotty's more radical assesment advances the view that protectionism was in essence a conspiracy against both the consumer and the 'surplus' population which emigrated.[71] At the very least, even the most sympathetic analysis of the 1930s concludes that the success was only partial and that most of the economic objectives were not achieved. What is not assessed is why this was so and what were the circumstances which prevented growth.

Between 1932 and 1938 some major blockages to industrial development had been removed. The political commitment to industrial protection and tillage, the economic war with Britain, and the general internal situation in 1932 permitted a greater flexibility than heretofore in policy making. The changed nature of state intervention was crucial to the success of the policy initiatives during the 1930s. Without an activist state it is unlikely that development would have been as significant as was the case. While the obstacles to growth which existed in 1932 were weakened, they did not disappear. The Department of Finance never accepted the protectionist position and, though its influence had been weakened between 1932 and 1936, it retained considerable power and authority. Institutionally the balance of power moved against Finance but its importance remained largely intact. This is also true in the case of the export economy and the graziers who gained most from trade with Britain. Though economically powerful, the graziers were unable to mobilise the political resources to reverse either the tillage programme or the economic war. Moreover, even within the general opposition to Fianna Fáil, the grazier sector was unrepresentative, as can be seen from the failure of the Blueshirt movement or the more strictly economic opposition expressed in the refusal of the large farmers to pay rates.[72]

Despite the weakening of power blocs opposed to protectionism, other obstacles to economic growth existed. The Department of Industry and Commerce remained the only major dynamic force attempting to promote change in the economy. Moreover, while circumstances worked in Industry and Commerce's favour up to 1936, thereafter the situation was more uncertain. Political issues defined the limits of policy. Once the economic war continued, protection could be given a patriotic flavour and remain relatively immune from criticism. De Valera's primary concern was his interpretation of sovereignty; all economic issues were subordinated to that consideration. However, when relations improved with Britain and the possibility of an agreement on outstanding issues arose, Lemass's strategic position was in danger of being weakened.[73] The nature of Industry and Commerce's developmental programme was such that the consequences of further changes after 1936 would have brought it into conflict with other groups in the society.

Ireland had not become an industrial society by 1937, nor had the industrial sector become a dominant dynamic force. Further progress implied deeper state involvement. Yet agriculture remained the main economic sector in terms of employment, exports, and output. In social terms agriculture continued to influence the political culture far more than industry or even urbanisation. The Coal-Cattle pacts had re-established a basis for stabilising the cattle trade, and this was to be reinforced by the 1938 Trade Agreement. Even prior to the 1938 agreement the Minister for Finance, Sean MacEntee, circulated a memorandum based on notes prepared by McElligott which questioned the soundness of government policy. MacEntee was concerned at the fiscal consequences of the fall in exports even though demand in Britain was rising. The memorandum criticised virtually every element of government policy and particularly those most closely associated with Lemass. Ireland's difficulties were attributed by MacEntee to a range of policies which included increased state expenditure on 'non-economic' and 'uneconomic' projects, an urban bias, and the neglect of exports.[74]

Finance essentially recommended a return to the status quo ante, a return which would have involved concentrating resources once again on the export of cattle to the British market, a minimalist state, and close control over expenditure. Finance's challenge came at a crucial moment in Irish policy making. The new constitution had been enacted in 1937, discussions were under way which would lead to a trade agreement with Britain, and perhaps most importantly Industry and Commerce did not have a set of clear objectives which could be placed in opposition to those of Finance. It also appears that Industry and Commerce had come to share many of the assumptions which shaped Finance's thinking. The Department accepted that agriculture would remain the backbone of the export trade, that Irish assets held abroad would continue to help the balance of payments, and that the monetary link with sterling would remain.[75] These assumptions constrained the Department in pursuing a more active and interventionist policy. For these reasons alone, the expansion achieved by 1937 would be limited by the need to maintain the more traditional elements of government policy. It may have been possible to move in a more radical direction, but departmental assumptions prevented this, as did electoral considerations. However, the problem was deeper than this. The nature of the Irish industrial bourgeoisie, its ability, and the environment within which the entrepreneur operated conjoined by the end of the 1930s to obstruct further rapid expansion.

Contrasting policy responses can illustrate the differences between institutions even when self-sufficiency remained the general goal. Lemass wished to continue industrial expansion, while the industrialists wished to maintain profitability by excluding all pressure on their earnings. Lemass informed the President of the Federation of Irish Industries in August 1937 that he wished to initiate the second phase of his industrial policy. This involved investment in the raw materials and semi-manufacturing sectors, until then largely catered for by imports. Lemass recognised the lack of enthusiasm among industrialists for this policy, as it would involve breaking their existing arrangements for importing these materials. He therefore approached the Federation in an attempt to gain support in advance of any public statement. The main initial objection of the Federation was on the question of cost. Whereas the industrialists demanded unrestricted tariffs for their products, they now suggested caution in deepening the industrial process.

The reasoning behind this was clear. If raw materials and semi-manufactured goods were produced indigenously, then Irish industrialists would be obliged to purchase them. This would increase their costs, and affect their profit margins. The danger for the Federation was that it would appear anti-national if it opposed the proposals. Support, according to Walsh, should be forthcoming only if effective consultation between the Minister and the industries affected could be agreed. Although only implied, such an approach could easily amount to a veto on any further developments. Little had been achieved by 1940. Indeed during the sitting of the Commission on Vocational Organisation, Senator J.G. Douglas, Vice-President of the Federation, indicated that whatever merits an indigenous raw material and semi-manufacturing sector might have 'existing factories might feel that their present supply of raw materials and its source were quite satisfactory and that it was not desirable that it should be interfered with.'[76]

The industrial bourgeoisie has often been characterised as a revolutionary force in modern society. In Ireland they certainly did not fulfil these expectations. As a social stratum, they were insignificant prior to 1932. To describe them as entrepreneurs would be too strong, for they demanded effective and total protection from all external competition. They owed their position to the state, and rather than develop an industry capable of competition, they lobbied the state to reinforce this effective monopoly.[77] Their lack of dynamism is evident from the tension between the representatives of Irish industry and the Minister:

> Differences of opinion frequently arose between firms already engaged in industry and the Department as to whether there was room for new entrants in a particular line of manufacture. It was the interest of existing firms to restrict competition while it was the Minister's duty to see that there were ample supplies of all classes of goods and such competition as would safeguard, to whatever extent was possible, the consumer's interest in respect of both price and quality.[78]

Central to this was the conflict over whether foreign companies should be allowed to invest in the Free state. The Federation of Irish Industries strongly objected to any foreign company operating in the state. They protested to the Minister when he supported the establishment of Irish Ropes. They demanded that in future the Minister should consult them, and ensure that Irish nationals be given an opportunity to establish any new industry.[79] These concerns led to demands for a revision of the Control of Manufactures Act, 1932. British firms, the Federation maintained, were evading the Act, and there was considerable difficulty in prosecuting the offending concerns. In particular, a number of companies had either established subsidiaries in the country or had agents producing the products, and this was interfering with the progress of native industrialists. The obstacles to continued penetration were not enough, therefore more stringent methods had to be utilised. Accordingly, the Federation recommended that every manufacturer in Ireland should be registered with the Department and only allowed to operate under licence. Interestingly, the FII strongly recommended that the Department should adapt the United states Industrial Recovery Act, which was later to be declared unconstitutional by the American Supreme Court, to Irish conditions.[80]

The draconian recommendations of the FII did not prove acceptable to Lemass. The amendments contained in the 1934 Act met some of the industrialists' concerns, but reflected the broader appreciation of the Minister that a certain degree of flexibility would be necessary. The revised legislation did not meet the industrialists' objections in full. The Federation compiled evidence on companies they believed did not comply with the Acts, and urged the Department, not only to prosecute but legally to procure information from the companies to allow prosecution. Both suggestions were rejected. Leydon wrote that the industrialists had misinterpreted the Minister's powers under the Act and subsequently maintained that there was in fact no evidence to justify prosecution.[81]

By the end of 1930s, however, the industrialists continued to complain about foreign competition. The Federation insisted that Irish industry would find it difficult to continue production in the absence of high tariffs. They continued to insist that foreign companies should not be allowed to compete on equal terms in the Irish market with Irish companies. In the opinion of the industrialists, the Anglo-Irish Trade Agreement of 1938 placed them in an invidious competitive position. The reduction of the tariffs on textiles and the restriction of quotas severely limited the capacity and output of this industrial sector.[82]

The end of the economic war, the Anglo-Irish Trade Agreement, and the saturation of most Irish markets by Irish produced goods offered the first significant challenge to the new industrialists. The newly-elected President of the Federation, J.J.Walsh, captured their fears in January 1938 when he warned that certain industries would be threatened if tariffs were lowered. The evidence suggests that Irish industry was vitally dependent on the level of tariffs for survival. The response of the Federation in 1938 and later was to demand further protection from the state. In particular, Walsh demanded that further controls should be imposed on those firms located in Ireland, but externally controlled. He estimated that some 10 per cent of the major concerns in Ireland were under such control.[83] The Federation believed that Irish nationals should have control over all Irish industry whenever the industrial concerns were established. It proposed that all shares in foreign companies should be transferred to Irish nationals over a fifteen year period. However, Walsh realised that access to the Minister was an absolute priority if Irish industrialists were to achieve their objectives. He believed that they had not generated adequate pressure to achieve these ends:

> The Minister for Industry and Commerce did not think much of the Council, and rightly so, because we were acting like 'jellyfish'. The Minister could not hold out against public opinion in this matter. The passing and the publication of the resolution, he said, would be a good thing for the country. It was not right or just that the freedom for which much sacrifice and suffering was endured should be used for the benefit of aliens.[84]

Despite this, access to Lemass was limited and on terms dictated by him. He refused to extend the right of veto to the Federation over his policies. Although prepared to consult with them on specific issues, he frequently rejected their claims. According to Lemass, the fears concerning foreign penetration were unfounded.[85] Walsh appears to have been one of the few to recognise that Irish industry was completely dependent on the goodwill of the Minister. The industrial constituency was narrow, and without substantial political leverage. In a still predominantly agricultural economy, the concessions to industry were frequently criticised. If circumstances changed, or if the actions of industry did not contribute to achieving government policy, there was always a danger that the concessions might be withdrawn. The majority of industrialists did not appreciate that protection was not intended simply for their benefit. The primary reason for this was that Irish industrial expansion was the product of protection. The Irish industrialists were protectionist in outlook, looking to the government to maintain their profitability and their existence. After the initial spurt of industrialisation, which amounted to guaranteed profits for those involved, the industrial sector became increasingly stable. Even prior to the Second World War, Irish industry appeared to lack dynamism. Import substitution had been the easiest phase of the process, and for most industrialists the only one.

The response of the Federation was essentially defensive. Although not always apparent, the objectives of the state and the industrialists were not the same. The state sought to generate industrial development on a wide scale. This involved the promotion of Irish industry by tariff subsidy, and other methods. The dynamic element was the state, not the industrialists. Very quickly the industrialists sought equilibrium within the initial phase of the policy. They resisted new entrants to specific sectors, because this competition would cause difficulty for those already in operation. In effect, the various sectors attempted to regulate entry and operation within their particular sectors.[86] The size of the market obstructed further internal development. Even when this was recognised, alternatives were not seriously considered. Textile producers contrasted Ireland with Denmark, and discussed the limitation of output without a world market. Despite this, they never considered expanding their production beyond the existing arrangements.[87]

This is not to suggest that the obstacles to growth were non-existent; they were very real. However, the industrialists were not prepared to go beyond the established practices. The Irish industrial bourgeoisie were a product of Fianna Fáil policy in the 1930s and owed their existence to them. They were consequently far less autonomous in terms of influence than the farming community or the working class. Without the support of the state, the industrial bourgeoisie would not be able to contain the strength of organised labour or meet competition. In effect, the state was substituting itself for the market. In a market economy, an Irish industrial bourgeoisie would have had considerable difficulty in existing. Only when the state reordered the market mechanism within the national state could an industrial bourgeoisie emerge. At no time prior to the Second World War did they represent an independent force in Irish society. Their displacement by the state, but without socialism, means that Ireland's economic experience differs from that of Britain or other industrial nations within Western Europe.

Irish industrialists frequently complained that they were not given access to the Minister, or given certain rights over policy. It is hard to see why a Minister should do so. The industrialists remained weak, their self-image was poor, and they acquired a fatalistic attitude to the environment in which they functioned:

> Our industrial history is part of our national history. It is an accepted fact that industrial development in Ireland was hampered, prevented, and in some cases, definitely forbidden by the positive penal legislation of Great Britain. When therefore we began after native government to develop our industries, many problems arising from historic difficulties, internal and external causes, immediately presented themselves, and not the least was the deplorable

> mentality which could not see that Irish-made goods might be purchased to advantage of all concerned. Externally, industrialists were faced with higher protection than would otherwise have been necessary.[88]

This strong sense of pessimism pervades the thinking of industrialists throughout the 1930s. They acknowledged the lack of an industrial tradition in Ireland, yet appeared at a loss to rectify the difficulty. There was a shortage of trained executives and skilled workers, but no moves had been undertaken by 1939 to cope with this difficulty. By that date, the number of apprentices had fallen off. Frequently, foreign skilled labour had to be attracted to Ireland, because no one could carry out the particular industrial functions. The industrialists, under pressure at the oral hearings of the Commission on Vocational Organisation, conceded that the difficulties of Irish industry were the fault of no one and everyone: 'The fault cannot be said to lie in any particular direction. It is a combination of failure on the part of the worker, the factory, and the particular industry.'[89] This defensiveness reflects the isolated condition of Irish industry. The industrialists accepted this position, but were sensitive to any threat to it. In particular, they recognised, but accepted, the predominant role of agriculture in the Irish economy. By accepting this pre-eminence of agriculture, they excluded themselves from playing a more dynamic role in development.

One reason was that the industrialists wanted costs and wages to be maintained at those prevailing in agriculture. A deeper reason involved a sense of inferiority towards the stronger agriculture sector. This implied a commitment to balanced growth: that in the process of development, industry should not handicap agriculture. In the case of Ireland, this would entail little or no further development after 1938.[90] The external markets for agriculture had been restored and demand consequently grew for its products. An equilibrium within the economy had been established. Any further growth for industry necessitated unbalanced growth. This would have entailed a commitment by the state and the industrialists to sustain growth within the industrial sector, whatever the short term costs to agriculture. It could lead to further learning opportunities for industry, and further expansion. This appeared to occur during the economic war, but this had been an historic accident: a by-product of de

Valera's conflict over sovereignty. The equilibrium was re-established in 1938, reinforcing the continued underdevelopment of Irish industry.[91]

The Secretary of the Federation, Erskine Childers, TD, was the only member to recognise the dilemma. As a politician, rather than an industrialist, Childers' observations tended to move outside the concern for survival. In his critique, he recognised that national income had not expanded under the Fianna Fáil government. The reasons for this were more fundamental than the exigencies of party rule:

> For the first twenty-five years [sic] of our independence we have made very little progress economically and any social benefits we have conferred on our people have been with the aid of borrowing and transfer of revenue from one group of persons to another.[92]

Childers subsequently provided an elaboration of his views for the Commission. The cause of Irish difficulties, he maintained, could be located in a deficiency of 'national and social discipline'. This he attributed to the adoption of a political system which presumed the existence of considerable wealth in the economy. The parliamentary system in Britain could be used to benefit all sections: in Ireland it led to distributional struggles concerning the division of a static national income. Childers suggested that the party system and the accompanying distributional conflicts were luxuries which the country could ill afford. Agricultural methods were, he added, out of date, while there was a basic ignorance about the functioning of industry. All of these difficulties were reinforced by a widespread belief among people that the state would provide adequate welfare for all. The solution accordingly was to confront Irish society and:

> Point out to them their duty as citizens, the absolute necessity, on their part, of increasing output and of working harder than they have ever worked before in their lives, especially in the early stages of an industry. Unless one does that one tends to spoil them.[93]

He was closely questioned by the members of the Commission as a result of these remarks. Under this pressure, he agreed to revise some of his comments. In particular, he accepted that the responsibility for low output could not be attributed solely to the workers, but was due to the general lack of experience of both managers and employees.[94] Whatever about the specific elements of Childers' critique, he did address points of substance. The Commission's report, in fact, ignored them and presented a reasonably positive section on industry.[95] Alone among the membership of the industrialists' organisation, he recognised that economic development had only been partly successful. He drew attention to the dilemma posed by this: there was a contradiction between the pursuit of short-term gains and the creation of an expanding industrial economy. Whereas most sections of Irish society were committed to stability by 1940, Childers recognised the flaw in that belief. Nor can it be said that his political colleagues shared his view, satisfied as they appear to have been with the achievement to date. Lemass remained one of the few who shared Childers' approach, if not the actual criticisms made.

The industrialists believed that the level of wages paid to workers in Ireland should approximate to those paid in agriculture. It was estimated that Irish wage levels were around 15 per cent higher than those prevailing in Britain, whereas the cost of living was approximately 10 per cent higher in Ireland than in England. Senator Douglas maintained that the high wages could be accounted for by the ability of trade unions to force employers to comply with their demands. The Federation believed that government intervention was required to regulate trade union activity. In a detailed submission to the Department, it recommended a fundamental shift in the basis of labour relations, involving a revision of the 1906 Trade Union Act and the enforcement of certain legal conditions on trade union activity. Some of these were to be embodied in the Trade Union Act 1941. Lemass, however, believed that even with these changes there was no guarantee that it would weaken the negotiating strength of the trade unions. Indeed, he cited the system operating in New Zealand, which he believed strengthened the trade unions rather than the employers.[96]

The trade union movement had benefited from Fianna Fáil policies throughout the 1930s. Lemass proved to be far more sympathetic to the working class than his predecessors or, indeed, some of his colleagues. This can be partly attributed to electoral considerations, but it is also due to his belief that an increase in working class consumption would expand the market for Irish produced goods. These considerations were reinforced by the nature of Fianna Fáil's socio-economic policies, which in urban Ireland can only be characterised as social democratic. Protection and industrial expansion created suitable conditions for the expansion of the trade union movement. Whereas during the 1920s state policy had restricted the development of a strong trade union movement in the Free state, Fianna Fáil's policies during the 1930s enhanced the opportunities for expansion.

Unlike the new industrial bourgeoisie, which owed its existence to state policy, the trade unions were already in existence prior to 1932. Though weak, the unions had acquired independent status and were thus less dependent on the state than the industrialists. Despite this independence, the trade unions owed much of their success to the new environment. The government provided an institutional framework congenial to the expansion of trade union membership as well as social reforms which improved the living standards of a significant proportion of the working class. The housing programme provided both employment and improved living conditions for many trade union members. Through the Unemployment Assistance Bill, the Workmen's Compensation Act, and most importantly the Conditions of Employment Act 1936, the government demonstrated its willingness to respond to trade union and working class pressure. The government's economic and social package reflected in large measure the policies enumerated by many individual unions and by the Irish Trade Union Congress (ITUC). As a consequence, relations between the trade union movement and Fianna Fáil were close, even though many leading trade unionists supported the Labour Party.

However, there was a limit to what Fianna Fáil, and Lemass in particular, was prepared to concede to either corporate grouping. Though Lemass was prepared to use the state to adjust the economic circumstances to benefit both groups, he also demanded cooperation from them. This was only partially forthcoming from either group; each of them demanded to be treated as a special case and for its interests to be given priority. Lemass's perspective was national rather than sectional and there was no guarantee outside the short term that national and sectional interest would coincide. Industry and Commerce shared some of the fears expressed by the industrialists, but the emphasis was somewhat different. The Department recognised that the control exercised by the state in economic and social matters was unprecedented in democratic countries, yet despite this the trade union movement continued to uphold the voluntary system of collective bargaining and resisted all attempts to legislate in this area.[97] The absence of state interference in industrial relations appeared incongruous in a context of extensive state involvement in other areas.

The introduction of protection, increased welfare benefits, and the sympathetic approach to labour meant that the traditional reasons for free collective bargaining, a free market system, no longer applied. Trade unions could not dictate impossible terms, but they could certainly increase the closed shop, push up wage rates in urban centres, and also expand their membership. The new collective conditions of action also gave trade unions an advantage over the less well organised business community. The unions tended to evade the conclusion that as state intervention in the economy increased so would the demand for coordination of the various producer groups for the benefit of the society. Yet if the government is not simply an instrument of capital or labour then its behaviour is more complex in that it will seek to defend what it considers to be the national interest, which may diverge from what either capital or labour believe to be the case. This implicit tension did not come to the fore until after 1937. Congress's failure to persuade Lemass to amend the National Unemployment Insurance Act to ensure that the rate of pay for a specific job would be uniform throughout the state demonstrates the limits of trade union influence over government policy. If Congress had been successful this would have limited industrial development to the large urban areas, whereas Lemass believed that a differential wage rate would promote conditions for industrial expansion in rural and western locations.[98]

The trade unions take on an essentially defensive position by the end of the decade. Public ownership is usually advocated as a means to defend existing employment rather than to stimulate further industrial expansion. Indeed by this time there is an assumption among delegates to the ITUC annual conference that the limits of protection had been reached, and that a policy of stabilisation should be pursued which would guarantee the benefits which had been derived from that process.[99] This sense of pessimism may have prompted Lemass's criticism of the trade unions in the Dail for what he believed was their indifference to unemployment. Lemass suggested that the behaviour of trade unions was preventing further employment creation. While Congress reacted angrily to Lemass, there was an element of truth in what he claimed. In a heavily protected economy, organised labour was in a strong position to obtain maximum advantage from its market position. In addition, restrictive practices, demarcation disputes, and tension between British and Irish unions were matters of growing concern to the Department. It was claimed that various actions and disputes had led to loss of production on a number of occasions. Lemass had threatened the unions with state action if these problems were not resolved.[100]

While the trade unions had welcomed economic nationalism and the benefits which the working class derived from it, they tended to evade the consequences of the changed policy. The unions sought to maintain their traditional institutions and structures, and to avail of the opportunities to pursue its economic objectives which involved increasing the wage level. As such the trade unions could be considered sectional in the sense that they represented a narrow section of society: an unpropertied class in a proprietorial democracy. Unions were placed in a weak position when their traditional behaviour was criticised as an obstacle to economic growth.

This was the precise charge made against the unions in the Senate on 14 March 1940, when James Douglas proposed the establishment of a court to regulate industrial relations. Ten days later Sean MacEntee, who had succeeded Lemass as Minister for Industry and Commerce, responded favourably to the Douglas initiative, although doubting that the problem could by solved by judicial means. Strikes, he suggested, were a cause for public concern, particularly those caused by inter union disputes. He identified the cause of this problem as the multiplicity of unions in the state.[101] This situation gave cause for concern on a number of grounds. The decentralised nature of trade unionism ran against the interests of national development, as did the labour unrest which ensued. Furthermore, the presence of British based unions was an affront to the isolationist and autarkic nature of Irish policy and possibly in 1940 could be seen as a threat to neutrality. Thus for both short- and long-term reasons the attempt to reform Irish industrial relations was placed on the agenda.

The conservative nature of Irish trade unionism reflected in large measure that of Irish society. As such it was fairly predictable that Industry and Commerce would attempt to direct it as it had other sections of society. Unlike the industrialists, though, the conservatism of Irish trade unionism had only an indirect effect on the industrial process. Its impact was negative to the extent that the unions accepted the industrialists' view of the limits of protectionism. It was also unlikely that the unions would have accepted the cost of a deepening of the industrial process, especially if this had involved a disruption of traditional methods of collective bargaining. Because of their common stake in the system as it had developed by 1937, both the industrialists and the trade unions were, notwithstanding their rhetoric, deeply committed to stability and as such suspicious of any further change.

The actions of industrialists and trade unions, though explicable in terms of human behaviour, placed serious obstacles in the path of any further development. These obstacles were not insurmountable. While difficulties could be foreseen, it is within the bounds of probability that a coherent industrial strategy could have been implemented. By 1939, Industry and Commerce were certainly edging towards a further phase of industrial development, but it is not at all clear that a political consensus existed within Fianna Fáil to mobilise resources to achieve this. Indeed by that date there are three broad groupings within the party with quite different objectives: the industrialisers are represented by Lemass and support continuing state intervention; the fiscal conservatives are represented by MacEntee, the Department of Finance, and some sections of the party and this group attempts to reverse the expansionary policies of the 1930s; the marginal agrarians are represented by a section of the western TDs whose main concern was with securing the income and livelihood of the marginal farmer who had been affected negatively by the rise in the cost of living and by the economic war. These were not tight coalitions. The last in particular tended to be fluid and in policy terms often incoherent. However, the existence of all three meant that radical changes in policy were problematic. If these developments promoted a more conservative environment, so did the new constitution enacted in 1937. It gave full expression to the main values of Irish political culture: nationalism, religion, language and property. The constitution also reinforced the sense of achievement prevalent during the 1930s, a sense which probably helped advocates of consolidation rather than change.

The final variable which postponed further development was the decision to end the dispute between the United Kingdom and Ireland. The economic war had broken the connection between the international economy and economic policy making in Ireland. Between 1932 and 1938 national considerations were dominant and autarky was the main objective of policy. It had been assumed by Fianna Fáil that the benefits from autarky would outweigh those to be derived from participation in the international economy. De Valera believed that the loss of the British market and the possible destruction of the Irish cattle industry should be welcomed.[102] Surprisingly, perhaps, Lemass took a much more cautious view and appears to have been one of those Ministers urging a compromise on de Valera. He may have recognised that whatever short term benefits might be derived from autarky, the cost of autonomous development could be very high indeed. While the economic war certainly helped legitimise a policy of industrial expansion based on import substitution, the benefits from this connection could be short lived. Industrial development did not sustain a dynamic for further expansion and industrial expansion, and employment in industry constituted a relatively small proportion of the work force by 1937. Moreover, the failure of agriculture to respond to state policy, particularly tillage, reduced government flexibility in economic matters. Without a radical re-orientation of agricultural production and a dynamic industrial sector the pressure to re-negotiate trading relations with the United Kingdom remained strong.

This was certainly the Finance position from an early stage in the dispute, and one which Lemass came to adopt by 1936.[103] Despite the apparent convergence, little could be achieved in economic matters until de Valera had satisfied himself that a political agreement could be reached on all outstanding disputes. For de Valera and for the British, particularly Chamberlain, the political and the financial issues received priority over trade.[104] Without a political agreement there was little hope of a trade agreement. The tortuous negotiations between November 1937 and April 1938 demonstrated that while there was a willingness to reach agreement, neither side were prepared to jettison their principles. The concessions made on both sides allowed the two states to settle the main matters of dispute but also determined the future of bilateral trade.

The Irish had two main objectives during the trade

negotiations: to secure entry to the British market on terms analogous to those received by the dominions; and to ensure continuing effective protection for Irish industry. The first objective was achieved following tough negotiations between the Irish Minister for Agriculture and his opposite number. This was probably the easier to achieve as both sides believed they had a considerable amount to gain from a revival of the Irish export trade in cattle. On the industrial question the margin was much closer. The British required special advantage for coal in the Irish market, preference for British goods over other countries, and the moderation of protection to allow British imports to compete in Ireland. The British were concerned that any special concessions to Ireland would lead to objections from the dominions, who might believe they were not being treated as well as Ireland.

Lemass's aim was to secure, in so far as circumstances permitted, the right to continue to protect native Irish industry against foreign imports. Lemass was in a weak negotiating position. The British were conceding on the agriculture issue and this put pressure on him to make concessions to British industry. Lemass argued that special factors prevailed in Ireland, but conceded that:

> It was the intention of the Éire government that in the case of fully established industries, protection should be afforded only at such rates as would be of benefit to industries which were efficient. But it was essential that the presentation of this undertaking should be such that Éire industries should clearly realise that, provided they were efficient, they would have a reasonable chance of maintaining their existence.[105]

Lemass was fairly successful in realising these objectives. The British withdrew a clause from the draft agreement which obliged the Irish government to protect only those industries '... which are reasonably assured of sound opportunities for success'. If this had been accepted it would have posed serious difficulties for any further attempts to industrialise.[106] The differences between the two sides were resolved by Lemass's willingness to establish a Prices Commission which would function as a review body for protective duties in the event of dispute between British and Irish producers. The Department of Industry and Commerce recognised that this concession could have serious consequences, but believed that the overall advantages bestowed by the agreement outweighed individual disadvantages:

> Every trade agreement involves a restriction of the freedom of both parties to it and each party when making the agreement must satisfy himself that he is getting an adequate return for whatever concessions he is making on whatever obligations he undertakes. From this point of view the trade agreement last year is a good bargain for this country.[107]

The various agreements signed in 1938 bestowed differing benefits on Ireland. Politically, the conclusion of the negotiations draws attention to the changed nature of the relationship between Britain and Ireland. In essence, this relationship is now post colonial. There is a clear recognition by the British negotiators, especially Chamberlain and MacDonald, that Ireland had to be treated separately from the dominions and its view of sovereignty recognised. Moreover, by 1938 the British had in effect accepted the Irish view of the relationship between the two states; but not between Ireland and Northern Ireland. The outcome enhanced the maturity of the relationship between a newly independent state and the former imperial power. There would be further grounds for tension, but the integrity of its independence was recognised, even during the Second World War.

The consequences for agriculture were the most significant economically. Agricultural production quickly reverted to its traditional focus on cattle and exports to the British market. The effect on manufacturing industry was less clear cut. Lemass had successfully defended the state's right to determine its industrial evolution, but important concessions had been made which might limit further growth. This was certainly the view of the industrialists. Yet this is not where the main problem was located; the Department of Industry and Commerce retained considerable flexibility in interpreting the agreement which would permit it to dictate the overall direction of policy. The power of initiative remained in Ireland. The main difficulty which faced policy makers was the return to normal trading relations in agriculture. This removed the main obstacle to the reassertion of conservative assumptions in policy making. If cattle for export became the main focus of policy, then the policy instruments required would differ from those utilised between 1932 and 1938.

Fiscal conservatism, the level of wages, the cost of living and a strong rural bias would increase the importance of Finance and reduce that of Industry and Commerce. The onset of war in 1939 disguised this outcome, but in the circumstances the elaboration of a developmental strategy by Industry and Commerce would encounter more serious obstacles than at any time since the late 1920s.

5

The Failure of Radical Alternatives: Policy Formation 1939–48

When John Maynard Keynes delivered the first Finlay lecture at UCD in 1933, his views complemented those of the Fianna Fáil government. He offered qualified approval for economic nationalism on the grounds that liberal free trade, once the dominant economic orthodoxy, no longer fulfilled its promise. On balance, he tended to welcome this strengthening of self-sufficiency. It was a cautious welcome, for Keynes believed that in a small country, such as Ireland, there were clear limits to self-sufficiency. These limits had to be appreciated if the community's standard of living was not to decline drastically. He also warned his listeners that there were dangers associated with the doctrine of economic nationalism. The first danger involved ignoring the actual economic environment in which policy is formulated. A government should not confuse the rhetoric of opposition with the tasks of government. The other dangers were haste and intolerance. If indulged in, each would imperil the positive achievements of economic nationalism. Notwithstanding these objections, a gradual and constructive policy had considerable merit.[1]

Keynes's views, or at least the positive ones, were as unwelcome to orthodox economists as they were welcomed by unorthodox social scientists in Ireland. Alfred O'Rahilly in his major economic work, *Money*, expressed his intellectual debt to Keynes, but in nearly 700 pages never adverts to the reservations.[2] Nor were these reservations shared by the main beneficiaries of economic nationalism: the new Irish industrial bourgeoisie. There was another Keynesian in Ireland, one who shared some of this caution. By 1939 Lemass had recognised some of the dangers which Keynes had identified in 1933. Whereas in 1933 the warnings could be ignored, by 1939 a more reasonable assessment of the experiment could be undertaken. More worrying from the government's point of view, many citizens, particularly industrialists but including government supporters such as O'Rahilly, continued to believe the rhetoric of opposition and tended to be intolerant of the views of others. Alternative views were at times seen as unpatriotic. Despite this, Lemass remained apprehensive concerning the progress of industrial policy. He warned the country, shortly before the Second World War, that:

> It was never conceived as possible that the state could be made completely independent of foreign trade or locked into a watertight compartment cut off from the current of international life ... Now their industries had passed beyond the infancy stage and were capable of facing comparison with industries in other countries, and they would have to be prepared to face that comparison.[3]

Such a choice was to be postponed by the war, although it is probable that the idea of choice, at this stage, remained unrealistic. The intervention of the war changed radically the environment in which decisions were taken. Lemass left Industry and Commerce to establish the Department of Supplies, with the mammoth task of ensuring that Ireland's necessary requirements could be procured and distributed. The political and economic survival of the state was the primary aim of policy making until at least 1943. By this date, the Irish government had overcome the worst of its isolation, had asserted its neutrality despite the hostility of the allies, particularly the United states, and had mobilised its resources to sustain the economy. Thus 1943 was a time for decisions, those pertaining to the post-war period as well as to the remaining years of hostilities. Ironically, perhaps, as Lemass and the Fianna Fáil government prepared for the end of the war with their commitment to self-sufficiency relatively intact, Keynes was laying the foundations, along with Cordell Hull and other liberal internationalists, for a new economic order which would challenge the certainties of Irish industrial policy and the security of economic nationalism.[4]

The war prevented further expansion of the economy, but it did not essentially change the ideological commitment to self-sufficiency. Lemass's remarks did not challenge the certainties of economic nationalism. It may be that 'Lemass in 1939 frequently sounded like the Lemass of 1959', but despite the similarities there were considerable differences.[5] Lemass was not in 1939, nor indeed in 1948, questioning the veracity of economic nationalism. When he talked of comparison with industries in other countries, he meant just that: comparison. This had been a traditional rule of thumb with the Department: Irish industry should be roughly comparable in quality, price, and output with its potential competition. The speeches of 1939 were a reminder of what was expected of Irish industrialists, not a conversion to free trade. Lemass in 1939 remained committed to self-sufficiency, but not autarky. Autarky, certainly as outlined by O'Rahilly and others, involved a complete break with the international trading system and the treatment of Ireland as a self-contained unit. Self-sufficiency, for Lemass, implied a passive approach to international trade, but not a full break with it. In this context, it is possible to promote economic development behind tariff barriers, without losing some of the benefits of international trade.

There is no evidence during the first years of the war that the government or the Department of Industry and Commerce were contemplating a change in industrial policy. Nor did Lemass's departure from the Department, or his replacement by Sean MacEntee, reflect any such reassessment. The Department reiterated its policy in July 1940, when it outlined to the Cabinet Committee on Emergency Problems the prospects for future industrial expansion. The Department had been considering sixty-seven proposals, in forty-five sectors, for new industries when the war occurred. Although most of these proposals had to be abandoned as a consequence, the Department was confident that they would be revived once hostilities concluded. Most of the schemes required high protection, as the objective was to substitute home production for imports. The only really large-scale project was the building of an oil refinery in Dublin Bay. Most other proposals appear to have been small scale in terms of investment capital and employment potential. The evidence available points to a mopping up of certain areas, rather than the inauguration of a new and dynamic phase of industrial development. It also appears that the role of the Irish industrialist was diminishing by this stage. It is possible to identify thirty-five of the sixty-seven promoters as non-Irish or, in the case of Dunlop, a British firm complying with the Control of Manufactures Acts. The nature of the proposals imply that import substitution did not have any considerable potential by this stage, and that Irish nationals do not appear over-active in promoting new schemes.[6]

The war and the evidence from experience gave Lemass the opportunity to reformulate his approach to industrial policy. This did not involve a radical change in objective: as the war progressed he concluded that more active methods would have to be applied if his economic policies were to be achieved. The Department of Supplies provided an institutional setting for this reassessment. During the Emergency, Lemass was placed at the centre of economic decision-making. When, in August 1941, after a Cabinet reshuffle, Lemass became jointly Minister for Industry and Commerce and Supplies, his influence over the economy became dominant. This joint authority provided him with a perspective with which to assess the future progress of the economy. The experience of directly managing the economy, albeit in a war situation, led to a number of policy decisions on his part. He recognised that Ireland's economic position in the post-war world would be difficult and that traditional policy might not prove adequate. There was an added concern that the war conditions might return, and it would prove necessary to retain or reactivate the wartime institutions. But, as a departmental official recognised at the end of the war, there were more direct reasons for invoking the wartime experience:

> During the Emergency the Department of Supplies had to exercise an unprecedented measure of control over a wide range of industry. The experience of the Department in this respect should be useful in connection with such control of economic activity as may be necessary in the post-war years.[7]

The Department was in a position to regulate production, distribution, and sale of essential commodities throughout the war. This unprecedented power, Lemass felt, could be used to direct the Irish economy when its most immediate justification had disappeared.[8]

In the longer term, Lemass recognised that neutrality, which was essentially political, had economic consequences. Thus, the attempt to secure a comprehensive agreement with the United Kingdom, regulating trade and supplies for the duration of the war, foundered on the British demand for transhipment facilities at Irish ports.[9] This failure to reach an agreement did not have serious consequences until the winter of 1940, when Ireland was effectively cut off from all sources of supply except those of the United Kingdom. The establishment of Irish Shipping to secure supplies from Spain and Portugal, the creation of the Emergency Scientific Research Bureau, and close cooperation with industrialists, secured a minimum quantity of necessary commodities. The experience of war reinforced rather than diminished the commitment to self-sufficiency. It became clear that the relationship with Britain was fraught with difficulties, there being no guarantee that Britain would respond favourably to Ireland after the war. The war itself had suspended the 1938 Trade Agreement, and again there was no guarantee that its benefits would continue to be available. Ireland's isolation was also evident in its continued dependence on imported raw materials and semi-manufactured products. These difficulties demonstrated that the cost of self-sufficiency to the state would be higher than perhaps had been previously considered.

Lemass was in a stronger institutional position to direct the economy and to influence policy. A new type of state company was also available as a model for the future. Although companies such as Irish Shipping, Tea Importers (Éire) Ltd and Fuel Importers (Éire) Ltd, were established as a specific response to the war, their organisation served to demonstrate certain possibilities. The logic of each, if continued after the war, was to weaken if not break the dependence on British merchants for imports.[10] These organisations also allowed the Department to cooperate closely with either the trade association or the principal firms in each sector. At first, the Department had been reluctant to intensify state intervention during the war. The progress of the war and the behaviour of certain sections of the business community persuaded Lemass that government intervention was necessary to regulate purchasing, distribution, and pricing. This occured as a consequence of the business community's failure to procure the necessities for national survival in wartime. Centralised state organisation then took over the task of importing most of these requirments.[11]

It cannot be concluded from this that the wartime experience transformed Lemass. However, it can be inferred that there were three major consequences. The behaviour of the British reinforced his commitment to self-sufficiency, leading him to respond cautiously to international trade developments at the end of the war. He believed that further state intervention would be required if development was to continue. He also seems to have recognised the weakness of the Irish business community, and concluded that their role in this process would be partial. In addition, the internal organisation of the Department of Supplies demonstrated some of the weaknesses of the Civil Service structure. Within Supplies, the usual bureaucratic methods of work were suspended, and a more rapid decision making machinery developed: speed and efficiency were valued over traditional office routine or hierarchial structures. More directly, Lemass was made aware of the complex interaction between the separate elements of the economy. He recognised that the collapse of imports and the severe restraints on exports could continue well into the post-war period. Inflation and unemployment remained central concerns, though the worst effects of unemployment were overcome by emigration and military service. Events in Britain concentrated his mind on the question of full employment.

As the war progressed, Lemass's sentiments on these matters concretised. He began to formulate detailed objectives to meet the challenge of war-time and, more importantly, that of post-war reconstruction. In June 1942, he took the opportunity to provide the Taoiseach with a memorandum on labour policy. The proposals mark a departure from previous policy. Heretofore, Industry and Commerce confined its labour policy to specific matters of trade union law, industrial relations, and factory legislation. The Trade Union Act 1941 had demonstrated the willingness of the Department to deepen its involvement in orchestrating the trade union movement. That Act had been an attempt to centralise the trade union movement, to concentrate power in the hands of a selected number of unions, and to amalgamate the disparate trade unions into a number of large and well organised unions. Its other objective was to reduce the influence of, if not to eliminate, British trade unions in Ireland. Although most of the aims of this Act were not achieved, it did demonstrate the government's willingness to intervene in the traditional relationship between the state, business, and labour. On his return to Industry and Commerce, Lemass actively promoted the new legislation. The memorandum extended these centralising tendencies, and advocated the establishment of a separate Ministry of Labour which would order and direct all aspects of labour policy. This further extension of state intervention marks a clear break with the more passive arrangements that had characterised relations between government, business and labour during the 1930s. At a Cabinet meeting on 30 June 1942, the need for 'systematic planning for the Emergency and the post-war period' was accepted. This decision placed such planning within the context of national development, which was precisely the point that Lemass had been stressing.[12]

Lemass insisted that the controls imposed during the Emergency should be continued when the war ended:

> It is contemplated that the general scheme of control of labour, introduced to cope with the circumstances of the Emergency, should be retained after the Emergency has passed and become a permanent feature of the state's labour organisation. The idea of amalgamating the social services into one Ministry might be implemented after the Emergency through the Ministry of Labour.[13]

There was also a growing awareness that the relationship between government and business would have to be revised in the light of new conditions. Lemass was also conscious that obstacles to growth and full employment would have to be removed. This was a view shared by de Valera who in a speech, prepared by Maurice Moynihan and delivered to the Fianna Fáil Ard Fheis in September 1943 reaffirmed the government's commitment to self-sufficiency. He added that to reduce unemployment, the government could not depend entirely on the contribution of the business community: their efforts would have to be supplemented by the state.[14] In a speech to the Dublin Chamber of Commerce a year earlier, de Valera suggested that there would be no rapid return to 'normality':

> For many years after the war we should be forced to depend almost exclusively upon our own resources, as we are being gradually forced to do now.

In a sense, he was making a virtue of necessity, and it is difficult to judge if he welcomed the spartan nature of wartime, which gave him the opportunity to indulge his propensity for self-sufficiency in the extreme. Yet even he was aware of the changed circumstances in which Ireland found itself, and he reflected once again Lemass's views when he added that: 'The state would continue to accept responsibility where before the war it accepted none.'

International trade, de Valera maintained, would continue to be broadly bilateral in focus.[15]

The war constrained, even further, the already restricted market economy in Ireland. To coordinate post-war planning it became clear that labour, the most independent variable in the equation of economic development, would have to be controlled or at least coordinated. De Valera's views were general; Lemass's were explicit and far-reaching. For him, labour policy was 'an Aim and a Plan for the control and direction of the nation's resources of labour'. Such a strategy would be necessary in the short term to overcome the dislocation caused by war, while in the long term it would assist in the coordination of post war labour requirements.[16] Radical policies were required, Lemass added, to implement this labour policy. As a result of the war there was a body of uncoordinated legislation which could continue to be utilised. However, insofar as labour was controlled, this was not a result of any coherent strategy:

> The government has not yet provided itself with sufficient powers to enable it to apply effectively any labour policy which might be decided upon.

Despite this, the powers which Lemass had at his disposal were considerable, if not actually draconian. They certainly provided a core of legislation which, if used in peace time, would have been closer to those of the Mediterranean dictatorships, than to Ireland's liberal democratic neighbours. Wage control had been instituted. Restrictions had been placed on emigration: thus, individuals in rural areas, or those under twenty-two, or anyone in employment, could not obtain an exit permit, except under exceptional circumstances. Individuals who refused employment or who left employment without due cause could be penalised. Unemployment assistance might be refused to them. These direct controls were supplemented by what might be called voluntary measures of 'social responsibility'. Arrangements for work sharing were concluded between employers and employees. Where this occurred, the regulations for receipt of unemployment assistance would be modified. Local authorities were encouraged to promote schemes with a high labour content. The Construction Corps was established for young men; refusal to participate could result in loss of benefit.

To coordinate these elements of control, a new Ministry was required. In the first place, the Ministry of Labour would take over a number of functions administered by Industry and Commerce: emigration control, wage policy, and industrial relations. It would also deal with unemployment benefits and insurance. The new department would be staffed by the relevant sections of the Departments of Industry and Commerce, Local Government, Agriculture, and the Board of Works. The Ministry of Labour would, if established, function as the only government institution dealing with labour and labour policy. Presumably, Industry and Commerce would deal with the business community in much the same way. A new department was required, Lemass stressed, to formulate a coherent labour policy during the war and to continue to coordinate it in peace time. For the remainder of the Emergency, the Ministry would control all labour in industry and agriculture. It was suggested that a 'pool' system be operated; the only members of the labour force not under control would be those outside the pool. Membership of the pool received certain benefits, but were placed under clear obligations. Each member would receive a basic wage whether work was available or not, but individuals had to agree not to emigrate and to work in any part of the state deemed necessary. The implications of this were not lost on Lemass. He suggested that the government should obtain trade union cooperation; if this was not forthcoming, then action should be taken to prevent trade union obstruction.

Once such a policy was in place, Lemass did not envisage any dramatic change during peace time. Such an approach would be justified because the revival of Irish industry would be hampered by restricted access to raw materials and plant and machinery. This constraint would be compounded by labour disputes, wage claims, and consequent inflationary pressures. The return of unskilled labour from the United Kingdom would add to these difficulties, while skilled workers would remain in Britain until the economy improved. Finally, Lemass believed that agricultural activity would not expand, and that the turf development schemes would cease. To offset these multiple difficulties, a programme of development would have to be undertaken which would include rural electrification and an ambitious construction expansion. The state would play a directive role in this:

> The labour needs of each industry would be calculated. As workers returned from the United Kingdom they would be allocated to their appropriate pools or left in the general class to be absorbed on unskilled labouring work in connection with the developmental plans referred to above.[17]

Nor did this exhaust the work of the Ministry of Labour. It would have the power to ensure that other developmental agencies coordinated their plans with those of Labour. It would also function as the agency for coordinating demobilisation. These proposals were the first recognition during the war that economic and industrial policy had to be more effectively coordinated than hitherto. The control of labour during wartime could be justified as a response to the Emergency; to advocate continuing such policies in peace time suggested that a more fundamental change was involved. A programme for development could prove ineffectual if labour remained outside the control, or at least the influence, of the state. Although a Ministry of Labour was not established during the war, the explicit commitment to control remained central to Lemass's policies until well after the end of the war. Draft legislation on industrial relations in 1944 continued to reflect this concern, though the specific legislation modified some of the more radical proposals discussed above.[18]

During 1942 and 1943, Lemass began to concentrate on the future organisation of the economy. Labour policy was the first of a series of specific policy proposals by him. These might be contrasted to the more general exhortations to economic development by de Valera. Raymond J. Raymond describes de Valera and Maurice Moynihan as Ireland's two chief planning executives who by early 1944 had put together a significant developmental programme: 'The nature and purpose of the plans evidence a revolution in Irish socio-economic aspirations and in the government's willingness to meet them.[19] The evidence from the files on which this conclusion is based is neither convincing, nor does it sustain these specific conclusions. In July 1942, de Valera wrote to Lemass requesting details of 'major projects of national development', drawing attention to the need for systematic planning. In his reply, Lemass discussed the possibility of expanding peat production and some of the difficulties associated with this. Later in the same year a detailed list of projects for development was forwarded to the Taoiseach's Office.

In the interim, the Cabinet Committee on Economic Planning was established. This Committee consisted of the Taoiseach, Tanaiste, and the Minister for Industry and Commerce. Its main purpose was to examine the various proposals for post-war development. However, its authority was clearly restricted: its decisions were not equivalent to those of the Cabinet, nor did its deliberations replace the detailed preparation of legislation by individual departments.[20] The Committee probably owes its origins to Lemass's belief, contained in the memorandum on labour policy, that initiatives should be taken which would prepare Ireland for the postwar world. It provided the opportunity to discuss in detail policy initiatives in advance of full Cabinet evaluation. The Department of Finance believed the authority of the Cabinet had been abused by the Committee, and it may be possible to infer that Lemass hoped to utilise the Cabinet Committee as a sort of economic war cabinet. To some extent, he achieved this aim as the minutes of the Committee reveal discussion on a wide range of topics.[21]

However, caution is necessary. It is important not to conclude that because there was a discussion in the Committee that anyone, particularly the government, was committed to action. The evidence from the files indicates that Lemass, not de Valera, played the significant role in the operation of planning. After the Taoiseach's initial correspondence, he does not play a central role in the deliberations. On virtually every issue, the initiative comes from Lemass. De Valera's ideas were general, particularly where economic development or industrial policy was considered. His interventions tended to reiterate policy rather than initiate it. In March 1944, de Valera discussed the possibility of continuing the government's policy of land division, suggesting that 50,000 acres per annum should be distributed in this way. At a meeting in May, Lemass was – to say the least – unsympathetic to de Valera's approach.[22] De Valera's generalised statements neither made nor formulated policy except in a general way; he lacked a comprehensive view of the Irish economy. Throughout the war Lemass was the only Minister with such a conceptual framework. De Valera's role was restricted but important: if he had opposed development, then it is unlikely that much would have been achieved. The Taoiseach's Office established the overall guidelines for policy. But even here, Lemass's influence can be detected. In a number of speeches on post-war development, de

Valera echoes ideas formulated earlier by Lemass and Industry and Commerce.[23]

There is also a gap between public statements and the output of the government throughout the years 1942-48. It is not possible to detect the creation of a systematic planning mechanism at governmental level. What emerges from the Cabinet Committee on Economic Planning are proposals for infrastructural investment. By 1944, the Taoiseach's Office had prepared plans for post-war investment costing £96 million. To conclude from this, as Raymond does, that 'under de Valera's aegis, Ireland began to move towards a managed economy ...' is to misread what was actually happening and to misunderstand the basic concept of economic management. Virtually all the proposals were infrastructural. While capital investment is important, it cannot be reduced to industrial policy or economic planning. The management of modern economies usually implies a concerted plan to promote industrial expansion, with capital investment for infrastructure playing a supportive if important role in this.[24] Capital investment is facilitative rather than central to the plan. In this case, there appears to have been no linkage between these general proposals and those of Industry and Commerce for post-war industrial development. The reason for this is that both industrial policy and infrastructural policy were part of a process already under way in the 1930s. Insofar as one can describe Ireland as a managed economy in the 1940s, the policy instruments for management were already in use during the 1930s.

De Valera's intervention in 1942 does not mark an innovation, but the continuation of a policy disrupted by the first years of the war and Lemass's concerns at Supplies. If the proposed capital outlay is broken down the elements of continuity are evident: 30 per cent of the investment was reserved for housing development, while a further 35 per cent was to be used for rural electrification and other electrical development. Moreover, the remaining 35 per cent of proposed investment would go towards traditional areas, such as roadworks, hospital expansion, and tourist development.[25] It would be mistaken to conclude that this investment was misplaced or unnecessary. A strong case can be made for the value of each proposal; however, it does not amount to planning or systematic management of the economy. It would be difficult to compare these examples with the forms of intervention available to the Vichy regime, or to the post-war planners in France.[26] Consequently it is possible to exaggerate the amount of change that occurred, or indeed de Valera's influence over the process.

It would be erroneous to deny that Ireland faced a challenge during the war. Changes occurred, but many of these were external and Irish policy-makers hoped to cope with them in a traditional fashion. With Lemass, however, there is perhaps more than simply a change in emphasis: he recognised the long-term problems and wished to confront them. It is possible to detect a certain uneasiness in his thinking as the war progressed. Lemass became the driving force in the government during the war: his organisational ability, his policy initiatives and his use of the state placed him in a commanding position. It would be premature to conclude from this, as Brian Farrell has recently done, that Lemass's experiences established 'the need to move beyond protectionism in order to provide economic development', and that 'behind the seemingly immutable commitment to ideals spelled out in the mid-1920s, Fianna Fáil was being pushed into a range of new policies and options', or that there was 'a progressive shift from the pre-war emphasis on creating Irish industry to the post-war emphasis on the need for competitive efficiency'.[27] There is a general confusion in these quotations. It is correct that Lemass became committed to a more interventionist role during the war. This should not imply that he was prepared to jettison either protectionism or native Irish capitalism. It was not a question of protection or economic development, or Irish industry or competitive efficiency. In retrospect it may appear that this is so because of the difficulties of the 1950s, yet this dichotomy was not in Lemass's mind in 1945, nor in 1947. What Lemass still sought to achieve was self-sufficient economic development which also had the merit of being efficient. Efficiency and self-sufficiency are not necessarily incompatible; they may be, but this depends on the specific circumstances.

It is from Lemass that one would expect a revolution in policy-making. After all, his experience at Supplies had forced him to reconsider his general approach: the memorandum on labour policy is a clear indication of new thinking. As the Minister responsible for economic affairs, particularly the promotion of industry, it might be expected that changes would be detectable here. The renewed activity of Industry and Commerce (supplemented by Supplies) cannot be denied. What is questionable is whether the Department was committed to any fundamental change in direction. The policy objectives contained in labour policy were compatible with those conceptualised during the 1930s. The goal of economic policy generally, and industrial policy in particular, remained self-sufficiency. The commitment to this end remained undiminished, although wartime conditions constrained its full implementation.

Late in 1942 Industry and Commerce once again reviewed the possibilities for industrial expansion. There is no hint of a policy change. The main difficulty facing Irish industrial expansion was the shortage of raw materials and plant. These shortages prevented the implementation of projects the Department had been considering in 1939. Continued import substitution remained the objective. This was to be supplemented by the promotion of specific industries of national importance, such as an oil refinery, a chemical industry and a fertiliser industry. The Department believed it would be difficult to procèed with these schemes in the immediate future, but recommended that consideration should be given to them once conditions allowed:

> The Department intends in the light of the experience gained during the Emergency, to pursue energetically the extension of existing industries, with a view particularly to reduce to the minimum the dependence of this country on outside sources of supply.[28]

In January 1943 this approach was endorsed by the Cabinet Committee on Economic Planning. The Committee further authorised the Departments of Supplies and Industry and Commerce to prepare information on industries which could be established or expanded. This policy aimed at maintaining self-sufficiency at the highest possible levels.[29] By April 1943, the Department reiterated the continuity of policy. The general strategy was to maintain the policy pursued between 1932 and 1939. However, it was now considered necessary to adopt a more interventionist approach. Accordingly, the Industrial Credit Company:

> Have decided that in the postwar period it would not merely examine and, if approved, adopt proposals for

> financing industrial undertakings ..., but promote entirely the establishment of companies to be financed by the ICC.[30]

This more interventionist approach continued throughout 1943. In a comprehensive report in November, the Department outlined its plans for promoting expansion. A questionnaire was circulated to over 2,000 firms, inviting them to supply information on the current state of their industrial activity, future plans, and any support required. When replies were received, departmental officials frequently visited firms, particularly when a small number were involved, to gather further information on the opportunities for expansion and any possible obstacles which such expansion might encounter.[31] Once this information became available, the Department could act to resolve any difficulties, particularly those of a financial nature. Once cooperation was forthcoming from the industrialists the Department was prepared to facilitate their demands for state support. Closer cooperation between Industry and Commerce and the ICC was also envisaged, while the ICC had given an undertaking that it would assess applications sympathetically. Industry and Commerce attempted, at this time, to bring the ICC into a more central relationship with the Department's plans for industrial expansion to eliminate overlapping or duplication of effort.

These were the broadly facilitative views of the Department. More important were the directive elements under consideration:

> The practice, current over a period of years, of endeavouring to interest individuals or groups in the promotion of industry for whose products there seems to be an economic market, will be continued. The field of these operations is indicated generally in the Import List, on the basis of an assumption that government policy will, in the postwar period, still aim at the production of whatever goods or semi-manufactured materials, previously imported, can be manufactured in this country on an economic basis.

The Department intended to supplement this approach by promoting development where existing firms were not involved. The production of raw and semi-manufactured materials for use in existing industries was a particularly neglected area. The Department believed that the existing firms would not, unaided, establish the conditions for expansion. Furthermore, many companies were unwilling to dispense with their current non-Irish suppliers. It was thus necessary for the Department to promote these industries by inducing a combination of Irish companies to produce what was required. Before the war, Irish industrialists had not been enthusiastic concerning Lemass's proposals to initiate a second phase of industrialisation. If this opposition continued:

> The ICC would be asked to explore the possibility of promoting a company for the purpose, independent of the cooperation of the firms using the materials.

This implied removing the opportunity to import the requisite materials. The Department recognised the difficulty of making such proposals in a fluid economic and political situation. The nature of the postwar economic environment would dictate the circumstances for economic activity. Industry and Commerce believed that international trade would retain a protectionist bias. Thus, bilateral rather than multilateral trade was considered to be the main future form of international exchange. This in turn justified the belief that the importation of certain commodities would no longer be in private hands, but reserved to a public corportion or at least an organisation with monopoly power. Barter arrangements would permit national purchasing through centralised machinery and facilitate the use of Irish shipping. The net result could be decidedly in Ireland's interests:

> Apart from the possible necessities of buying only in certain countries on a barter basis, large-scale buying should lead to better terms of purchase and lower freight and insurance charges, and so assist towards a reduction in the cost of the final manufactured article.

Given these assumptions, the continued application of the Control of Manufactures Acts to foreign capital was considered. Surprisingly, departmental officials appeared unsure as to its future application:

> While it is not possible to anticipate the conditions in the postwar period to the extent of being able to forecast what changes, either in the direction of tightening up or loosening the terms of these Acts in respect of foreign participation in industry, it is very necessary to reconsider, as a matter of general policy, the principles contained in these Acts.

In general terms, the working of the Acts had demonstrated to the Department that certain amendments were necessary: these were left undefined. However, reference is made to a sub-committee of the FIM which had been examining the functioning of the Acts. If Industry and Commerce were to accept the FIM position on this legislation, the logical outcome would have been to tighten up the details, if not explicitly to exclude any foreign penetration of the Irish economy.[32] The obstacles to the further growth of existing indigenous industry was a matter of additional concern to the Department. The cost effectiveness and the quality of Irish production required investigation if greater efficiency was to be achieved.

Existing methods of distributing manufactured goods would also undergo close scrutiny. During the 1930s, the Department had decided not to disrupt the existing mechanisms to ensure that goodwill between manufacturer and distributor would be maintained, and employment safeguarded. Most of the distributors pre-dated the period of industrial development, and had resisted the protectionist policies:

> A point was reached, however, even prewar, when the effect of this policy was rather to increase, to a certain extent unnecessarily, the cost of some home produced goods by the commissions and profits of middlemen.

The Distributors Association demanded, in a submission to the Commission on Vocational Organisation, that the manufacturers should not be permitted to undercut their business by selling direct to the retailer. This body estimated that there was a 10 per cent difference between a product sold to the retailer, without the intervention of the distributor. This was not acceptable to them:

> We want to compete on an equal footing with the manufacturer. If he sells to a retailer he must sell at a price at which we can sell also and must give us a margin between the retail and wholesale prices.[33]

Industry and Commerce had been criticising the role of distributors since the 1920s. There was a general belief, even then, that they, rather than the Irish manufacturers, were the cause of higher prices for industrial goods. Indeed in this case, the distributors appeared to be asking for a 10 per cent rise in the manufacturer's price, to keep the distributors in business. As a consequence, it was recommended that steps be taken to overhaul the distribution system, and reduce to a minimum the real cost to the consumer.

Related to this was the need to reduce manufacturing costs. This would be necessary if post-war competitiveness was to be achieved and export markets won. Specialisation of output was one method of achieving this end. The main objection to the way Ireland had industrialised during the 1930s centred on the large variety of products produced by even the smallest concern. Specialisation in a limited number of products could lead to increased efficiency, lower unit costs, as well as greater output and quality. Resistance could be expected to any proposals as they would involve dictating which firm would make what. Therefore, as voluntary agreement might be absent legislative powers would be required to give effect to this proposal. However, it was maintained that standardisation, rather than specialisation might be the most appropriate method of achieving these aims. The proposals to give effect to this marked a greater degree of departmental intervention in the micro-economy than hitherto. The Department was well aware of the implications:

> Consideration is being given to the possibility of enforcing efficient production by requiring firms to install up-to-date plant and use every organisational device to reduce costs. The only control over industry in the prewar period to improve efficiency was the threat to remove or reduce tariffs, which was to a large extent ineffective because of the repercussions from the unemployment which would be created in consequence. It may prove necessary, in the postwar period, to schedule industries in which new concerns could not operate without a licence to which conditions as to general efficiency, variety and price of products, standardisation or specialisation, might be attached. There would be the further advantage from such a licencing system that productive capacity could be confined to the extent of the potential market.[34]

The memorandum on labour policy and that on industrial development mark a shift of emphasis. Whereas, during the 1930s the Department facilitated Irish industry in the belief that it could generate industrialisation, it was now preparing to increase intervention to achieve these objectives. This can partly be attributed to the war experience. Lemass and his officials appreciated more fully what could be achieved by the discretionary use of the state apparatus. We can detect here also the genesis of Lemass's policies for labour and industry which he attempted to implement after 1945. It also indicates certain misgivings concerning the autonomous development of Irish industry. Although unstated at this time, there is an implication that, unaided, there would be little further development. The outcome of the policy documents on industry sustained the view that the Department was encountering difficulties, or entertaining doubts in this area.

Surprisingly, perhaps, the main proposals for post-war investment which the Cabinet received from Industry and Commerce concerned infrastructural schemes. Various projects were outlined, including rural electrification, harbour improvements and the development of an Irish mineral industry. Industry and Commerce did estimate that there would be a substantial spin-off from rural electrification. This, it was suggested, would involve an expenditure of at least 4 million by rural residents to wire their premises. In turn, this would expand the home market for electrical goods. It was estimated that an extra 4,000 would be employed per annum over a ten year period to carry through the scheme. These proposals would only have an indirect effect on industrial policy, though the employment created would be welcome.

By mid 1944 the Department had received 500 replies to the questionnaire circulated a year earlier. At this stage, Industry and Commerce remained reasonably optimistic that further expansion would occur.[35] At the Taoiseach's suggestion, Industry and Commerce began to prepare White Papers on development projects; these were to contain general outlines for future development, rather than specific details. This appeared to be the ideal opportunity for the Department to expand its approach to industrial policy. In March 1945, the Department reported to the Taoiseach that a number of proposals were under consideration. The success of these would depend on the level of assistance and the extent of protection which would be available. If these proved adequate, Industry and Commerce continued to be optimistic that the home market could be secured and an export trade built up. The memorandum concluded:

> These questions will involve decisions on important matters of policy affecting the general control of industrial activity

> and the Minister has these matters under examination at present. Meanwhile, the preparation of a memorandum on industrial development cannot be completed, as it is felt that, if it is to serve any useful purpose as a White Paper, it must contain an outline of the measures which the government propose to undertake to encourage the expansion of existing industries and the erection of new industries in the country.[36]

The subsequent publication of a number of White Papers resulting from these discussions indicated that a change in industrial policy was no longer a central objective for post-war plans. Industry and Commerce believed that no useful purpose would be served by the publication of a White Paper. Those that were published were either general in outline or specifically related to proposals on construction, infrastructure or welfare. The Committee, in fact, had only discussed these proposals in outline, and therefore instructed the departments to prepare the detailed documents for publication. In this form at least, Industry and Commerce did not avail itself of the opportunity to do so.[37] Industrial policy had not become less important for the Department, consideration of alternatives reinforced the commitment to the broad outline established during the 1930s.

Industrial policy for Lemass was a means to an end. It was designed in the late 1920s to promote the maximum employment possible for the Irish people. The absence of a White Paper reflects his inability to persuade his Cabinet colleagues to take the steps necessary to deepen the industrial process and create the conditions for full employment. At the 6 December 1944 meeting of the Cabinet Committee on Post-war Planning, Lemass's view on the need for an employment policy was agreed. Two years earlier, Lemass had been authorised to prepare an examination of the Beveridge Report on full employment.[38] From June 1942 until January 1945, Lemass applied himself to finding a solution for Ireland's employment problems. In his first major analysis in June 1942, he recognised the need for an integrated industrial, labour and manpower policy. However, with the publication of the Beveridge Report and the policy debate in Britain, Lemass appears to have moved beyond the simple and rather crude suggestions in this memorandum. The specifics were jettisoned, but the core was retained. The objective of policy should be to provide adequate productive employment for all the population. Events in Britain had a greater influence on Lemass than other Ministers. As an industrialiser, he naturally looked to Ireland's neighbour for policy initiatives which would enhance Irish industrial development. More importantly, he had been sensitive since the 1920s to developments within the mainstream of British social democracy and to policy developments based on these ideas. His officials also appeared to share this view, quoting various British thinkers in defence of their ideas.

In a speech to the William Rooney Fianna Fáil Cumann in early 1943, Lemass declared that the government was committed:

> To end involuntary unemployment. . . . Its solution will be found if we get a new conception of their responsibility by the state, employers and trade union movement. Unemployment is mainly a symptom of defective industrial organisation. It is not an inevitable feature of an economy based on private enterprise or organised on democratic lines.

It was necessary to overcome what Lemass described as the Beveridge giants: want, disease, ignorance, squalor and idleness. There was only one way to achieve this: 'The solution to unemployment is work. [The] solution for poverty is more production.'[39] Lemass recognised that Irish welfare was inadequate, but argued that redistribution would not suffice if the Beveridge giants were to be overcome. This would require considerable expansion of production: he was now proposing to enlarge national income, rather than a more equitable distribution of existing wealth. Policy during the 1930s had been distributional in impact, involving a shift in wealth from agriculture to urban centres. National income, moreover, had been fairly stagnant during this decade. Lemass now recognised that wealth creation should become a major policy objective.

To achieve this, Lemass applied himself to the 'new economics' of Keynes and his associates. If he had been an 'instinctive Keynesian' during the 1930s, Lemass became a literal and literate one during the 1940s. In absorbing Keynesian economics, Lemass followed the path of many British civil servants and politicians.[40] The Department of Finance did not respond to the impact of Keynes as positively as Lemass. The British White Paper on employment, it suggested, was not an adequate model for Ireland. In what was obviously a defensive response to a threat from a new source, Finance welcomed the White Paper in general terms, but offered a policy which undermined its foundations. The Finance recommendations, if accepted, would have returned economic policy to the 1920s. In particular, Finance recommended that '... a comprehensive review should be undertaken of all existing controls, tariffs, quotas, etc., with the object of removing unnecessary restrictions on trade and whatever makes for higher costs of agricultural produce'.[41] The Department of Finance also advised against any further commitment to expanding welfare. In reality, Finance believed that Ireland could not afford the type of commitments envisaged in Britain. In this they may have been correct. Unlike them, however, Lemass believed that the existing conditions were not the only ones available. He believed that an increase in production could expand national income, and undermine the conditions which sustained Irish poverty. Finance represents once again the pre industrial elites, anxious to reduce costs and maintain their own wealth through trade with Britain.

Lemass quickly responded to Finance's challenge. Towards the end of November 1944, he circulated his observations on the Finance memorandum. In this, he rejected the entire Finance philosophy. He rejected the view that Irish emigrants were attracted by higher standards of living abroad. Lemass believed that the working class in other countries were not necessarily better off than those employed in Ireland: the problem in Ireland was associated with lack of opportunity and insecurity. To provide employment and remove these threats:

> It is just as important for us to devise methods of maintaining total expenditure as it is for the British ... a similar examination of measures which might be effective in maintaining total expenditure in our circumstances, appears desirable.

Such a policy would necessitate breaking with conventional fiscal policy. In particular, the object of the budget should no longer be a rigid commitment to balancing it. Lemass was recommending a revolution in policy-making and one which would undermine Finance's control over the budgetary process. The annual budget should be devised in the light of economic conditions, with the main consideration being the state of trade.

These proposals were radical enough, but he supplemented them by proposing that state control over the economy be increased. This would involve emergency employment measures in the short term: in the longer term he believed the state should take powers to make it compulsory to retrain the unemployed. In addition, the policy of regional industrial expansion should be discontinued and industrial location should be concentrated on urban areas. Finance capital should be made available to commercial firms and the role of the ICC should be expanded. Industry should be encouraged to scrap all outdated machinery as quickly as possible. He concluded these observations by rejecting the entire Finance approach, adding that policy would be defined by politicians not by civil servants, whose function was to administer not design that policy. In sweeping terms, Lemass challenged virtually every canon in Irish economic policy, even those over which he had presided. Everything, he believed, should be open to question:

> If the principle of manipulating state expenditure, and controlling private investment, so as to regulate total purchasing power in relation to the state of trade, is accepted, every method of achieving the desired result must be considered in combination.[42]

Lemass internalised the basic elements of Keynesian economics. As might be expected from an active politician, he was more attracted to the policy prescriptions than to the niceties of economic theory. Yet, he had a clear understanding of what Keynesianism implied for policy makers. In January 1945, Lemass produced a remarkable document: the only extensive outline that I have discovered of the evolution of his ideas. It is systematic in that it integrates his long-term concerns for full employment with available economic techniques to achieve this end. The attraction of the new ideas for Lemass was that they allowed him to pursue a policy which was based on modern developments in economic thought and which did not conflict with a commitment to democratic government. Although recognising that his policy might be improved, he challenged his Cabinet colleagues to offer realistic alternatives. Any alternative would have to incorporate two essential conditions which Lemass outlined:

> (a) that the total outlay on the products of Irish industry should always be high enough to set up a demand for such products which cannot be satisfied without using the whole

> output capacity of the country; and (b) that the output capacity of the country should be so expanded that on the basis of the most efficient production methods it will require, when fully utilised, the employment of the whole available manpower.[43]

In terms of Irish economic development, the consequences of these proposals were radical. Keynes provided Lemass with the intellectual tools to expand on his under-consumptionist views and to justify his belief that a rise in public expenditure could benefit the economy. Acceptance of Keynes had other radical consequences: Lemass considered that full employment implied no unemployment and was prepared to accept the consequences of this. It also involved sweeping changes in the agricultural economy. Such changes involved rejecting the Fianna Fáil policy of maintaining the largest number of producers on the land irrespective of output and efficiency. Output and efficiency would therefore be the criteria for assessing policy. For agriculture:

> Policy must be directed to ensuring that ownership will be confined to persons willing and capable of working them adequately.

Two major policy proposals arose from this. The state should not provide support for farmers with low output or without the means to develop and expand production. Once farming had been re-organised, then guaranteed markets for the output should be provided to eliminate the cyclical element in farming. This challenge to private property was met by the Minister for Agriculture, who noted that any disturbance to the existing property relations would lead to agitation and serious disturbances. Dr Ryan was worried about votes as well as property. However, in contrast to Lemass, he did not outline an alternative strategy. The existing system was adequate and the focus of production should remain Britain. Government policy should concentrate on maintaining the price level offered for Irish cattle in the United Kingdom.[44]

Lemass believed that the major difficulty facing Irish producers was inefficiency, particularly in agriculture. In his opinion, there was a danger that Ireland would lose export markets, or be unable to regain those already lost. The loss of the export market for butter was a case in point. The cost per cwt of butter varied from as little as 20 shillings to 50 shillings (£1 to £2.50) depending on the creamery. The lower price should be the required one for the industry: uneconomic units should be eliminated. This was all the more important as the export of cattle was limited to prewar levels and increased output and exports should be sought elsewhere. The market system could not adequately generate these changes within agriculture. Only the state could ensure that production was directed into efficient channels. A more active state policy remained the imperative for a successful agricultural policy. Lemass recognised that the nature of Irish agriculture led the state to reinforce the existing tendencies, rather than to promote change. A less passive approach was required.

Industry faced different obstacles to growth, consequently state intervention would take a different form. Lemass used the concept of industry loosely: it involved most economic activity outside agriculture. The state would provide the financial services required for growth and continue to control imports to ensure that where necessary, demand would continue to be met by Irish producers. In other cases, the state would intervene directly and establish large scale industry, particularly in the engineering, metallurgical and chemical sectors. In these cases monopolies would be awarded for production, but control would be ensured by the government controlling the equity of the company. Lemass noted that in certain cases foreign companies had been awarded monopolies in the past; this should be avoided in future.

In this area of policy there is considerable continuity with the 1930s. Lemass wished to continue his earlier policies, but by different methods. He now realised it was necessary to expand the role of the state if economic goals were to be reached. The regulation of the economy had become urgent, because the free play of market forces, even in the protected economy, had not eliminated unemployment or emigration. Whereas during the 1930s the state supplemented the market, Lemass now believed it was necessary to direct the market in an overtly corporatist manner. This politicisation of the market remained an important element in his thinking until at least 1948. Lemass also recognised that some changes were necessary in the detail of policy. During the 1930s, the Department was satisfied if the internal market demand was absorbed by Irish producers. In a small market, import substitution had certain limitations. These had been recognised, and it had become necessary to promote exports of industrial goods as well as agriculture. Exports were of value in themselves, but Lemass believed that it was preferable for a country to make up the balance between exports and imports by improving the volume of exports, rather than relying on the earnings from capital invested abroad.

Lemass's memorandum was corporatist, integrationist and activist. Each level of policy was structured to achieve specific ends. However, his coporatism was of a specific kind. It was not the corporatism recommended by the Commission on Vocational Organisation, but promoted massive intervention by the state in the internal affairs of the coporate groupings. This had already been attempted in the Trade Union Act 1941. That Act was to be supplemented by an even more vigorous approach:

> A full employment policy is incompatible with the old practice of settling wage rates by direct negotiation between employers and trade unions, or by strikes and lockouts and that in return for the removal of the fear of unemployment, the workers must be willing to accept the supervision of wage rates by a public authority charged with the responsibility of protecting the real value of all wages against depreciation through the inflation of prices following higher wages in some occupations.

Although he recognised the right to organise and negotiate, Lemass believed such rights should be curtailed if they ran counter to the public interest.[45]

This approach would not be limited to trade unions. Despite his belief that the state should not actively intervene in privately owned industry, the logic of his position impelled him in that direction. He proposed that the state should actively promote industrial organisation to achieve the highest level of output and efficiency. Any obstacles to technical innovation should be removed:

> In a protected economy the effect of competition in inducing technical progress is lessened, and it is necessary to supplement it by pressure of another kind. This added pressure must be provided by the state.

Profit control had been the main prewar form of control of private industry. The control of prices rather than profits would now be emphasised; higher industrial profits were to be welcomed, rather than condemned as heretofore. These profits would be based on the companies which adopted the most efficient forms of production. It would also involve: '... the elimination of industrial concerns which are unwilling or unable to operate profitably at these reasonable prices.' To achieve these ends, the tax system would have to be overhauled to allow industrialists to invest and re-equip.

The next step for Lemass involved the establishment of a foreign trading organisation to promote exports and to make available export advice which could identify potential markets and products of benefit to Irish industry. An important element of the 'new economics' forced Lemass to recognise that self-sufficiency could not sustain full employment, at least under democratic government. An expanding export base would be required to achieve full employment. A complete overhaul of existing thinking on export strategy was necessary: exceptional measures would be required if the volume of exports was to be increased significantly. Anticipating developments at the end of the 1950s, Lemass suggested that the government should not insist on national control of industries which export most of what they produced, nor should foreign technicians be excluded simply because they were foreign. Both these suggestions were important developments as they challenged a widely-held view that Ireland could achieve complete autarky. Lemass had a more limited approach to self-sufficiency, recognising that the export of industrial goods could supplement the expansion of productive industry for home consumption.

Budgetary strategy was also to be radically transformed. Accordingly, when total demand did not create the conditions for full employment, the state should intervene in a number of ways. Imports should be reduced and Irish goods substituted. An increase in state expenditure and a reduction in taxation were also proposed. Such an approach was based on accepting deficits and increased borrowing. This would involve more direct control over the banking system. It would also involve using production criteria rather than fiscal or monetary ones to determine policy. The budgetary strategy was derived directly from Keynes.

Despite this novel approach, I would suggest that Lemass retained a conceptual framework informed by his experiences of the 1930s and his ideological formation during the 1920s. Although prepared to alter elements of his previous policy, Lemass was not willing to concede economic sovereignty to international agencies. The commitment to protecting Irish industry remained, particularly where production for home consumption was concerned. A more active export strategy supplemented protection: it did not replace it. Implicit in his memorandum was the belief that Ireland could expand the volume of its agricultural and industrial exports while continuing to protect the indigenous economy from imports. It is not clear if Lemass was aware of the direction in American and British policy concerning the future of the international economy. As indicated in previous memoranda and speeches, he appeared to believe that barter or other forms of bilateralism would continue for the forseeable future. He also did not recognise the task that faced him. The transformation of agriculture alone amounted to a call for social revolution. His Cabinet colleagues quickly dissuaded him from this suggestion.[46]

His policy proposals in other areas were no less radical. Virtually every economic interest group would have been destabilised by his proposals and it is unlikely that his political party, or his Cabinet colleagues, would have welcomed this threat to their Dáil seats. More importantly, however, the policy may have had defects which Lemass did not recognise. He believed that Irish exports would increase to meet external demand, yet there was no tradition of industrial exports. Ireland did not have export markets for industrial goods, nor was the skill available to capture and retain them. Lemass recognised that state intervention was necessary, but was unwilling to recognise a degree of lethargy in Irish industrialists. Even more seriously, perhaps, was the possible impact of deficit budgeting in a protected economy. There was a danger that this could initiate an inflationary spiral and suck in imports if Irish producers proved unable to meet demand. Finally, the level of state regulation required, particularly after a world war, was probably unsustainable. It would certainly have been politically difficult to justify.

Yet it is a mistake to conclude that the period 1939 to 1945 '... was inevitably a sterile epoch in the development of Irish economic policy'.[47] Notwithstanding the problems which beset the economy and the obstacles which Lemass encountered when he attempted to devise a more active strategy, the war had made a difference to the way in which he addressed these problems. While protectionism remained central to policy formation,

Lemass was absorbing new thinking. He had yet to reformulate essential policy, but his concern for full employment laid the basis for his immediate postwar legislative programme.

While Lemass's policy proposals were both ambitious and radical, his ability to implement these policies remained more problematic. The latent resistance to his expansionary programmes had not been diminished by the end of the war. If anything, conservative forces were stronger in 1945 than they had been in 1938. In this Ireland can be contrasted with the experience of most Western European states. In common with most other European states, the Irish economy revived immediately after 1945, but the contrast becomes clear when Ireland's growth tapers off and sustained economic growth is not achieved. While Europe shared in the unprecedented economic growth which characterised the postwar era, Ireland suffered economic stagnation until the early 1960s. Ireland's GNP expanded by 7.6 per cent between 1949 and 1954 while the average for all OEEC countries was 29 per cent.[48] All European states faced a dilemma in policy making after the war:

> Which should receive preference, existing levels of domestic output and employment or the *possibility* of expanding foreign trade through a system which might leave levels of national employment and output much more vulnerable to events in other economies.[49]

The choice was never clear cut for any economy; in general, however, most states adopted a strategy which presupposed the liberalisation of trade and the multilateral system which accompanied this. Ireland was one of the few countries to remain apart from this process. Irish policy makers also recognised the need for growth, but chose to reinforce the achievements of the 1930s rather than the possibilities of the future. Whereas the Second World War proved to be a watershed for most states in social, economic and political terms, this was not the case in Ireland. The 1930s had been a decade of growth and consolidation for the new state and consequently continuity rather than change continued to be attractive. Nor did Fianna Fáil feel the need to change in 1945. It had won a convincing victory in the 1944 elections, despite losing some of its traditional support in the west. Its policy of neutrality had been vindicated, while the 1937 constitution had been accepted by most sectors of the society. Although difficult to quantify, it is possible that the wartime experience reinforced conservative-nationalist sentiment because, in the eyes of most Irish people, the state had successfully manoeuvered through a difficult time.

Lemass's policy initiatives and behaviour reflect this environment. Despite his absorption of Keynesianism little change in policy can be detected. There is no evidence that the Fianna Fáil government considered the possibility of introducing policies linked to deficit spending or to more general forms of expansionary budgets. Unlike his counterparts in Britain, Sweden, or the United states Lemass's political support base was relatively narrow and consequently he could not generate a large constituency for such policies. More important perhaps is the evidence that Lemass himself, despite his appreciation of the new economics, was forced by the post-war circumstances to continue his older policies. As early as July 1945 he wrote to de Valera noting that his:

> General objective will be to do everything possible to have trade and commerce restored to normal conditions on the general basis of this policy in the pre-emergency period of giving protection to native industry so as to secure maximum employment.[50]

Thus when faced with a choice between the uncertainty of innovation and the certainties of what was in place, he chose the latter. Nor had Lemass broken with what Bew and Patterson described as a 'narrow type of economic nationalism'. At the policy level, as distinct from some general remarks made at the time, the objectives of Industry and Commerce do not depart on any point of substance from the certainties established during the 1930s.[51]

The implications of the post-war environment for Irish industrial policy were not clear to Industry and Commerce. Without an alternative conceptual framework there was a strong incentive to continue implementing the policies successfully elaborated a decade earlier. Nor did Lemass differ from this when it came to day to day activities within the Department. He believed that it would be possible to promote industrial expansion using methods less drastic than had hitherto been the case. He also believed that there continued to be untapped potential for further economic expansion. There is also an emphasis on efficiency which had not been the case previously. However this did not mark a departure from the commitment to self-sufficiency; Lemass continued to believe that it was possible to have a high level of self-sufficiency and efficient industrial organisation. In pressing for efficient production methods Lemass had not embraced neo-liberal views of competitive advantage as a speech to the Dáil in 1946 makes clear:

> It will be common ground among us I think that the test of efficiency of any economic policy is the contribution it makes to the ending of unemployment and the abolition of undeserved poverty.

The criterion used for efficiency is compatible with a high level of protection, a point recognised by Lemass when he listed a large number of reasons for the continuing validity of protection. As these included market failure, national security and welfare considerations, it is safe to conclude that throughout the immediate post-war years Lemass's thinking and actions remained embedded in an essentially economic nationalist framework.[52]

This can be ascertained from a consideration of the detailed behaviour of the Department between 1945 and 1948. Traditional policies are maintained and sometimes extended, while new policy initiatives do not depart in degree from the central themes. The Control of Manufactures Acts had been the cornerstone of industrial policy during the 1930s and remained the method by which the Department controlled foreign investment until the early 1960s. Mary Daly has concluded that:

> In terms of its primary aim, which was to prevent the establishment in a protected Irish market of firms which were merely branches of external concerns and hence incapable of ever exporting, the Control of Manufactures Acts must be deemed to have failed.

Between 1945 and 1954 some 224 New Manufacturing Licences were awarded, compared to ninety-four between 1932 and 1940, thirty-nine of the latter having been cancelled.[53] Despite this, there was no 'open door' for foreign investment prior to 1948 nor is there any evidence that policy was being reconsidered. The acts remained in force and were applied with vigour. There are numerous examples of British companies being refused permission to locate in Ireland, the main grounds for refusal being associated with the protection of the home market and the fear by Irish industry that there would be unwarranted competition. These considerations were prominent in the minds of officials as was their commitment to regulate the capacity of each sector and to control entry once it concluded that the maximum output had been obtained. Employment and welfare considerations were of primary concern when decisions were taken at this time; if a foreign company could produce a new product or could produce for export the Department was generally sympathetic to the application, otherwise proposals were refused.[54]

The Department's main concern after 1945 was to maintain a high level of production and to sustain Irish producers already in existence. Departmental decisions were always based on these considerations; at times Lemass threatened Irish producers with competition or withdrawal of tariffs if they did not improve efficiency, but such threats appear never to have been actually carried out.[55] What is clear is that policy was interpreted flexibly to obtain the maximum results for the economy. In different contexts the policy is applied differently. Nor was the Department averse to utilising the threat of foreign competition to obtain certain guarantees from existing companies. The government had awarded Dunlop a monopoly in the production of rubber products as an incentive to locate in Ireland during the 1930s, yet Lemass remained unhappy with the behaviour of the company. Lemass was favourable to an application for a New Manufacturing Licence to produce plastic and rubber products – mainly for export – which Dunlop was not producing. He was concerned that Dunlop would object on the grounds of the earlier guarantee. The occasion was taken to put pressure on Dunlop, who were unwilling to export and to obtain from them commitments for the future:

> The Irish Dunlop Company should be informed formally that an application is before the Minister ... and that the Minister contemplates granting the licence. They should be asked whether they intend to undertake themselves the manufacture of rubber flooring on a similar scale (i.e. both for the home and export markets) and if so, any views they might wish to offer would be considered. Discussions with

> the promoters of the new proposal should proceed on the basis that a licence will be granted.[56]

The Control of Manufactures Acts cannot be deemed a failure on this account. It is true that the number of licences granted means that more foreign companies located in Ireland after 1945. However, the conditions remained stringent, and many applications were refused. It also demonstrates that there remained considerable scope for economic expansion but that Irish industrialists were either unable or unwilling to establish the new capacity. In this context foreign companies located by default. The continued investment in the Irish economy by foreign companies was prompted by the availability of investment opportunities and markets as well as the failure of Irish companies to invest. The Acts *could* have prevented most foreign investment, but in certain areas this investment proved necessary if any expansion was to take place. Lemass's concern was for industrial expansion and he favoured Irish companies to achieve this; where this was not possible he used his discretionary power to allow limited foreign investment.

The basic strategy required active support for Irish industrialists in promoting industrial expansion. Any radical departure in policy after 1945 would have required the dismantling of protection and accepting the dislocation that might follow. No such restructuring took place; indeed as international trade returned to normality in 1947 Lemass reintroduced virtually all the controls which had been in place prior to the war. Tariffs, quotas and other restrictions were imposed as each sector of the economy found its monopoly of the home market threatened.[57] One of the consequences of this approach was that the limit of Irish industrial expansion remained the extent of the Irish market. There is little evidence that Irish industrialists were planning to export at this time. Nor did the Department offer them an incentive to do so. Lemass's horizon may have extended beyond the home market in that he recognised the opportunities available, but the experience with Irish industry and his specific policy proposals did not enhance the possibility of exports. Lemass's successful campaign during 1946 and 1947 to obtain tax relief for industrialists probably reinforced the tendency to concentrate on the home market. Lemass promoted the industrialists' case on the grounds that profits should not be restricted to facilitate new investment in plant and machinery. Finance's criticism that such a concession simply increased the profits of companies without any discernible benefit to the community was probably correct.[58]

There is a substantial contradiction in Lemass's approach between 1945 and 1948. His actions reaffirmed the commitment to economic nationalism, thus signalling the industrialists that the support base for them would continue to be available. Simultaneously he recognised that if Ireland was to achieve the growth necessary to achieve full employment, then the state would have to play a more active role in promoting this growth. During the immediate postwar years trade liberalisation became a major objective of the leading industrial nations. High unemployment during the 1930s was attributed to the collapse of the international trading system. The majority of European states continued to experience high levels of unemployment up to 1939 even when, as was the case with Sweden, innovative recovery programmes were implemented. Postwar planners believed that an increase in international trade would contribute to the lowering of unemployment. Throughout the industrial world this proved to be the case.[59]

Ireland remained the exception, experiencing low growth, continuing unemployment and eventually falling victim to a major crisis. The decisions taken by the Irish government on economic and industrial policy after 1945 reflected the continuing commitment to self-sufficiency. The Department of Industry and Commerce's detailed decision making not only reflected this but reinforced the protectionist environment for native entrepreneurs. The most striking contrast after 1945 is between the reconstruction of the economic fortress and Lemass's failure to implement policies which reflected the theoretical insights of Keynesianism. When Lemass introduced new policies, these, in large part, reflected established norms. This is not to imply that Lemass did not pursue innovative policies after 1945, but it does mean that new policies did not involve a departure from the general policy framework already established.

Innovative policies can be detected in three areas: exports, industrial relations and industrial organisation. The main source of innovation was not in policy objectives, but in the extent to which Lemass was prepared to use the state apparatus to achieve these objectives. In late 1945 he circulated a bill to establish a foreign trade corporation; the aim of which was to regulate imports and to control Irish exports. According to Lemass exports would not increase without state assistance, due to the size of Irish companies and their lack of experience. Despite this, Lemass was not promoting an active export policy; his aim remained that of securing foreign markets for surplus Irish production. Moreover, the basic institutional structure of Irish protectionism would remain. Lemass assumed that foreign states would open their markets to Irish exports while accepting Irish restrictions on their own exports. The proposals met with sustained opposition not only from Finance, but from the Department of External Affairs which maintained that opinion in the United states remained hostile to state control of trade. Although there was considerable discussion on the issue, the legislation was subsequently withdrawn after Lemass suffered a series of defeats in the Cabinet on the structure of the new organisation.[60]

On the most favourable analysis Lemass's proposals were naive. At a time when foreign trade was being liberalised, he was attempting to secure greater control and this may be attributable to his belief, reinforced during the war, that state agencies were the most appropriate ones to direct economic growth. Notwithstanding this the proposals may also have been inappropriate given the continuing dependence on agriculture for exports. Finance was at pains to point out that industrialists would welcome state support in any field, but there was no guarantee that industrial exports would be promoted as a consequence.

Lemass also recommended further state intervention in labour policy and in business organisation. The Industrial Relations Act 1946 and the draft Control of Prices and Promotion of Industrial Efficiency Bill 1947 had as their objectives the coordination of business and labour to achieve the state's economic objectives. The Industrial Relations Act set up the Labour Court in an attempt to move wage policy beyond collective bargaining. Lemass continued to believe that full employment could be achieved if wage policy was linked to economic policy, and clearly hoped that the Labour Court would become the institution where wages and conditions would be regulated in the national interest. Divisions within the trade union movement, hostility to the judicial nature of the court itself, and the strength of traditional collective bargaining conspired to neutralise the ambitious hopes which Lemass had for the court. An informal wage round was negotiated in 1948, but this did not prove to be a departure from tradition.[61]

By 1947 Irish economic policy had largely returned to the patterns formulated during the 1930s. Industrial production continued to be heavily dependent on the state's good will. The Industrial Relations Act did not, contrary to expectations, provide the institutional conditions for an alternative approach to industrial relations and wage policy. Export policy suffered from similar drawbacks; Lemass's draft legislation proved unrealistic both in terms of its possible inducement effect and in its understanding of the changing international environment. Irish foreign trade was re-establishing its traditional patterns and these reflected the continuing dominance of agricultural production. Successful trade negotiations in 1947 and 1948 secured the British market for Irish agricultural exports, while simultaneously removing pressure to export from Irish industrialists.

In a major review of policy in October 1947, Lemass questioned the willingness of the main producer groups to obtain maximum benefits from the changing situation. He noted that while there were short term difficulties associated with capital and resource shortages, the real difficulties were long term and closely associated with the behaviour of producer groups:

> The general public is suffering at present from a seller's market both here and abroad which generally leads to lack of initiative on the part of producers, high profits on manufacture and distribution and, in the case of employees, demands for more wages and shorter hours. This mentality is a national danger and in operation causes an upward trend in the cost of production, which will render it more difficult to correct when normal conditions are resumed and goods are available on a competitive basis. At the same time, the seller's market offers ample opportunities which may never occur again of developing industry and export trade. Unfortunately there seems to be a tendency on the part of industrialists here to concentrate on the home market, whilst on the other hand numerous approaches have been made by outside concerns to start industries here with an eye to the export trade.[62]

Lemass recognised some of the difficulties, but was unwilling to change policy. He introduced a bill, however to establish an

Industrial Efficiency Bureau. This agency would absorb the functions of the Prices Commission and would examine the efficiency of an individual company or sector in the economy. A report would be prepared for the Minister and based on this he would require changes in the company's organisation to assure higher efficiency. Failure to comply could result in loss of state protection or other penalties. These proposals generated considerable opposition, particularly from the industrialists. The legislation fell when the Dáil was dissolved and the Inter-Party government did not proceed with it.[63]

Each of Lemass's main policy proposals after 1945 had one thing in common; their coercive nature. In each case Lemass sought to extend state regulation of producers and at times he also favoured direct controls. Up to 1948, when he left office, Lemass had acquired substantial institutional power, certainly more than he had had in 1932. His legislative programme reflected this. Despite these ambitious plans, policy making during the immediate postwar years was a failure. The status quo was reinforced rather than challenged. Lemass's own actions were ambiguous: he was proposing legislation which, if enacted, would destabilise the economy while simultaneously reviving older policies which would negate the impact of the newer ones. This ambiguity was based on a dilemma: Lemass was committed to attaining full employment and he recognised that further industrialisation was required to achieve this. He doubted the capacity of Irish industrialists to reach the output required to maintain high levels of employment, yet he was cautious when confronting them because of the possible impact on existing employment.

In a sense Lemass's postwar strategy was incomplete, reflecting a piecemeal or ad hoc approach rather than a coherent set of objectives. He knew what he wanted, but was not always clear on how to obtain this. He opted for what he knew best, state intervention, but in doing so he confronted all the main vested interests in the economy. These groups and their institutional and political allies were strong enough to neutralise Lemass's efforts to exercise control over them. Lemass may have been correct when he suggested before the war that Irish industry was by then beyond the infant stage; a continuing difficulty for him and his successors was that any proposal to remove the infant from the cradle was met with fierce opposition. In an increasingly stable economy the established interest groups were in a strong position to sustain a veto over policy. The election defeat in 1948 removed Lemass from his institutional power base, consequently preventing him from formulating alternative strategies for national development.

6

The Crisis of the Traditional Economy 1948–61

THE 1948 election dislodged Fianna Fáil from power for the first time in sixteen years. The consequences of this were more profound in political than in policy terms. The election introduced a period of political uncertainty which was to last for over a decade. It also demonstrated that there was an alternative to Fianna Fáil if all other parties cooperated. The emergence of a loose anti-Fianna Fáil coalition led in turn to the realignment of Irish politics in terms of Fianna Fáil versus the Rest, a feature which has continued to characterise the political system. The political significance of 1948 can be attested to by the failure of each incumbent to be re-elected between then and 1957. The cycle was to be broken in 1961 when Fianna Fáil was returned to office, albeit with a minority government. Table 6.1 outlines the shift in voting patterns between 1948 and 1961.[1]

Table 6.1 General Election Results: 1944–61 (percentage of vote)

	1944	*1948*	*1951*	*1954*	*1957*	*1961*
Fianna Fáil	48.9	41.9	46.3	43.4	48.3	43.8
Fine Gael	20.5	19.8	25.7	32.0	26.6	32.0
Labour	8.8	8.7	11.4	12.1	9.1	11.6
National Labour	2.7	2.6	–	–	–	–
Clann na Talmhan	10.8	5.3	2.9	3.1	2.4	–
Clann na Poblachta	–	13.2	4.1	3.8	1.7	–
Others	8.4	8.5	9.6	5.7	6.6	–
Sinn Féin	–	–	–	–	5.3	–

Source: Cornelius O'Leary, *Irish Elections 1918–77* (Dublin 1979)

PROPERTY OF
ST. MARY'S COLLEGE
STRAWBERRY HILL

This governmental instability disguises considerable continuity in policy making over the same period. Indeed this very instability may have contributed to continuity, as governments were unable to evaluate fully the need for change, and even if they did could not implement it without a further mandate. It may be no accident that the main departure in post-war economic policy occurred when Fianna Fáil was in power and received a further mandate. One contributory factor to continuity is thus the precarious nature of each government's majority. Another is the continuing influence of Fianna Fáil over policy-making even when out of office. Between 1932 and 1948 Fianna Fáil had acquired hegemonic influence over Irish policy-making in many spheres. The Inter-Party government which replaced it in 1948 did not attempt to reformulate the existing policy framework. The declaration of the Republic was the logic of de Valera's foreign policy; the welfare programmes were implicit in Fianna Fáil's traditional expansionary approach to such issues; while economic policy continued along lines well established by previous administrations.

The first Inter-Party government has usually been described as innovative, yet despite certain nuances by a number of Ministers there is little evidence for this. The introduction of a capital budget in 1950 is frequently cited as evidence for innovation, apparently committing Ireland to Keynesian demand management.[2] If this commitment was given in 1950, it was remarkably short lived. Subsequent budgets were deflationary, emphasising a continuing commitment to the balanced budget and the fear of balance of payments crises. Moreover, the 1950 budget can only be described as Keynesian in a very narrow sense indeed. The decision to commit a certain percentage of budget allocation to capital projects was important, but only if part of an overall process to facilitate growth in the economy. This was singularly not forthcoming in 1950, nor was it for the remainder of the decade. In other Western European states an ideology of growth emerged, and all policy instruments were utilised to achieve this end. This 'growth consciousness' was not simply an application of technical Keynesianism, although these techniques were important; it also involved mobilising the resources of the state through cooperation between government, management, and labour to provide the institutional means to achieve these ends. This involved, as Kuisel has shown in the French case, a shift in state objectives from stability to modernity in economic development. This was reinforced by the use of sophisticated techniques of economic management to ensure the planned development of the mixed economy.[3]

While economic management had been in operation in Ireland since the 1930s, by the late 1940s it was being utilised to preserve stability rather than to generate a modern industrial economy. Consequently the expansionary rhetoric of Irish policy-making between 1948 and 1950 has to be placed in a context where traditional policy making in all sectors was maintained. Notwithstanding Ireland's participation in the European Recovery Programme (ERP), the elaboration of a capital budget, or the absorption of Keynesianism by some officials, T.K.Whitaker's assessment of ERP that '... no one who took part in preparing the Recovery Programme (and that includes myself) ever looked on it as a development programme, but rather as an exercise that had to be undertaken to persuade the Americans to give us Marshall Aid' could be applied more generally.[4] The expansionary nature of the Irish economy at this time was due to extraneous circumstances and did not involve a commitment to planning or to new departures in economic policy. This can further be seen from the Irish refusal to participate in international agencies or to reduce its export dependency on agriculture. Moreover, the success of demand management elsewhere in Europe was dependent on developing a strong export base. The absence of this relationship between exports and budgetary strategy facilitated the conservative policies which were promoted during the 1950s.

Nor did the Department of Industry and Commerce provide a focus for change; continuity is also the main feature of industrial policy. The new Minister, Daniel Morrissey, was inexperienced and heavily dependent on his officials for advice. Though a strong protectionist, he did not possess the independence of mind which had characterised his predecessor. He internalised the presuppositions of his Department, but apparently proved unable to promote even its limited policy objectives within the Cabinet.[5] Consequently in the major policy areas the Department pursued a cautious approach. Morrissey continued to operate the Control of Manufactures Acts to prevent foreign penetration of the Irish economy, and on a number of occasions prevented Irish firms from linking up with external companies.[6] The Department continued to promote protection for indigenous industry, through tariffs, quotas and duties and to maintain or increase these levels. The government generally accepted Industry and Commerce's recommendations on these matters; usually only the Department of Finance objected. Thus, at this level as with fiscal policy, whatever about generalised declarations of policy, little actually changed in terms of policy intervention.

There was a general tendency for the Inter-Party government to respond to issues, rather than devising policies to achieve consistent objectives. Departmental files at this time contain many references to the need for exports, both industrial and agricultural. Despite this, industrial exports remained insignificant until the 1960s. Protection may have been an obstacle to this growth because industrialists did not have the knowledge or experience of external markets to identify export possibilities. It is questionable if this in itself prevented an increase in industrial exports. The West European market was expanding at a high level of demand by the end of the 1940s. Barriers to trade had begun to fall; the United states and Canada, for example, reduced tariff barriers at the first GATT meeting in Geneva in 1947. This was followed throughout the 1950s by a number of GATT meetings, all of which resulted in decisions to lower tariffs. Despite the tendency for trade barriers to fall, Irish industrialists did not take advantage of these opportunities. This weakness was compounded by the insistence of the British and American governments that Ireland's contribution to European recovery should be in the agricultural area. The higher prices and easier access to the British market achieved in 1948 reinforced the traditional agricultural export patterns.[7]

The failure to increase industrial exports can be attributed to a number of factors. As Lemass had recognised, industrial exports would not be generated unless the government provided the institutional support and specific inducements to achieve this objective. Nor did the government or the Department of Industry and Commerce actively inform potential exporters that profits from exports would not be subject to control. Export policy appears to have been passive: if the Department was approached it acknowledged that there was no control, but did not base a strategy for industrial exports around it. Lemass's attempt to promote a Foreign Trade Corporation had not been pursued, although the draft legislation had drawn attention to the need to stimulate exports. These proposals had recognised that manufacturing exports were necessary if Irish growth was to continue and attempted to devise policy instruments to achieve that end. The establishment of the Dollar Exports Advisory Committee (DEAC) in 1950 was a further attempt to achieve this. However, unlike the earlier Lemass initiative, this was a response to the general economic turmoil which resulted from the shortage of dollars in Europe. The United states Economic Cooperation Administration in Ireland pressurised the government to increase its dollar earnings, and the Taoiseach stressed the need to bridge the 'dollar gap' which would intensify when Marshall Aid was discontinued in 1952.[8]

A distinction has to be drawn between industrial exports as such and exports to dollar areas in particular. The DEAC was set up to stimulate exports, yet expanding exports remained secondary to the main objective of increasing dollars. An increase in industrial exports would have been welcome, but this was not in itself the main purpose of policy. In contrast, the Industrial Development Authority (IDA) maintained that the expansion of manufacturing exports should be the clear focus of any export policy. It proposed that an organisation to promote exports should be established to achieve national coordination of industrial exports. The IDA recognised the difficulties which existed:

> We hold the definite view that there is no likelihood of any appreciable increase in industrial exports on the basis of the individual effort of manufacturers. Our manufacturers as a whole have very limited knowledge or experience of export trade and apart from their reluctance to enter into an unknown and highly competitive field, the share of any particular manufacturer in export trade would be relatively so small that it could not bear the expense of an adequately staffed and operated export department.[9]

Industrial exports, the IDA added, would not be generated unless financial inducements were forthcoming. However, the Department of Finance was critical of these recommendations. Finance believed that the manufacturers themselves should establish the export body, and insisted that neither public finance nor tax concessions should be made available to exporters. There was, the minute continued:

> An air of unreality about this interim report of the IDA. It does not seem to come to grips with the problem at all. If, however, the government agrees to the proposals, there is not the slightest doubt that the manufacturers will receive the IDA with open arms. Why shouldn't they? The state will then be doing for them something which they should do themselves.[10]

This opposition is not surprising as the IDA proposals were similar to those outlined by Lemass in 1945, proposals which Finance had vigorously opposed at the time.

Whatever merits an export organisation might have had either for dollar exports or for industrial exports, little was in fact achieved. The DEAC issued a number of detailed reports, including one which recommended a state-funded export organisation. The circulation of the reports was followed by considerable disagreement between various departments. The Department of Industry and Commerce questioned the validity of concentrating on dollar exports, while Finance believed that agricultural exports should be the main source of dollar earnings. Both Finance and the Revenue Commissioners questioned the amount of capital required for the organisation. Nor did the establishment of Coras Trachtala (CTT), as a promotional agency for Irish exports, in December 1951 meet the recommendations of the IDA or the DEAC. CTT was basically an advisory body, and did not have the finance or the power to induce industrialists to export.[11] By the time Marshall Aid terminated, dollar exports had not increased significantly, nor had industrial exports. The main difficulty remained one of finance. In a deteriorating fiscal situation, Lemass (who had returned to power in 1951) refused to commit himself to tax remission on export profits:

> It is under consideration but, while it has, as you might expect, my sympathetic interest, it offers very substantial difficulties from the viewpoint of the Minister for Finance. He fears, and with some reason, that if the principle of tax remission is conceded for one desirable purpose, it will be difficult to resist it for other purposes.[12]

The desirability of exports in general and for dollar exports in particular should not disguise the real obstacle to expanding Irish exports during the 1950s. A major obstacle was the continued dependence on agricultural exports to the British market. All governments assumed that agricultural exports would remain the mainstay of foreign trade. This might not have been mistaken during the 1920s and 1930s when, with the exception of the economic war, Ireland was in a strong position to maximise its proximity to and relationship with the UK market. The benefits from agricultural exports and the British market were not as clear cut during the 1950s. The 1948 Trade Agreement with the UK secured Irish entry to the British market on reasonable terms. One consequence of this was that Britain remained the sole focus for agricultural exports. There was no attempt to diversify exports during the late 1940s or 1950s, nor was there an attempt to generate other forms of agricultural products which could be exported. Under these circumstances there was little likelihood that agriculture would provide the stimulus for an expansion of the export trade.

This left the industrial sector as the main possibility for exports. There was much greater flexibility in this sector than in agriculture. The export of industrial goods accelerated rapidly in global terms throughout the 1950s, a process which continued during the 1960s. This phenomenon contributed significantly to the long term boom under way. Those countries which experienced high export growth also had the highest levels of GNP growth. International demand thus proved to be an extremely important stimulant for the growth of a manufacturing sector in many states.[13] Despite these possibilities, Irish industrial exports remained marginal for most of the 1950s. This can be attributed to a number of factors. There was little export consciousness among industrialists; without inducement they would not export. In a rapidly changing international economic environment, industrialists preferred the security of the home market to the challenge of an uncertain foreign market. The government was reluctant to participate in the new international agencies, such as GATT, because it was recognised that this would weaken Ireland's economic sovereignty. The decisions taken between 1945 and 1957 by successive governments reinforced the national rather than the international focus of economic policy-making. This in turn separated Ireland's economic development from that of the rest of Western Europe. These difficulties were compounded by the weakness of Morrissey as Minister between 1948 and 1951, as well as the dominance of conservative Finance criteria during 1951 and 1952, a factor which precluded Lemass from playing a more positive role at this juncture.[14]

Without government intervention it was unlikely that many manufacturers would develop an export trade. The success of import substitution and the continuing expansion of the protected sector indicated that further possibilities for internal growth remained available. Morrissey drew attention to the high level of imports in 1950, estimating that £60 million worth could be replaced by Irish products and 45,000 new jobs created. There was still considerable scope for further industrial development within the protected economy, he claimed.[15] Morrissey's remarks were made during the second stage of the IDA Bill, the IDA itself having already been in operation for nearly a year. During the 1960s and 1970s, the IDA proved remarkably successful in attracting foreign industry to Ireland, becoming one of the major institutional supporters of free trade. It would, however, be mistaken to interpret the establishment of the IDA as a break with traditional industrial policy. It was not an alternative approach, but a method of supplementing the framework already in existence.[16]

A memorandum by Sean MacBride stressed the objective of self-sufficiency and independent industrial development. He recommended that an independent body be established to evaluate tariffs and quotas, to examine applications for protection, and to assess the implications of these for the cost of living and balance of trade. MacBride's proposals were accepted by the government and formed the basis for the legislation which established the IDA. They did not mark a break with Fianna Fáil policy, but were presented as an attempt to extend the earlier framework. The new government, in fact, criticised Fianna Fáil for its failure to meet its own objectives, not for the policy it pursued.[17] The Department of Finance criticised MacBride's memorandum, believing that it impugned the integrity of the Civil Service and questioned the usefulness of an independent body for assessing industrial policy. However, the Minister, Patrick McGilligan, while agreeing with this criticism, did note that part of the policy would involve attracting large foreign industries to locate in Ireland. The IDA was given authority to encourage new industry and expand and modernise existing ones. It was also empowered to examine the effects of protection, and applications for tariffs. The proposals contained in the 1949 Act were wide-ranging, but certainly less radical than those of Lemass's Industrial Efficiency Act of 1947.[18]

Morrissey believed that the main function of the IDA would be the promotion of new industry. If this was the case, the new legislation did not provide an adequate basis for achieving it. The IDA took over responsibility for virtually all aspects of industrial development, but it had no executive authority. As a result, the lines of communication between the Minister for Industry and Commerce and the IDA were more complex than those which had existed between the Civil Service and the Minister. The IDA could make recommendations to the Minister, which would then be considered by him and subsequently forwarded to the Cabinet. This made decision making a difficult and drawn-out process. Nor was there much contact between Industry and Commerce and the IDA; John Leydon informed the government that, although both bodies maintained a common registry, the Department had no knowledge of what the IDA was investigating, nor did the IDA inform the Department.[19]

The aim of the act was certainly ambitious: it involved removing most industrial policy functions from the jurisdiction of the Department of Industry and Commerce. However, the IDA encountered serious difficulties from the beginning. When the members of the Authority started work, they found a large number of tariff and quota applications waiting for their attention. In addition, the functions of the Trade Loans (Guarantee) Acts, the Prices Commission, and general questions of industrial policy were transferred to them. Without executive power and finance, the IDA quickly became an overworked institution which could not develop policy. The Chairman, J.P. Beddy, quickly recognised these limitations and suggested that increased staff, adequate capital resources to promote industries, and authority to erect factories should be made available as a priority. He maintained that the IDA could not fulfil its prescribed tasks without these resources. Although Beddy was supported by MacBride, the Taoiseach with the support of the Ministers for Finance and Industry and Commerce refused to consider the proposals or to circulate them to other members of the Cabinet. The consequences for the IDA of this decision were serious: it was expected to perform many of the functions of a government department without having access to the requisite resources or authority to achieve its objectives.[20]

The decision to establish the IDA weakened the Department of Industry and Commerce, while at the same time placing inordinate pressure on the Authority. It is difficult to disagree with Lemass, who charged Morrissey in the Dáil with reactivating the Tariff Commission. This, he maintained, reflected a Fine Gael mentality opposed to industrialisation. Lemass further questioned whether the government was prepared to continue protection, and suggested that the new Authority was a method of weakening the strength of the industrial sector. Lemass was mistaken in some of his charges; whatever about some members of the government, the IDA at this stage was not opposed to protection. The procedure imposed on it, however, meant that each application for protection was examined closely, frequently involving visits to the factory. This had rarely been undertaken when Industry and Commerce had control over policy and it was an approach which alarmed many industrialists.[21]

Lemass's opposition to the IDA in 1950 and his commitment to abolish the authority appears incongruous in the context of his belief in state intervention. Bew and Patterson have concluded that: 'In view of his radical ideas of 1945, it is difficult to believe that he wholeheartedly supported opposition to the IDA,' and suggest that it was a public attempt to reconcile Fianna Fáil to the industrialists alienated from it in previous years.[22] While there is some strength in this view, it would be mistaken to conclude that Lemass was compromising with conservative forces. At its simplest level Lemass was a party man, and his opposition can be construed as the response of a politician in opposition. But his criticism has more weight than this. He rightly concluded that the division between the IDA and Industry and Commerce would weaken policy coherence. Without clear lines of authority Lemass recognised that it would be difficult to devise new policy instruments, a point confirmed when an analysis of the department's policy output for 1948–51 is made. The ambiguous nature of the institutional arrangements between the IDA and Industry and Commerce also weakened the integrity of the civil service. This was a major consideration for Lemass; after all he remained a statist, one who believed that the state should be utilised for development. As Industry and Commerce was the major vehicle for such developments, any weakening of its institutional power would be suspect to Lemass.

Despite these criticisms the IDA itself was closer to Lemass than perhaps he suspected. Beddy remained a protectionist and opposed Ireland's participation in the general liberalisation of European trade. Like Lemass, Beddy wished to induce greater efficiency among Irish industrialists but within a protected framework. When the Foreign Trade Committee recommended that Ireland should join the International Trade Organisation (ITO) and the International Monetary Fund (IMF), the IDA countered the suggestion vigorously. The IDA argued that the ITO presented a danger to Ireland's national independence and its industrial economy. The benefits from international free trade were not available to Ireland, and the organisation was designed to favour the major industrial states. Ireland had a very low level of industrialisation as well as social problems which differentiated it from the major industrial states:

> Ireland is endeavouring to improve these unsatisfactory features by developing her resources and in particular by providing for her own requirements in many respects. She is thus one of a number of less developed countries, is engaged in expanding her economy and has not yet progressed sufficiently to withstand world competition, particularly in industrial products.

The ITO effectively collapsed following the United states Congress's refusal to ratify a radically revised version of its structure, but the option to join GATT remained. The divisions within the government on both issues were largely the same: the Departments of Finance, Agriculture, and External Affairs recommended membership, while the Minister for Industry and Commerce, supporting the IDA, was opposed. Support for liberalisation was not accompanied by any strategy for Irish industry; consequently Morrissey was able to persuade the Cabinet to continue to support Irish industry within the context of the national economy.[23] Far from being an agency for free trade, as it is sometimes characterised, the IDA in fact continued to represent the interests of Irish industrial development within a framework based on protection.

Lemass's charge that the Department of Industry and Commerce had been dismantled by the Act may have been exaggerated, but it had a strong element of truth. On his return to office in June 1951, he set about dismantling the IDA. The IDA took this threat seriously: one of its members, Kevin McCourt, resigned and joined a private company believing that Lemass would carry out his promise. The other members of the Authority attempted to persuade Lemass to retain it. Beddy successfully justified its existence to the Minister and he decided to retain the Authority while restricting its activities considerably. Henceforth, it would be concerned exclusively with the promotion of new industry where it had not previously existed. All other aspects of industrial development and protectionism were then returned to the Department. This narrow focus was of central importance to the future development of the IDA; it could now concentrate on developing policy and attracting investment in specific sectors. Despite this, the Authority had been weakened by the uncertainty surrounding its future, and there was a drop in morale during 1951 which was not restored for some time.[24]

The IDA still had no clear conception of its role. For most of the 1950s it was experimenting and responding to changes in the international economy and within Ireland. It did recognise at an early stage that the Control of Manufactures Acts obstructed attempts to attract foreign companies to Ireland. The Authority recommended that these Acts should be amended to ease the restrictions on foreign capital entering the country. In the interim, they attracted investment from whatever source was available, whether foreign or indigenous. The Undeveloped Areas Act 1952, which established An Foras Tionscal, provided the finance for the first time to attract new companies to specified areas of the country. The Industrial Grants Act 1956 extended the use of these grants to other areas of the country. Specific tax concessions on profits from exports were conceded in this Act also. Between 1952 and 1957 An Foras Tionscal received 249 applications, of which seventy-five were approved and thirty-nine were fully realised. It has been estimated that 1,700 jobs were created at an estimated cost of £460 per head. Foreign companies, including those in joint participation with Irish companies, constituted 64 per cent of the total companies receiving grants between 1952 and 1967. Although the data available do not permit a firm conclusion, it is probable that most of the earlier grants between 1952 and 1957 were paid to Irish companies rather than to foreign ones. Throughout the 1950s, the IDA encountered considerable reluctance on the part of foreign companies to locate in Ireland. Most of these companies had not considered the possibility of locating in Ireland, while those who had were frequently discouraged by the Control of Manufactures Acts.[25]

The IDA was probably the first institution in Ireland to recognise that export-led industrialisation was the only way to develop the Irish economy. This also required changes in the institutional environment. Although it is difficult to detect exactly when the change came, Lemass had begun reformulating his ideas during his period of office between 1951 and 1954. The Chairman of the IDA exercised considerable influence over his thinking at this time. Beddy was closer to Lemass in ideological terms than either were to the traditional advocates of free trade. As a protectionist, Beddy could offer advice on the importance of new policies which Lemass would treat with respect.[26] A distinction may have been drawn by both men between external investment in Ireland and the removal of controls over that investment. As late as May 1953, Lemass could welcome investment from abroad but refused to consider amendments to the Control of Manufactures Acts.[27] The process seems to have been gradual but cumulative. An Foras Tionscal could only award grants within the congested areas up to 1956. This was an attempt to decentralise protected industry rather than a challenge to it. At the same time, the IDA was acquiring experience in its new tasks; it was coming into contact with foreign investors and learning what they required. The IDA did not have a grand strategy during the 1950s, but its activities began to influence policy makers and politicians once its attempts to attract foreign capital proved successful, as was increasingly the case by the end of the decade. Its role consequently became more important: the Authority accumulated experience which could prove invaluable to policy-makers and politicians once consideration was given to new strategies for development.[28]

The IDA's influence was long term and did not make a direct impact on Lemass until 1957. A report on the Irish economy produced by IBEC Technical Services Corporation, otherwise known as the Stacy May Report, exercised a more direct influence. The report had been generally favourable to Irish industrial strategy, but criticised agricultural and fiscal policy. Its critical remarks drew a quick response from the Departments of Agriculture and Finance who demanded that the report should not be published. Lemass was in favour of publication, but was not without his own criticisms. The main focus of the report was on Irish industrial competitiveness. Irish industry was compared unfavourably to that of the United states. While Irish industry had grown impressively after the Second World War, *per capita* income remained lower than the average for Western Europe. This was attributed to agriculture's poor performance. IBEC believed that the close trading links with Britain restricted Ireland's flexibility in developing a strong export trade. It also found that material costs were too high and value added too low in comparison with manufacturing competitors. *Per capita* value added in industry was also low, which contributed to low income. This could be directly attributable, the report argued, to a lack of capital investment in Irish industry. While the report was not hostile to import substitution, it stressed the need to utilise technological developments to enhance competitiveness and develop an export trade in manufactures. It also suggested that the government should attract foreign and particularly American capital, drawing particular attention to the approach adopted by Puerto Rico.[29]

Lemass rejected the direct comparison between American and Irish industry, but did commit himself to review existing tariffs in comparative context. However, he remained cautious about radically changing the tariff policy:

> The principle laid down is very sound in theory. If this test were to be rigidly enforced, however, it would, in all probability, discourage industrial expansion in this country, in as much as in many industries, particularly those where mass production methods can be applied, our highly industrialised competitors, producing for large markets, would be bound to have a competitive advantage over our relatively small scale industrial base.

Lemass was able to cite the report itself in support of a continuing policy of import substitution, reinforcing his view that Ireland was still under-developed industrially:

> The process of industrial development, in the conditions prevailing here, is a slow and difficult one. While it may be possible for some of our manufacturing industries to produce at world competitive prices, it can hardly be expected that industrial development should be confined to industries which can satisfy this test. Hitherto, when industrial proposals have been submitted to the Minister by

> private initiative, it has not been the practice to demand detailed costings or evidence to show that the commodities concerned can be produced at prices as low as elsewhere. If, on going into production, an undertaking applies for protection on the grounds that the sale of its products is being adversely affected by imports, it is then required to furnish particulars of comparative prices, etc. There may, and there often are, factors which make it impossible for the undertaking to bring its costs and prices down to the levels prevailing in other countries, and if such a test were universally applied, there is little doubt that industrial development in this country would receive a definite setback.[30]

Notwithstanding Lemass's continuing support for protection, he recognised that Irish industry faced numerous difficulties. IBEC had drawn attention to the low productivity of Irish industry, and attributed this to the low level of investment in plant and machinery. Lemass added that the provision for depreciation in Ireland was lower than virtually every other OEEC country. He therefore recommended that income tax allowances be made available for the purchase of capital equipment, that the depreciation allowances on plant and equipment be liberalised, and that an allowance should be made for depreciation on buildings. The Department of Finance countered each of these on cost grounds and on the basis of the protected nature of Irish industry. At a Cabinet meeting in May 1953, the government agreed to establish a committee to examine the question of industrial taxation. This was followed by a protracted exchange between Finance and Industry and Commerce on the terms of reference for the committee. Lemass used the Cabinet Committee on the Provision of Employment to advance a permissive course, while Finance used its bureaucratic position within the Civil Service to restrict this approach. Finance insisted that any concessions should take into account the loss of revenue to the Exchequer. Industry and Commerce believed that such an emphasis would neutralise the reasons for tax exemption. John Leydon maintained that the Department of Finance drafted the terms of reference 'to create a bias against any sort of concession to industrialists'. He also warned that Finance might use its institutional position to influence the composition of the

Commission and neutralise its effectiveness. The terms of reference were finally agreed in September 1953. There was little change over the original Finance draft, but Lemass did succeed in altering the emphasis on Exchequer considerations.[31]

The contrasting approaches of Finance and Industry and Commerce to the question of taxation reflects a much deeper division between the two Departments. Industry and Commerce remained, particularly under Lemass, the main source of institutional support for economic expansion and industrialisation. Despite an apparent shift in emphasis in 1950, the Department of Finance retained its traditional hostility to economic experiment, to protected industry, and to an unbalanced budget. If anything, Finance was becoming more conservative during the 1950s, rejecting all the main initiatives promoted by Lemass.[32] Lemass was not only an industrialiser, he was also an urban politician who rejected a status quo still based on the dominance of agriculture. He argued that agriculture was not contributing to the Irish economy and that it appeared to be stagnant.[33] His proposals to reform taxation were based on the assumption that industry could provide a means of overcoming the slow-down in the economy, if given adequate support. More fundamentally, during 1952 he attempted to roll back the consequences of that year's budget, a budget which has been described as 'inappropriate in the prevailing economic condition'. Furthermore:

> By the time the 1953 budget was introduced, the balance of payments situation was fully under control and the economy was ripe for renewed growth. However, there was to be no return until after 1958 to the expansionary fiscal policy that characterised the first five years or so of the post-war period.[34]

Although accurate as far as fiscal policy is concerned, this fails to appreciate the rapid recovery in industrial employment after the 1952 downturn. The 1952 budget can be interpreted as a convincing victory within the government for Sean MacEntee and the fiscal conservatives. Between 1952 and 1954 Lemass counter attacked. He was concerned at the effect which fiscal conservatism was having on unemployment. Even prior to the 1952 budget, he recommended that the Department of Finance should not be allowed to delay the imposition of tariffs: if that, or other departments, did not quickly make known their objections to a tariff then the government should be circulated forthwith. Lemass believed that Finance was procrastinating on the issue; on one occasion it refused to place an item on the Cabinet agenda.[35] In June 1952, Lemass decided to alter the Department's policy towards tariffs. He noted that all applications since 1945 had been examined with considerable care before any recommendations were made. The severe economic environment which had resulted from the recession justified a change in policy:

> It was, therefore, desirable that any delay should be avoided, where possible, in dealing with tariff applications. The Minister's feeling was that where a *prima facie* case existed – and he was disposed to accept that such a case existed in many instances, particularly of applications for the restoration of suspended duties – the tariff might be imposed preparatory to any detailed examination of the extent and nature of that now carried out before applications were submitted to him for a decision. He directed that all applications on hand and all applications submitted in the future should be dealt with on the foregoing lines.[36]

It does not appear from this that Lemass had any serious misgivings concerning the efficacy of tariffs; he continued to believe that protection offered the best method for advancing economic development. Given the restricted fiscal climate, he utilised available policy instruments in an attempt to expand employment opportunities. This concern with continuing unemployment was shared by de Valera who circulated a minute in February 1953 proposing that employment be stimulated. In response, Industry and Commerce drew attention to its successes in expanding employment and industry. Between April 1951 and February 1953, 144 new industries had been established, while a further 200 proposals were under consideration. The use of tariffs and quotas had secured or increased employment in a number of industrial sectors. These developments were supplemented by the discretionary grant awarding power which Bord Failte and An Foras Tionscal had acquired under legislation enacted in 1952. The Department also estimated that £23 million of public expenditure had secured 46,000 jobs in the period 1952–53.[37]

The tight fiscal policy had a more serious impact on building and construction than on other sectors of the economy. The building programme and local government expenditure had been the mainstay of this sector; the withdrawal of financial support led to a loss of 6,000 jobs between 1951 and 1955. This led to a meeting between the government, the ITUC and the Labour Party in July 1953 to discuss the matter. Lemass rejected the view that Ireland faced a depression, citing evidence for an increase in national income and personal consumption. Employment in the industrial and service sectors, moreover, was increasing. He conceded that it might be possible to expand the state capital programme, particularly as there were considerable resources available in 1953.

This meeting had an immediate impact on Lemass: the following day he circulated a memorandum advocating increased state expenditure to stimulate the economy. He recognised there were a number of outstanding difficulties, but dismissed the possibility of a balance of payments crisis. He recommended an investment of £10 million in public works. This would boost the economy, but he accepted it would not create the necessary number of extra jobs. The long-term aim of public investment should be to reduce unemployment to a stable level, considered by Lemass to be in the region of 5 per cent. To achieve this end a minimum of 25,000 new jobs would have to be created. Lemass continued to believe that the Irish experience differed from that of other European countries, and that any economic strategy had to accept these differences. The cycle of unemployment and emigration and the consequent declining population meant that the level of private capital investment was inadequate to induce expansion. Lemass wanted to break this cycle by increased state investment:

> The scope for expansion of investment in new production to replace imports is diminishing. Many forms of production are now at the limits of existing market needs. Increased export possibilities, so far as manufacturing industry is concerned, are not substantial enough to produce investment on an adequate scale. Only a rising population, with rising living standards, will create a situation in which the expansion of industrial and commercial activity will involve a regular expansion of private capital investment to a degree that will prevent abnormal unemployment.[38]

Lemass's policy proposals in 1953 do not differ in substance from those enumerated twenty years earlier. The state remains the focus of policy and the option of interdependency is not considered. The policy framework continues to embody under-consumptionist principles blended with aspects of Keynesianism and placed within a protectionist context. For Lemass in 1953 as in 1932 the key remained the extent to which state intervention would reduce unemployment by increasing income and demand.

The balance of political power, which had favoured MacEntee in 1951 and 1952, now moved in Lemass's direction. Despite frantic opposition from MacEntee, the government seriously considered the possibility of expanding capital expenditure. Lemass also won crucial support from Frank Aiken, who recommended the establishment of a National Development Fund (NDF) which could operate as a counter-cyclical agency to stabilise employment at a high level. MacEntee objected to the continued commitment to protection, arguing that it prevented Irish industry from seeking export possibilities. He accused Lemass of limiting his view to the Irish economy, and of being mistaken in his belief that Ireland could generate growth to absorb the unemployed. The logic of MacEntee's position was the dismantling of protection and the promotion of competitive exports on the world market.[39] While this was the logic the reality was somewhat different. Neither MacEntee nor Finance provided a strategy to obtain benefits for Irish industry from exports. The strength of their position rested on the recognition that Ireland could not provide employment for its population. This position was weakened by a failure to elaborate a realistic strategy to obtain this objective. The suspicion must remain that MacEntee and Finance did not take Irish industry seriously and continued to believe in the dominance of agriculture.

The Department of Finance continued to oppose any scheme, arguing that the government was committed to a balanced budget and price stability. This, it continued, would be in jeopardy if the National Development Fund was established. Finance also stressed the non-productive nature of the investment, dismissing its value as of short-term significance. The Finance view was also given a powerful boost by the circulation of a blistering sixteen page attack on the NDF from the Central Bank. Like the Department of Finance, the Central Bank continued to believe that agricultural exports should be the mainstay of the economy and therefore any expansion of capital expenditure might endanger the stability of this sector.[40] Despite these objections, the government accepted the need for the fund. Once a National Development Committee was set up to administer the fund, Lemass vigorously proposed a wide range of infrastructural schemes, including holiday resort development, harbour works, and road works in depressed rural areas. The collapse of the government in 1954 led to the deferral of investment and, significantly, the National Development Committee had still to meet nine months after the new government entered office.[41]

Lemass may have had some reservations about tariffs in 1953, but unlike MacEntee he continued to believe that protection could play a role in the Irish economy. His proposals in 1953 bear a strong resemblance to the under-consumptionist views which had been a feature of his intellectual apparatus since the 1920s. The NDF would have provided the finance to increase domestic demand, which could in turn provide a focus for new industries. Although he recognised the limits of protection in 1953, it is possible to infer that Lemass believed he could expand these limits by capital investment. The alternative for him was neither free trade nor protection, which seems to have been the case with MacEntee, but the best method of securing the existing capacity and expanding Irish industry further. Lemass continued to believe that Irish industry operated in a precarious environment; as an underdeveloped economy it had to protect itself from the more mature industrial states. What Lemass did not recognise in 1953 was that the limits of protection had been reached in another way. There is little question that protection could have been deepened if Irish society was prepared to pay the cost. The replacement of imported raw materials, chemicals, or capital goods by home production remained one option. Unlike the earlier phase of protection, this deepening of the industrial process would require more capital investment and state promotion than had hitherto been the case. Such an approach could also lead to a conflict of interest between the users of imported commodities and state policy. These obstacles were not insurmountable, but they were very real.

Most attempts to promote these deeper linkages failed. In an agricultural country the provision of fertilisers would appear an appropriate vehicle for investment. Not only would its production in the home market provide an essential input for agriculture, but it would provide additional employment. Home production did not meet demand throughout the 1950s. The use of fertilisers generally was on the increase, although by international comparison it was under-utilised by Irish agriculture. The Departments of Agriculture and Finance maintained that the most appropriate means of increasing the use of superphosphates involved bringing the price down to that prevailing in the world generally. Industry and Commerce predicted that this would lead to the collapse of the existing Irish capacity and prevent any further expansion. Industry and Commerce's room for manoeuvre was restricted, not only by Finance's commitment to free trade, but also by the reluctance of agricultural producers, strongly supported by the Department of Agriculture, to pay a higher price for this input. This reinforced a conventional view of the Department of Agriculture: that Irish farmers could only compete if its inputs remained low. Little consideration was given to an approach which emphasised quality, expanded output, and the processing of basic agricultural output prior to export. Another case in point is the failure of forestry policy. Climatically, Ireland is suitable for an extensive forestry programme. Yet the cost, resistance from farmers, and the reluctance of the paper industry to develop that end of the process, neutralised any attempts to generate new linkages.[42] By the time Lemass left office again in 1954 the possibility of further industrial expansion remained in question. Despite his efforts to generate expansion, most proposals were ineffectual or were neutralised by opposition. Although Lemass was not aware of it in 1954 Ireland would remain underdeveloped unless there was a more radical approach to policy, one that would also have to question his own commitment to autarkic structures.

Nor did the second Inter-Party government of 1954–57 adopt a radical approach to policy. Although it had some achievements to its credit, the government did not revise the institutional structures dealing with the economy. An imaginative approach to industrial policy may have been possible, but it was not forthcoming. Fiscal policy continued to be restrictive and there was little support for promoting economic expansion. The new Minister for Finance, Gerard Sweetman, endorsed his Department's orthodoxy, as had his predecessors. It appears that without Lemass in a Cabinet the centre of gravity on economic matters moved sharply to the right. In 1954 the budget was balanced by reducing expenditure and achieving economies. However, Finance urged that economies continued to be necessary, particularly if food subsidies were to be introduced. The balance of payments crisis in 1955 did not improve matters, and in July 1956 the deteriorating situation was met by an increase in import duties.

The 1956 duties, though they restricted imports, were not introduced to extend protection: the aim of this policy was to improve the balance of payments. The British government agreed to waive their privileges under the trade agreements, and allowed Ireland to increase duties on previously exempted items. During the early 1950s the Board of Trade had reversed its long-standing pressure on Ireland to facilitate British entry to its markets. Britain took an increasingly passive approach to Ireland as a market for its exports. Despite this, Finance believed the situation continued to be serious. The long-term problem for the Irish economy, according to a Finance analysis, was that the terms of trade were moving against agricultural products exported from the country. Finance believed that this was not a short-term difficulty, but one which could not be resolved easily. By 1957, the economy was in the depths of its worst depression since the foundation of the state. Despite Finance's analysis of the weakness of Irish agriculture, there is no evidence that the Department recognised the implications of their observations for the future of the economy.[43]

The crisis of 1957 and 1958 has often been seen as a crisis for protectionism. This was not essentially the case; within specified limits protection had worked quite well. The depression was a result of the fiscal policies pursued by the government in the short run; in the medium term it was a result of the failure of agriculture to increase exports and expand national income. In the longer term, it was a consequence of the failure of Irish society and economy to respond to the dilemma it faced, all factors emphasised by Lemass since 1945. On the one hand, the society wished to retain traditional patterns of economic organisation, particularly in agriculture. On the other, it demanded an end to emigration and full employment with rising incomes. These were incompatible aims. There was a certain logic in the Finance position, given this set of assumptions. Finance remained committed to an agricultural economy throughout the 1950s, and its defence of external reserves had a certain rationality within this context. Nor had the Department of Industry and Commerce a realistic alternative at this time. It displays a cautious and defensive attitude between 1954 and 1957, insisting that protected industry should remain so. In 1955 it took a vigorous stand against trade liberalisation within Europe, arguing that that any Irish commitment to reduce tariffs imperilled the security of Irish industry and its future prospects. Ireland, it believed, had 'little to gain from liberalisation in Western Europe'. If anything, Ireland had become more protectionist, mainly because the British government was not prepared to exercise its rights under the trade agreements to secure the abolition of existing quotas.[44]

Nor had this view changed when the Cabinet discussed the practicality of participating in a European Free Trade Area in 1957. In a special report written by the Secretaries of the Departments of the Taoiseach, Agriculture, External Affairs, Finance, and Industry and Commerce, a gloomy future was predicted for the Irish economy whatever decision the government took. The report concluded that there was no future for the Irish economy, unless exports were expanded. However, the Department of Agriculture believed that exports in that area probably could not be expanded. Industry and Commerce submitted that Irish industry required permanent protection, while it believed that there was little prospect of generating industrial exports. Industry and Commerce provided an appendix to the report reinforcing its case, citing the main reasons why protection should continue. It claimed that without protection 60 per cent of industrial employment would disappear. This objection was recognised in the report and a cautious approach was advised. More dramatically, the report drew attention to the dangers inherent in the state of the economy.

> Ireland has reason not merely to be worried about the setting up of a Free Trade Area but about her future economic and political prospects generally. It is obvious that we can avoid economic stagnation and continual loss of population only by making the most strenuous and urgent efforts to raise the efficiency and volume of production both in agriculture and in industry. If a Free Trade Area is established and we had to accept from the start the full obligations of membership, those existing industries which

> need permanent protection (and therefore could not adjust themselves over the transitional period) would go to the wall. Few new industries could be established in the absence of a protective shield and a guaranteed home market.[45]

This report, produced at the height of the recession, reflects the stagnancy in policy formation by this time. It is surprising that such a report makes no attempt to offer positive proposals but continues to insist on the primacy of traditional policy.

It is usually assumed that *Economic Development*, written by the Secretary to the Department of Finance, T.K. Whitaker, was the catalyst for the changes in policy which were initiated shortly after.[46] The influence of the report on the subsequent success of the economy, however, may have been exaggerated. The distinction drawn between capital and current expenditure was not a new one, although the emphasis on capital investment was important. A major aim of the document involved restricting demand which, in the circumstances of 1958, could only have been calculated to continue the recession in the medium term. The report did not treat the industrial sector in any detail, but continued to stress the need to improve the competitive position of agriculture. The document may have provided a psychological boost at an opportune moment for the economy, but the economy remained in recession for a further two years. The causal relationship between the production of *Economic Development* and Ireland's economic expansion during the 1960s is, to say the least, tenuous. It is also difficult to attribute the changed direction of the economy to it, except in an indirect fashion. Its main predictions and recommendations had little relevance to the experience of the 1960s. In retrospect, *Economic Development* might be seen more accurately as a transitional document, one that attempts to face up to the complex aspects of a changing society, but finally opts for the traditional policy style and approach of the Department of Finance.[47]

If *Economic Development* is compared with the first *Programme for Economic Expansion* there are numerous similarities. The Programme, published as a White Paper, was essentially a political publication unlike the earlier document. Lemass appears to have played a dominant role within the Cabinet Committee set up to draft it. Without the political intervention of Lemass, at this stage and subsequently, it is unlikely that economic buoyancy would have been achieved during the 1960s. From a strictly economic perspective, *Economic Development* had recommended the coordination of government machinery preparatory to directing the economy in a planned fashion. The objective of planning should then be to concentrate resources on expanding exports. These general views, as distinct from the more specific recommendations, were broadly compatible with Lemass's perspective. Lemass's emphasis was different; even in the *Programme for Economic Expansion* he put his own stamp on the document, somewhat to the chagrin of Whitaker.[48] He also differed fundamentally from Whitaker in that he continued to believe that industrial expansion was an essential precondition of economic expansion. Moreover, he remained an economic nationalist, if not a protectionist, throughout his political career. The development of Irish economic resources remained his primary objective, though he became increasingly flexible in his attempts to achieve this aim.

Even before *Economic Development,* Lemass had reconsidered an essential feature of industrial policy. When Fianna Fáil returned to office in 1957, Lemass had to face the contradiction in the defensive approach which he had previously maintained. He recognised that existing investment and output were not sufficient to maintain the level of demand he believed necessary to obtain full employment. In the absence of a policy to develop linkages within the economy, he opted for export-led growth. Unlike the conventional view on exports, Lemass believed that the promotion of industrial exports was the best way to achieve this. The evidence available to him suggested that indigenous industry could not fulfil this objective; therefore he proposed to amend the Control of Manufactures Acts and use other available institutional devices to attract foreign investment to Ireland. In the Dáil he made a forceful case for reconsidering these Acts, but added that home industry would remain the main motor for change. However, he announced that export growth was absolutely necessary and this could only be achieved if foreign participation contributed capital, technology, and experience to Irish industry. Lemass was prepared to remove all restrictions on inward investment if the companies exported most of their production. Although he believed that multinational companies would always play a marginal and supplementary role in the economy, the decision to amend the Acts had more than symbolic value. In the decade following, the IDA succeeded in attracting an increasing number of foreign companies to locate in Ireland. It is arguable that without the amendment this strategy would not have been as successful.[49]

The decision to attract foreign investment should not be equated with the end of protection. The policy followed remained a cautious one; Lemass retained control of tariffs, and it was not until 1963 that the first major tariff cuts were introduced. This generated the momentum which led to the Anglo-Irish Free Trade Agreement and the official end of protection. In the interim, the economy expanded rapidly and industrial exports began to play a significant role in this expansion. This did not occur spontaneously, and the economy remained in depression until 1960. If anything, the policies contained in *Economic Development* and the first *Programme for Economic Expansion* continued the deflationary spiral. This policy was continued through 1958, but began to be reversed in 1959. This seems to have been accompanied by a policy change within the government. Whereas the projected Public Capital Programme for 1958–63 envisaged an expansion, within that social investment would contract in real terms as well as in relative terms. What actually occurred was that both social and other investment expanded at an accelerating rate from 1959. While social spending declined relative to capital spending, it expanded in real terms.[50] One possible explanation for this is the changes which took place within Fianna Fáil in 1959. Lemass replaced de Valera as Taoiseach and quickly accelerated the pace of development. For the first time he acquired the power to implement his policies in full, although in circumstances quite different from those of the 1930s.

Lemass's economic philosophy had not radically changed subsequent to his 1945 memorandum on full employment. What had changed was the emphasis he placed on different aspects of the process for achieving this. In 1958 and 1959 there was an even greater urgency to act, given the nature of Irish unemployment. The aim of economic policy, he maintained in 1961, was to achieve both economic development and social objectives:

> The aims of the Programme are to bring about such a rate of economic progress in all sectors that unemployment and unnecessary emigration will cease and that the living standards of the people will be progressively improved.

These aims did not differ fundamentally from what Lemass had been saying in 1927, 1945, or 1953. Nor had his emphasis on the motor force to achieve them:

> In Irish economic development the role of the government is predominant. Nobody believes that, in the circumstances of this country economic progress on the scale which is needed is likely to be realised otherwise than through the medium of a strong and sound government policy directed to that result. This does not mean reliance solely on an extension of direct state-sponsored activities although state enterprise may have a considerable part in it. It expresses also our understanding that the vast dynamic of growth which is inherent in free private enterprise cannot be fully availed of without government drive and leadership.[51]

However, the methods to achieve them had. In 1959 Lemass received the power for the first time to apply the lessons of Keynesianism which he had absorbed during the 1940s. The decision to expand both social and capital expenditure is a cogent reflection of this. During the early 1960s economic policy moved further to the left than at any time since the 1930s. Rapid economic growth complemented a more egalitarian social policy, each actively promoted by the state. More importantly, perhaps, was the decision to opt for export-led growth and the policy consequences of this. It was recognised by the end of the 1950s that Ireland would have to revise its attitude to free trade and particularly to liberalisation with Britain and Western Europe. The reciprocal nature of export led growth clearly brought into question the continuing legitimacy of protection as a policy instrument.

The legitimacy of protection had been raised by T.K.Whitaker in 1956 when he questioned the continuing dependence on protection for economic growth. He argued that industrial output in Ireland was considerably less than the OEEC average, and wondered how firmly based many aspects of industrial development actually were. The answer provided by Whitaker was that protection should be modified, and internationally competitive industrial exports promoted.[52] Whitaker's criticisms of protectionism were to be embraced enthusiastically by the modernisers during the 1960s. As a result there has been an unquestioned belief that protection had failed during the 1950s, if not earlier, particularly because Irish industry had not generated a sizeable export potential. The problematic decade is considered to be the 1950s: critics of protectionism concede that there was some strategic value in protection during the 1930s, while the Second World War and economic recovery thereafter might have warranted continuation up to 1949 or 1950.[53] The general consensus appears to be that something went wrong with industrial policy during the 1950s which required a dramatic change of direction, a change which was effected between 1958 and 1966 and stimulated by *Economic Development.* In this sense, the 1950s have been characterised as transitional, leading not only to free trade but to what has been described as the 'economics of independence' which are associated with free-trade policies.[54]

A more accurate description of this decade would be one of crisis leading to a transition from protection to free trade. The economics of free trade cannot accurately be equated with independence. Economic independence had been achieved after 1932 when the Fianna Fáil government asserted its economic sovereignty by implementing an independent developmental strategy. That this strategy did not always fulfil its objectives does not invalidate this conclusion. Even prior to the Second World War this had been conceded by Britain and reinforced during the 1938 and 1948 trade agreements. More importantly, the policies pursued after 1932 laid the institutional basis for the changes which took place after 1958, providing policy makers with experience which would not have been available without protection. Without protection there would have been very little industrial growth in Ireland between 1932 and 1963, and it is questionable if an industrial strategy would have been considered in 1958 without this experience. Although industry was not the most important sector of the economy in 1958, its very existence and its dynamic nature provided the focus for further planning.

There are three elements to Irish protectionism which require evaluation. The first concerns the overall success of the policy; the second addresses the criticism that protectionism failed during the 1950s; while the last examines the reasons why indigenous industry failed to make a successful transition to free trade and industrial exports. Protectionism can be counted a success on a number of grounds. Employment in manufacturing industry, which accounted for 4.6 per cent of the labour force in 1926, had reached 14.3 per cent by 1960. During the 1930s and 1940s, the industrial base expanded and absorbed a substantial number of rural migrants. In addition, the policies pursued meant that Ireland had not experienced a serious depression during the 1930s. In contrast with the 1920s, however, the growth of GNP after 1932 was slower. It has been estimated that real GNP at factor cost expanded at an annual average rate of 2.4 per cent between 1926 and 1931, 0.3 per cent between 1931 and 1939 and 0.1 per cent between 1949 and 1958.[55] It might be argued that without protection the outcome for the economy would have been far worse than was the case, at least up to 1949. Protectionism pointed Ireland in a new direction and in the short to medium term, secured a number of benefits from the economy, but also raised the possibility of reorganising the economy and benefitting from further industrial expansion.

Table 6.2 Average Yearly Employment in Sectors Enumerated by the Census of Industrial Production, 1947–60

	All Industries and Services	Building and Services	Transportable Goods Industries
1947	159,946	59,864	100,082
1948	172,433	67,964	104,469
1949	179,693	70,111	109,582
1950	193,411	74,481	118,930
1951	197,334	74,623	122,711
1952	191,827	73,465	118,362
1953	195,137	72,468	124,644
1954	199,363	69,465	129,898
1955	200,701	68,725	131,976
1956	192,939	63,429	129,510
1957	178,570	53,159	125,411
1958	176,461	51,019	125,442
1959	179,852	51,612	128,240
1960	186,501	52,527	133,974

Source: Census of Industrial Production 1958-60, in *Irish Trade Journal and Statistical Bulletin*, December 1962

A more serious case can be made against the policies pursued during the 1950s. The Irish economy as a whole did not perform well during this decade; growth rates and employment prospects were poor, both in comparative terms and historically. Despite this, it would be premature to attribute this to the failure of protected industry. Whereas the labour force had expanded during the 1930s, it contracted throughout the 1950s. Unlike the 1930s, industry could not absorb the surplus labour available during the later decade. Between 1949 and 1961 the labour force contracted by 174,000 members. Of this reduction, 84 per cent can be accounted for by losses in the agricultural sector. While industrial employment failed to absorb these workers, its record was not as bad as is at times suggested. The annual average employment level for concerns enumerated under the Census of Industrial Production between 1947 and 1960 is given in Table 6.2. Between 1947 and 1955 the trend for all industries and services is upwards, while decline is evident thereafter. If, however, the examination is limited to the transportable goods industry, an upward trend is perceptible throughout the period.

Table 6.3 Employment in Protected Industry

	1938	1949	1952	1954
1. Food, Drink and Tobacco	17,262	20,677	22,704	24,024
2. Textiles	6,218	8,547	8,289	10,981
3. Apparel	20,699	24,992	22,451	25,784
4. Leather	985	1,394	1,354	1,545
5. Manufactures of Wood	6,996	7,272	6,764	7,036
6. Metal Manufactures and Machinery	1,918	2,249	1,977	2,303
7. Iron and Steel	4,832	5,081	5,078	5,657
8. Vehicles	3,216	4,534	3,859	5,652
9. Chemicals, Oils and Fertilisers	3,156	3,725	3,614	3,996
10. Papermaking and Printing	7,201	8,616	9,461	9,843
11. Building Materials Clay and Concrete	2,998	3,615	3,848	4,161
12. Miscellaneous	3,061	4,783	5,121	6,086
Total	78,542	95,476	94,556	107,067

Source: SPO Employment in Protected Industries, S.11219 A and B.

The selected data available on protected industry for the years

1938 and 1946 to 1954, contained in Table 6.3 supplement the trends in Table 6.2 and show a similar tendency for industrial employment to expand. Employment in the industrial sector is therefore more impressive than either an examination of general employment or selected years would permit. The problem of unemployment remained largely that of agricultural employment and, to a lesser extent, the construction industry. The use made of unemployment statistics at times does not allow a comprehensive assesment of the issue. To compare years of growth (for example 1953–55, when industrial employment had reached a post-war high) with years of recession is neither justifiable nor does it evaluate the overall trend. Alternatively, if 1950 is compared with 1955, and if both are compared with 1960 (all years of expansion) the overall upward movement is clear. If 1952 is compared with 1957 or 1958 (all years of recession following balance of payments crisis) an upward trend is still visible. The overall number in industrial employment during the recession of 1957 and 1958 remains considerably higher than the years of expansion in 1949 or 1950.[56]

It is arguable that protected industry during the 1950s continued to fulfil the objectives which policy had formulated for it. Low wages and emigration cannot be attributed to a sector that was continuing to provide employment. The malaise in the Irish economy can be more readily attributed to agricultural policy and to conservative monetary policy. Both these policies continued to reinforce traditional approaches; the failure of each reinforced the general crisis by 1957 which was only resolved when these policies were discarded. Nor did agricultural exports expand or change direction in a context where the terms of trade were against it. It can also be suggested that during the 1950s there was no 'domestic engine of growth' to allow the economy maximise on the opportunities available to it from the general buoyancy of international trade. Irish exports grew at an annual rate of 3.7 per cent between 1950 and 1961: a third of the rate for Austria and a quarter that of Greece. These countries, particularly Austria, developed domestic engines of growth which Ireland was unable to do until the 1960s. This outcome can be attributed to the failure of policy makers to develop alternative policies, rather than to protection itself.[57]

It is true that industry did not develop an export capacity at this time and this can be considered a failure. Using other variables, industry made a significant contribution to the economy. The volume of production expanded by an average of 3.5 per cent within manufacturing industry between 1953 and 1960, while total employment in the manufacturing sector increased by almost eight thousand. Industry's share of Gross Domestic Product expanded throughout this period, while that of agriculture contracted. By 1955 agriculture's share was down to 26.9 per cent while industry stood at 30 per cent. Although most economic indicators in Ireland compared badly with the expanding European economy, Irish industry performed better than the general variables indicate. Taking the Census of Industrial Production, where protected industry was concentrated between 1949 and 1961, the volume of output expanded by 4.5 per cent and productivity growth by 2.7 per cent annually.[58] It is difficult therefore to conclude that protectionism failed during the 1950s.

In 1961 Fianna Fáil was returned to power as a minority administration. It was to last four years, at the end of which decisive changes had taken place in the society and in the economy. Ireland's long decade of stagnation which had continued from 1948 to 1961 had ended, to be followed by its short boom from 1961 to 1973. The 1961 election was the first which Lemass fought as leader of Fianna Fáil and Taoiseach. His failure to win an overall majority did not prevent him from generating an ambitious developmental programme for virtually every aspect of the Irish economy. Moreover, his strategy was successful. During the first half of the 1960s the economy performed extremely well, with high growth rates, increasing exports, and rising employment. For the 1960s, at least, the cycle of low output, low incomes, short term expansion followed by balance of payments crises appeared to be broken. Lemass's government adopted the ideology of growth more comprehensively than any other government since 1922. Not only this but for the first time political, institutional, and social resources were orchestrated and directed towards a common aim.

During his short period as Taoiseach, Lemass shifted the balance of power within Irish society. His administration initiated the most comprehensive attempt at modernisation which had occurred in Ireland. In a broad sense Ireland acquired 'modernity' during this decade, becoming increasingly industrialised, secularised, urbanised and bureaucratised. In retrospect the achievements of the 1960s were partial; more traditional norms quickly reasserted themselves, yet the achievements were real. The crisis of the mid to late 1950s was not simply an economic one, it was also a crisis for traditional Irish society. The recession questioned the validity of political independence as a method of enhancing national welfare. Lemass used the crisis to press successfully his view that a radical departure was necessary. The success of the industrial sector during the 1960s coupled with an expansionary fiscal policy and a commitment to export led growth appeared to justify Lemass's belief that political independence could be used to generate increasing welfare for the society. The one irony in this process, and one that concerned Lemass increasingly prior to his retirement, was the state of indigenous industry and the role which it would play in economic development. If, to a large extent, Irish industry had fulfilled the objectives set for it between 1932 and 1961, its role in the new economic environment was to be more problematic and insecure. Whereas between 1932 and 1961 the interests of the state and Irish industry largely coincided, thereafter this was no longer inevitable. It was possible that national interest as defined by the state would no longer coincide with the interests of native Irish industry. For protected Irish industry the 1960s were to be a period of considerable challenge, and a challenge which was not to be effectively met.

7

Towards an Industrial Economy

THE EVENTS of the 1980s in many ways recall those of the 1950s. Economic crisis, large-scale unemployment, emigration and government instability carry the reminder of an earlier era. Ireland's boom was short lived, lasting until 1979 at the very latest. The confidence generated by this expansion has now dissipated to be replaced by an all too pervasive pessimism. Yet it is important to emphasise the contrast between the two periods as well as their similarities. The Irish economy has been transformed since the 1950s. It is now an industrialising economy with many of the social and cultural characteristics appropriate to that mode of production. The crisis of the 1950s was an Irish crisis, a result of the internal dynamics of that society. It was still overwhelmingly an agricultural society with an industrial enclave, and one which reflected this dominance in its culture and social structure. The earlier crisis was an agricultural crisis, a result of the failure of a traditional society to move beyond the limits imposed by this. Even then, industry was the motor force for change; the modern, if not the modernising, sector of the economy. In contrast, Ireland's crisis in the 1980s is an industrial crisis. The enhanced linkages between Ireland and the industrial world economy mean that Ireland could not be immune to the recession which has affected Western Europe in particular since 1974.

This is Ireland's first industrial recession and much of the confusion in policy making is due to a lack of understanding of how to respond to such a set of problems. If the crisis of the 1950s was essentially national and agricultural, the 1980s can be characterised as a crisis resulting from interdependency; in that participation in the world economy facilitates the transfer to each state of instabilities in the system. However, in the case of Ireland the international recession has been reinforced by continuing difficulties within the national economy. One of the striking features of the current recession internationally has been the diverse and contrasting national responses to economic instability. There may be objective circumstances to which every state has to react: energy prices, inflation, or competition, but the reaction depends on the decisions taken by the nation state. These in turn are dependent on the relationships between the different social groups making up the society. The options available to a government and its flexibility in the face of change are in the end structured by the political culture. The decisions taken to adopt an ambitious industrial strategy as the mainstay of economic development in Ireland was understandable, but the premises on which it was based changed quite quickly. Decisions taken during the 1960s established a new framework for policy, but also constrained policy makers thereafter. The inadequacy of policy making in the 1980s can be attributed to decisions taken between 1958 and 1969.

The decision to end protection was not taken easily, and there was some resistance to this policy. Until well into the 1960s Lemass continued to express goodwill towards indigenous industry. This should not be surprising as Irish industry continued to be the primary focus of policy in the new developmental process. This would be export based and over time protection would be removed. What Lemass envisaged was that traditional protected industry could make the transition from supplying the home market to producing internationally competitive goods for export. For the lifetime of the first *Programme for Economic Expansion*, at least, serious consideration was given to the method by which this could be assured. The Committee on Industrial Organisation (CIO) was established to review each sector of the protected economy and to recommend an adequate response to the international competition which a free trade and export based economy would have to meet.

The CIO concluded that the sectors examined were not adapting to the new economic environment. It found that most industrial sectors were not internationally competitive, that they concentrated on production for home consumption, and that unless adjustment took place there would be a considerable loss in employment.[1] This adjustment did not take place despite the willingness of the state to provide advice and finance to aid the transition. Few of the companies examined by the CIO continued in existence two decades later. The Committee on Industrial Progress concluded in 1973 that traditional industry had not adapted to free trade. Employment growth in this sector was below the national average between 1958 and 1973; after 1974 most of the decline in industrial employment occurred here. Moreover, indigenous industry failed to make the transition from the domestic to the export market and continued to produce for local demand.[2] Most of the protected sector consequently limped through the 1960s and disappeared following the recession of 1973–74.

It was during the 1960s, not the 1950s, that protected industry failed. Despite increased demand nationally and internationally, much of Irish industry retained its focus on traditional domestic markets. Indeed, the expansion of domestic demand may have induced a certain degree of complacency among manufacturers, disguising the long-term challenge. Its success on the home market prior to 1958 and the continuing profits to be obtained here in an expansionary period may also have prevented most industrialists from pursuing an export strategy. There was not an export consciousness among the industrialists, mainly because of the oligopolistic nature of the closed economy, but also because resources had not been available to promote exports since 1945. Moreover, to an increasing degree after 1961 government resources were directed to attracting foreign companies to locate in Ireland and less attention was consequently taken of indigenous companies.

It may also be the case that the nature of Irish protectionism itself prevented rapid change. Hirschman has suggested that 'Import Substituting Industrialisation' (ISI) encounters serious difficulties after the first 'exuberant' phase of development is over, thus leading to the view that ISI becomes exhausted because further momentum is not evident. This is what appears to have occurred in Ireland after the initial phase; further growth is severely constrained. However this is not inevitable. Further growth is possible if a number of criteria are met: the effective deepening of the industrial process through backward linkages and/or the development of an export trade. In the case of Ireland, and in a number of other post war industrialisers, this further phase did not occur. The obstacles are not inevitable, but they do exist. One constraint is the absence of an export horizon, given the dependence on the home market. The industrialist requires time and resources to adjust, and these are not always forthcoming. The existitng tariff level can also reinforce these constraints; this will leave producers to concentrate on home production but prevent them from moving into the more complex and capital intensive production of imported inputs if, as is normally the case, tariffs on these items are low or non existent. Consequently, the tariff policy itself may not provide an incentive to deepen the process.

Socio-political factors can also prevent development. If the national industrial bourgeoisie are politically weak, it is unlikely that they will have the confidence that their influence over economic policy is strong enough to achieve benefits. Accordingly:

> Only a cohesive, vocal, and highly influential bourgeoisie is likely to carry industrialisation beyond relatively safe import substitution to the risky export oriented stage.

Hirschman believes that there is a vicious circle here: industrialists do not export because they are not influential and they are not influential because they do not export. This is certainly relevant to the Irish experience. The agricultural sector, though weakened, continued to be the exporting mainstay of the economy and consequently retained considerable influence over policy.[3] It was not until the 1960s that the weakness of this dependence on agriculture was fully appreciated. The recognition that agriculture would not provide the motor to generate increased exports coincided with the findings of the CIO that Irish industry lacked an export horizon. This occurred at a time when the successful implementation of demand management was dependent on a substantial increase in exports; what has been described by Katzenstein as '... international liberalisation and domestic compensation, based on corporatist political structures'.[4] Without export growth domestic compensation would not be possible and liberalisation would have disastrous consequences. Neither agriculture nor indigenous industry appeared adequate to the demands placed on them by the state during the first half of the 1960s.

There were a number of alternatives available to the Irish state during the second half of the 1960s. The first of these would have involved deepening the planning process which had begun with the first *Programme for Economic Expansion* (1958–62) and was followed by another, the second (1963–68). The second *Programme* was far more ambitious and detailed than the first; yet its essentially macro-economic approach had limited if any real effect on the direction of the economy. However, implied in planning is the further possibility of state intervention to deepen the macro element and to influence directly the micro economy. This was a real possibility; after all the trade unions who were close to Lemass had been advocating further intervention to secure full employment.[5] Yet the cost of such action was considered to be too high to justify, for it would have required a level of state intervention unprecedented in Western Europe. It would also have involved the government in tasks to which it was not suited. In addition, the political consequences of such action were uncertain, as there could have been considerable instability in the political system as a consequence. A less radical step might have involved the government picking potentially competitive firms and allocating adequate resources to support them in order to achieve particular ends. This was not pursued for fear of reaction among other sectors of the economy and for the reasons stated above.

There was, however, a policy alternative available which could be pursued with little short term cost and with quantifiable benefits. As the decade progressed evidence accumulated that the main source of employment and exports in the Irish economy was to be found in a new sector, grant-aided industry. The grant-aided sector accounted for 70 per cent of new employment and 90 per cent of increased exports in the transportable goods industries.[6] Foreign companies comprised the bulk of the firms in this sector and proved to be the most dynamic sector of the economy for the remainder of the decade and throughout the 1970s. During the recession which began in 1973–74, manufacturing employment in indigenous firms remained stable, while that in foreign firms increased by a third.[7] While some of the employment figures have recently been questioned, the broad trend remains valid; much of the growth in the Irish economy since 1958 can be directly attributed to foreign investment in Ireland. The existence of this sector provided the basis for an alternative industrial strategy, and one which was relatively painless. The promotion of foreign investment obviated the need to take awkward political decisions such as would be necessitated by state intervention. This was reinforced by the fear that such action would not be welcomed by American investors on ideological grounds.

The decision to opt for this strategy, although based on economic necessities, led to the effective jettisoning of indigenous industry. Its failure to meet national needs led to its marginalisation within the policy process. Indeed policy making itself became de-politicised when the IDA in 1969 received effective authority to operate Ireland's industrial policies. This removed responsibility from the government for policy making. It also marked the end of the planning experiment as the third *Programme for Economic Expansion* (1965–72) was allowed to lapse. The decision to join the European Community has also to be interpreted in this context. At first membership was promoted in terms of markets, competition, and capital for Irish companies; but increasingly it was the presence of foreign companies in Ireland exporting to Europe which became the main reason. This was clearly important. Far more important was the promise of higher prices for farm products. Entry meant that Irish farmers could benefit from subsidies in the Community, which also meant that the Irish state did not have to subsidise them. The attractiveness of these options is reinforced when one considers that each could be introduced with few changes to the traditional political structure, to society or its culture. In the short term, Irish policy makers had achieved a positive sum outcome: benefits for industry, agriculture, employment and exports at little cost to the society or the political system. However, it can be suggested that these decisions, though understandable, did not prepare the society for the changes. Ireland became dependent on others to provide for its welfare without developing a society that could provide for itself.[8]

These decisions may have increased the blockages to growth in Ireland. The agricultural lobby has been so well organised since entry to the European Community that it uses the state to promote its case and this is generally accepted by the society. Lemass had to an extent circumvented the blockages during the 1960s but they had not disappeared. In a period of prosperity conflict could be reduced by distributive policies but, as Olson has shown, distributive coalitions by their nature restrict the ability of the state to change the environment. In the absence of a strong state able to coerce or disperse corporate interests, or a corporatist strategy for incorporation and consensual policy formation, it becomes very difficult to break out of a cycle of decline.[9] By discarding the strong state while not developing an adequate corporatist framework, Ireland's problems increased rather than diminished. Once the recession occurred there was strong pressure on the state from all sectors for protection from the impact of economic change.[10]

Despite these difficulties Lee has argued that an historic breakthrough had been made in 1957 by the leadership cadre around Lemass and Whitaker:

> It did succeed in bringing to an end the emigration that for more than a century has been the main scar on the social anatomy. Since 1957 a bridgehead had been established in the direction of a viable community. The past twenty five years have seen the creation of a dual society, a dualism that has resulted from the, however halting, advance of the productive forces and despite the resolute resistance of the parasitic forces.[11]

These achievements are clear: the average family has a standard of living some three to four times higher in real terms than that of a family during the 1920s. The patterns which have prevailed in Irish society for over a century have been undermined and a new society is in the process of formation. Moreover the essentially proprietorial and agricultural nature of that society has given way to a social structure reflecting modern industrial norms.[12] These trends have been supplemented in the economy by the dominance of industry; manufacturing exports constitute some 75 per cent of total volume, while exports are no longer concentrated on Britain but are divided among a number of markets. Tables 7.1 and 7.2 detail the important economic changes upon which these trends have been based, in particular, the central role played by manufacturing industry.

Despite these significant achievements, the Irish economy remains a developing rather than a developed economy. The analogy with the developing states in the Mediterranean and Latin America remains strong. The problems associated with development remain: high levels of unemployment (now at 20 per cent of the labour force); a huge foreign debt; increasing emigration, particularly of the skilled and educated. Moreover, indigenous manufacturing industry has not been the main vehicle for growth; this has been a result of investment by foreign companies. Between 1973 and 1980 employment in foreign companies expanded by 36.3 per cent while the figure for Irish industry was 3.3 per cent. While foreign investment has brought considerable benefits to Ireland it does not appear to have generated the linkages necessary for self sustained indigenous growth which would provide reasonable employment for those living within the state. These are not features of a developed society, but of one which has yet to utilise its resources, human, technological, and material, to full effect. While it is dangerous to exaggerate the historic success of the mature industrial economies, they, more than others, have successfully achieved this goal.

Table 7.1. Sectoral Employment 1966–80

	1966	1971	1975	1980
Agriculture, Forestry and Fishing	31.3	25.9	22.2	18.9
Industry	27.6	30.6	31.4	32.0
(Manufacturing Industry)	(18.6)	(20.3)	(20.9)	(20.9)
Services	41.2	43.5	46.4	49.1

Source: NESC Report No 67, *An Analysis of Job Losses in Irish Manufacturing Industry,* (Dublin 1983), p.9.

Table 7.2 Growth Rates in the Manufacturing Sector 1953–80

Period	Volume of Output	Employment
1954–59	2.3	–0.1
1959–66	6.2	2.7
1966–73	7.0	2.1
1973–79	5.1	0.8

Source: NESC Report No.66 *Policies for Industrial Development,* (Dublin 1982), p.3.

In most cases this has been accomplished by the elaboration of specific national strategies which could maximise not only national output, but also the benefits to be derived from the international economy. The White Paper on *Industrial Policy*, published in 1984, appeared to address this problem, but while its proposals marked a new point of departure little would seem to have been achieved since then.[13] The impact of the recession on Ireland has become more severe, while the decision to opt for retrenchment has driven the economy further into decline. Furthermore the casual acceptance of emigration by politicians and sections of the community challenges the reality of Irish independent policy making in much the same way that the recession of the mid 1950s did. What is not clear is whether an adequate response is available to the challenges not only of economic recession but of international change.

The Irish case demonstrates how difficult it is to promote self sustained and dynamic industrialisation. Even when the international environment is conducive to growth, there is no guarantee that such growth will occur in any individual economy; in a recession growth is even more problematic. It might be suggested that self sustained and dynamic industrialisation is not the norm. A small number of economies have experienced this process; but most have been characterised by partial industrial expansion accompanied by blockages to further growth. In the Irish case most blockages have been internal rather than external.

Blockages to economic growth remain. Unlike 1957 there is not a leadership cadre of the calibre of Lemass or Whitaker. The absence of vision in recent policy making is a consequence of the abdication of responsibiity by many politicans and a return to government by specialists, in particular accountants and economists. The cutbacks are aimed at the weakest targets, the working class and claimants; middle class benefits remain unaffected. Moreover the effectiveness of the agricultural lobby and the self-employed has prevented the development of an adequate tax system, which would not only be fair but which would provide incentives for growth and employment. Entrepreneurship has been much improved over the past quarter of a century, yet it is difficult not to believe that there remains many social obstacles to the growth of an expanding entrepreneurial culture. The continued use of polical means to defend sectoral interests remains widespread. Thus whether the defence of that interest is legimate or not, the activity excludes others from resources and binds the state to traditional powerful lobbies, particularly that of agriculture.

Once again there is a widespread consciousness that Ireland has become a zero sum society; one where resources are limited and the gain for one implies a certain loss for another. Not only is this perception socially divisive, but interest groups increasingly function as vehicles to obtain the maximum share of a stable national income without concern for the greater good. This is reinforced by the return to dominance of neo-liberal economics, which glorifies in individualism and the pursuit of self-aggrandisement. This, in turn, precludes the state from playing an active role in development. The refusal to accept that Ireland has a politically sophisticated society, but a developing economy means that alternatives to neo-liberalism are not entertained. The possibility of a moratorium on foreign debt is not discussed, not because it is the wrong policy – which it may be – but because the economic consensus accepts once again that economic policy is externally determined. Yet self preservation and prudence alone should warn that large scale unemployment and declining living standards will eventually destabilise the society with unpredictable consequences. Ireland therefore continues to require a strong state to direct the economy and to provide for the welfare of the society. This need not be socialism but, as in France or Japan, the realisation that in a changing environment a society has to consciously move to absorb the changes and work with them. In the absence of this direction, there is a danger that Ireland will, as in the 1920s, become the passive object of change and consequently will not benefit from it.

Notes

Chapter 1:
Politics and National Development (pp.1–10)

1. Eric Hobsbawm, *The Age of Revolution* (New York, 1962); Maxine Berg, *The Machine Question and the Making of Political Economy 1815–1848* (Cambridge, 1980).
2. In this and other chapters Ireland will normally be used to refer to the twenty-six counties which now constitute the Irish Republic. Northern Ireland will be used for the six counties of Ulster which remained within the United Kingdom. Southern Ireland or agrarian Ireland will occasionally be used in place of Ireland.
3. Joel Mokyr, *Why Ireland Starved* (London, 1983), pp.6–23, 278.
4. Sidney Pollard, *Peaceful Conquest* (Oxford,1981).
5. Mokyr, op.cit., p.291.
6. Padraig Pearse, 'The Sovereign People' in *Political Writings and Speeches* (Dublin, 1966), p.335 (Orig. ed. 1916)
7. For a recent analysis of Ulster cf. Liam Kennedy and Philip Ollerenshaw (eds), *An Economic History of Ulster 1820–1939* (Manchester, 1985).
8. George O'Brien, *The Economic History of Ireland from the Union to the Famine* (London, 1921), p.351. For a review of issues involved, cf. Eoin O'Malley, 'The Decline of Irish Industry in the Nineteenth Century' in *Economic and Social Review*, 13, no.1 (1981), pp.21–42.
9. Daniel Corkery, *Synge and Anglo-Irish Literature* (Cork, 1931), p.74.
10. For a comprehensive examination of nationalism see the essays in Leonard Tivey (ed.), *The Nation State* (Oxford 1981). For a discussion of political culture and its relationship to nationalism cf. Brian Girvin, 'Change and Continuity in Liberal Democratic Culture' in John Gibbins (ed.), *Politics and Contemporary Culture: New and Old Politics* (Sage: forthcoming 1989).
11. L.M. Cullen, *An Economic History of Ireland since 1660* (London, 1972), p.167.
12. Henry Patterson, 'Industrial Labour and the Labour Movement 1820–1914' in Kennedy and Ollerenshaw, op. cit. pp.158–83. For comparative purposes see Edward Lahiff, *Industry and Labour in Cork 1890–1921* unpublished M.A. thesis Department of Modern History, University College, Cork (1988).
13. Lennart Jobert, 'The Nordic Countries 1850–1914' in Carolo M. Cipolla (ed.), *The Fontana Economic History of Europe: The Emergence of Industrial Societies 2* (Glasgow, 1973), pp.375–485. For the conservative and defensive nature of much of Irish society by 1914,

cf. Tom Garvin, *Nationalist Revolutionaries in Ireland 1895–1928* (Oxford, 1987).

14. For over a century after 1850 Irish population declined continuously; the only time this did not occur was during the late 1940s and from the early 1960s through to 1979. The process of emigration has reappeared. The failure to provide for its citizens can be quantified in terms of those who can make a livelihood in the state.
15. Peter J. Katzenstein, *Corporatism and Change: Switzerland and Austria and the Politics of Industrialisation* (Ithaca, 1984).
16. The literature on imperialism, neo-colonialism and dependency is enormous. Representative examples would include: A. Gunder Frank, *Capitalism and Underdevelopment in Latin America* (New York, 1969); Paul Baran, *The Political Economy of Growth* (New York, 1957); Samir Amin, *Unequal Exchange* (Brighton, 1976); Roger Owen and Bob Sutcliffe, (eds), *Studies in The Theory of Imperialism* (London, 1972). For a trenchant criticism see Albert O. Hirschman, 'Rival Interpretations of Market Societies: Civilising, Destructive, or Feeble?' in *Journal of Economic Literature*, xx (1982), pp.1463–84.
17. Raymond Crotty, *Ireland in Crisis* (Dingle, 1986), pp.15–16.
18. Bill Warren, *Imperialism: Pioneer of Capitalism* (London, 1980); Nigel Harris, *The End of the Third World* (Harmondsworth, 1986). Both these authors stress the extent to which development has taken place and question the validity of dependency and associated theories.
19. Albert O. Hirschman, 'The Rise and Decline of Development Economics' and 'Beyond Asymmetry: Critical Notes on Myself as a Young Man and on some other Old Friends' in Albert O. Hirschman, *Essays in Trespassing* (Cambridge, 1981) pp.1–4, 27–33.
20. Bob Sutcliffe, 'Imperialism and Industrialisation in the Third World' in Owen and Sutcliffe (eds), op cit. pp.171–92 where very stringent criteria are applied to industrialisation.
21. Dudley Seers, *The Political Economy of Nationalism* (Oxford, 1981), p.83.
22. John A. Hall, *Powers and Liberties* (Harmondsworth, 1986) pp.15, 233–36; Mancur Olsen, *The Rise and Decline of Nations* (New Haven and London, 1982).
23. Nicos P. Mouzelis, *Politics in the Semi-Periphery* (London, 1986) for a thorough discussion of the concept. There is not a complete 'fit' between the case of Ireland and the examples cited by Mouzelis, but there is enough overlap between them to explore the similarities and the differences.
24. Peter Mair, *The Changing Irish Party System* (London, 1987) where the similarities between the Irish political system and those of Europe are stressed. For a more detailed discussion of these themes cf. Brian Girvin, 'Nationalism, Politics and the World Economic System',

paper presented to Joint History and Sociology seminar, University College Cork, December 1987. I am grateful to the participants at this seminar for their comments and criticisms.

25. Brian Farrell, *The Founding of Dáil Éireann* (Dublin, 1971) pp.ix–xx.

Chapter 2:
Independence and the Obstacles to Economic Development in the Free State 1922–27 (pp.11–46)

1. Patrick Lynch, 'The Economics of Independence: Some Unsettled Questions of Irish Economics' in Basil Chubb and Patrick Lynch (eds), *Economic Development and Planning* (Dublin, 1969), pp.128–44, quote at p.130.
2. M.A.G. Ó Tuathaigh, 'De Valera and Sovereignty', in J.P. O'Carroll and J.A. Murphy (eds), *De Valera and his Times* (Cork, 1983), pp.62–73.
3. Dorothy Macardle, *The Irish Republic*, (London, 1968, orig. ed. 1937), pp.838–43.
4. Brian Farrell, *The Founding of Dáil Éireann*, (Dublin, 1971), p.87; Patrick Lynch, 'The Social Revolution that Never Was', in Desmond Williams (ed.), *The Irish Struggle* 1916–26 (London,1966), pp.41–54.
5. Establishment of National Economic Council, 4 September 1920; SPO, DE2/40. Irish Industrial Scheme, March–April 1921; SPO, DE2/19.
6. First Memorandum on Irish Claims in Regard to Finance, 1921; UCDA, McGilligan Papers, P35A/2. Ronan Fanning, *The Irish Department of Finance* (Dublin, 1978), pp.120–22.
7. Correspondence Relating to Proposals of His Majesty's Government for an Irish Settlement [Cmd. 1502], H.C. 1921.
8. Economic Relations Committee, 1921; UCDA, McGilligan Papers, P35 B/26.
9. Memorandum by George O'Brien in ibid.
10. Memorandum by Riordan and Smiddy included in ibid.
11. O'Brien diary, cited in James Meenan, *George O'Brien* (Dublin, 1980), p.89.
12. Macardle, op cit., pp.785–91. Maurice Moynihan (ed.), *Speeches and Statements by Eamon de Valera* 1917–73, (Dublin, 1980), pp. 153–8.
13. David Johnson, *The Interwar Economy in Ireland* (Dundalk, 1985), p.20.
14. Raymond Crotty, *Ireland in Crisis* (Dingle,1986), p.60; other calculations derived from Census of Population,1926, *General Report* (Dublin,1928).
15. Mary Daly, *Social and Economic History of Ireland Since 1800* (Dublin, 1981), p.137.
16. The Banking Commission, *Final Report* (Dublin, 1926), p.10.
17. Fanning, op. cit., p.108.
18. Coffey to Cosgrave, October 1922, Cosgrave to Coffey, 27 Oct. 1922; UCDA, McGilligan Papers, P35A/4.

19. Fanning, op. cit., pp.103–4.
20. Fanning, op. cit., pp.106–7.
21. Memorandum, Patrick Hogan, October 1923; UCDA, McGilligan Papers, P35B/2.
22. Memorandum Patrick Hogan, 25 Jan. 1924; UCDA, McGilligan Papers, P35B/2.
23. Memorandum October Act 1923; UCDA, McGilligan Papers, P35 B/2.
24. Raymond Crotty, *Irish Agricultural Production* (Cork, 1966) p.111.
25. Fiscal Inquiry Committee, 1923; SPO, S.3107.
26. Draft speech for Dáil; SPO, S.3107.
27. Reports of the Fiscal Inquiry Committee (Dublin, 1923), Final Report cited unless specifically noted, paragraph 2.
28. Fiscal Inquiry Committee, paragraph 7.
29. Fiscal Inquiry Committee, paragraphs 9–11.
30. Fiscal Inquiry Committee, paragraphs 10,94,90–1
31. Fiscal Inquiry Committee, paragraphs 13–14
32. Fiscal Inquiry Committee, paragraphs 28–36.
33. Fiscal Inquiry Committee, paragraph 123
34. Fiscal Inquiry Committee, paragraph 130.
35. Fiscal Inquiry Committee, paragraph 96.
36. Executive Council C2/34, 18 December 1923; SPO, S.3107.
37. O'Brien diary, cited in Meenan, op. cit., pp.129,139.
38. Fiscal Inquiry Committee, paragraphs 134–7.
39. O'Brien diary, cited in Meenan, op. cit.,p.129.
40. ibid., p.128.
41. Memorandum to Executive Council on Fiscal Inquiry Committee by Minister for Industry and Commerce, 21 January 1924; SPO, S.3107.
42. All references to memorandum cited in footnote 41.
43. ibid.
44. Cited in Fanning, op. cit.,pp.203–4.
45. Department of Industry and Commerce: Reconstruction and Employment. Memorandum 6 December 1922. Cabinet decision, 12 December 1922; SPO, S.1906.
46. Department of Industry and Commerce: Unemployment. No date, from internal evidence late 1924; UCDA McGilligan Papers, P35.B/1.
47. Industry and Commerce: Secretary; SPO, S.2470A.
48. Industry and Commerce: Measures Enacted. No date, from internal evidence 1928; UCDA, Blythe Papers, P24/320.
49. All references to memorandum cited in footnote 48.
50. Gordon Campbell to Department of Finance, 29 February 1924; Department of Finance, F22/11/24.
51. Memorandum by McGrath, 29 February 1924; Department of Finance, F22/11/24.
52. Cited from memorandum ibid., 29 February 1924.

53. Appendix I in memorandum ibid., 29 February 1924.
54. All references from memorandum ibid., 29 February 1924.
55. ibid.
56. Memorandum by McElligott, 3 March 1924; Department of Finance, F22/11/24.
57. Campbell to McElligott, 19 March 1924, to Secretary Executive Council, 19 March, 1924; Department of Finance, F22/11/24.
58. Hogan to Blythe, 9 April 1924; Department of Finance, F22/11/24.
59. McElligott to Blythe, 10 April 1924; Department of Finance, F22/11/24.
60. Industry and Commerce: Measures Enacted; UCDA, Blythe Papers, P24/320.
61. Watching Committee on Tariffs, no date, from internal evidence late May early June 1925; Department of Finance, F22/44/25.
62. McElligott to Blythe, 19 June 1925; Campbell to Finance, 15 September 1925; Department of Finance, F22/44/25.
63. Dublin Industrial Development Association to Finance, 17 June 1926; Department of Finance, F22/44/25.
64. Tariff Commission Act 1926, memorandum 17 April 1926; SPO, S.4950.
65. ibid.
66. ibid.
67. Brief drafted for Blythe by McElligott, 22 October 1926; Department of Finance, F22/44/25.
68. Campbell to Smith, 25 April 1925; Smith to Campbell, 29 April 1925, 17 May 1925; Campbell to Smith, 2 June 1925; UCDA, McGilligan Papers, P35B/5.
69. Campbell to McGilligan, 19 July 1927; UCDA, McGilligan Papers, P35B/10.
70. McGilligan's notes on memorandum cited in note 69.
71. The Barrington memorandum on agriculture, memorandum by Campbell, 18 January 1927; UCDA, McGilligan Papers, P35B/9.
72. Cited from memorandum, ibid.
73. Industrial Banking: Industry and Commerce memorandum, 19 November 1924; UCDA, McGilligan Papers P35B/4. R.C. Ferguson, memorandum on flax spinning industry, 19 April 1927; UCDA, McGilligan Papers, P35B/11; for discussion cf. Mary E.Daly, 'Government Finance for Industry in the Irish Free State: The Trade Loans (Guarantee) Acts' in *Irish Economic and Social History* xi (1984),pp.73–93.
74. Industrial Banking, ibid.
75. Evidence presented by R.C. Ferguson to Banking Commission, 7 June 1926; UCDA, McGilligan Papers, P35B/20.
76. Evidence presented by T.J. Barrington to Banking Commission, 29 June 1926; UCDA, McGilligan Papers, P35B/20.

77. Industrial Banking, 19 November 1924; Notes by Campbell on Currency Bill, 12 April 1927; UCDA, McGilligan Papers, P35B/4, P35A/26.
78. Barrington to Campbell, 18 January 1928; UCDA, McGilligan Papers P35A/26.
79. Fanning, op cit., pp.178–86.
80. Campbell to McGilligan, 2 July 1926; UCDA, McGilligan Papers, P35/39.
81. Industry and Commerce to Finance, 13 January 1925; memorandum: ESB control, undated; Shannon Scheme: control, memorandum November 1925; UCDA, McGilligan Papers, P35/39, P35/66, P35/33.
82. Quote from Shannon Scheme: control; Shannon Scheme: organisation, no date; Shannon Scheme: future arrangements assuming a state system, no date; UCDA, McGilligan Papers, P35/33, p35/32 P35/39. cf. *Report of the Public Services Organisation Review Group 1966–69* (Dublin,1969), for a discussion on use of this form of organisation.

Chapter 3:
Fianna Fáil and the Challenge to the
Free Trade Economy 1927–32 (pp.47–87)

1. Raymond Crotty, *Irish Agricultural Production* (Cork, 1966), pp.108–32. Tony Varley and Chris Curtin, 'The Political Negotiation of State Agricultural Policy: Ireland 1922–39', paper read at Irish Sociological Association, Magee College Derry, April, 1980.
2. Albert Hirschman, *Essays in Trespassing* (Cambridge,1981), pp. 80–82.
3. Gordon Campbell, memorandum 18 January 1927. UCDA, McGilligan Papers, P35b/19
4. Hirschman, op.cit, p.96.
5. William Ashworth, 'Typologies and Evidence: Has Nineteenth-Century Europe a Guide to Economic Growth?' in *Economic History Review* xxx, no.1 (1977), pp.140–8. In particular see pp.153–5 for discussion.
6. I have adopted this concept from Nicos Mouzelis, 'Capitalism and the Development of the Greek State' in Richard Scase (ed.), *The State in Western Europe.* (London, 1980), pp.241–73.
7. Eugene Genovese, *The Political Economy of Slavery* (New York, 1967), pp.3–25, 160. Carlos Pelaez, 'The Theory and Reality of Imperialism in the Coffee Economy of Nineteenth-Century Brazil' in *Economic History Review,* xxix, no.2 (1976), pp.276–290.
8. Genovese, op.cit., pp.30–60, 244–60. Nathaniel Leff, *Underdevelopment and Development in Brazil*, (London, 2 volumes, 1982). Crotty op. cit., pp.84–107. For a comprehensive discussion of

the American South after the Civil War cf. D.W.Grantham, *The Life and Death of the Solid South* (Lexington, Kentucky, 1988).

9. James Meenan, *The Irish Economy Since 1922* (Liverpool, 1970), p.301. Commission on Emigration, *Reports* (Dublin, 1955), p.148.
10. Thomas Cochran, *Frontiers of Change* (New York, 1981), pp.5–16. Ashworth, op.cit. Maxine Berg, *The Machine Question and the Making of Political Economy* (Cambridge, 1980).
11. Meenan, op.cit., pp.275–6.
12. Barbara Solow, *The Land Question and the Irish Economy 1870–1903* (Cambridge, Mass., 1971) pp.194–204. Crotty, op. cit., pp.97–102, 119–21. Lennart Jorberg and Olle Krantz, 'Scandinavia 1914–70' in Carlo Cipolla, *The Fontana Economic History of Europe: Contemporary Economies 2* (Glasgow, 1976) pp.377–459.
13. Crotty, op.cit., pp.88, 108.
14. Evidence of Agricultural Credit Corporation, NLI, Commission on Vocational Organisation, MS.923 Q.4475–76, 4516–17.
15. Crotty, op.cit., p.90.
16. Crotty, ibid., pp.128–29.
17. Meenan, op.cit., p.275.
18. This figure is computed from census data and includes employers, those working on their own account, and assisting relatives. There may be some objections to including relatives assisting in the above figure. However, although they were not employers they were also not employees in the normal sense. For a study of the labour force in Cork which tends to confirm this approach cf. Edward Lahiff, *Industry and Labour in Cork 1890–1921* M.A. thesis, National University of Ireland (1988).
19. Agricultural Credit Corporation, MS.923 Q.4416–4538. Department of Agriculture, memorandum MS.941, document 197 NLI, Commission on Vocational Organisation.
20. Damien Hannan, *Displacement and Development: Class Kinship and Social Change in Irish Rural Communities* (Dublin, 1979) p.29. Department of Industry and Commerce, *Agricultural Statistics 1928–33* (Dublin, 1935).
21. Solow, op.cit., makes this general case throughout. Crotty, pp.126–29 for effect of de-rating.
22. Department of Agriculture, oral evidence to Commission on Vocational Organisation, NLI, MS.930 Q.2949–3020. Tom Garvin, 'The Sociology of a Nationalist Revolution: Ireland 1858–1928' (unpublished manuscript, April 1984) pp.40–1. The major study of economic values remains D.C. McClelland, *The Achieving Society* (Princeton, 1961).
23. Gavin Kitching, *Development and Under-Development in Historical Perspective,* (London, 1982) assesses the role of pre-capitalist economic units in the world economy.

24. Kieran Kennedy, *Productivity and Industrial Growth: The Irish Experience* (Oxford, 1971), pp.2–7. David Johnson, T*he Interwar Economy in Ireland* (Dundalk, 1985), pp.12–13. Dudley Seers, *The Political Economy of Nationalism.*, (Oxford, 1983).
25. Johnson, op.cit., pp.20–5. T.K. Daniel, 'Griffith on his Noble Head: The Determinants of Cumann na nGaedheal's Economic Policy 1922–32', *Irish Economic Social History*, 111 (1976), pp.55–65.
26. John A.Hall, *Powers and Liberties* (Harmondsworth, 1985), pp.233–8.
27. C.S. Andrews, *Man of No Property* (Dublin and Cork, 1982). *Brian Farrell, Sean Lemass*, (Dublin 1983), pp.21–4. Brian Girvin, 'The Dominance of Fianna Fáil and the Nature of Political Adaptability in Ireland' in *Political Studies*, 32 (1984), pp.461–70.
28. Richard Sinnott, 'Interpretations of the Irish Party System' in *European Journal of Political Research*, 12 (1984), pp.289–307.
29. Peter Mair, 'Labour and the Irish Party System re-visited: Party Competition in the 1920s' in *Economic and Social Review*, 9, no.1 (1977), pp.59–70.
30. Arthur Mitchell, *Labour in Irish Politics 1890–1930* (Dublin, 1974), pp.192–239.
31. Terence de Vere White, *Kevin O'Higgins* (Tralee, 1966: orig. ed. 1948), pp.228–229. Warner Moss, *Political Parties in the Irish Free State* (New York, 1933), pp.141–58.
32. Farrell, op.cit., pp.10–14.
33. Tom Garvin, *The Evolution of Irish Nationalist Politics* (Dublin, 1981), p.165.
34. See in particular the selection of de Valera speeches at the time in Maurice Moynihan (ed.), *Speeches and Statements by Eamon de Valera 1917–73* (Dublin,1980), pp.121–62.
35. Brian Girvin, 'Nationalism, Democracy and Irish Political Culture' in B. Girvin and R. Sturm (eds), *Politics and Society in Contemporary Ireland* (Aldershot,1986), pp.3–28.
36. M.A.G. Ó Tuathaigh, 'De Valera and Sovereignty' in P.J. O'Carroll and J.A. Murphy (ed.), *De Valera and his Times*, (Cork, 1983), pp.62–70.
37. James Meenan, 'From Free Trade to Self Sufficiency' in Francis McManus (ed.), *The Years of the Great Test 1926–39*, (Cork, 1967), p.72. Calculations from *Census of Industrial Production 1926 and 1929* (Dublin, 1930) and *Census of Industrial Production 1931* (Dublin, 1934). Mary Daly, *Social and Economic History of Ireland since 1800* (Dublin, 1981), p.144 cites a figure of 13,000 new jobs for this period. I have been unable to trace the source of this figure. The best estimate I have been able to obtain for employment in protected industries is contained in Table 3.4. It covers the years 1922 to 1927 and points to an increase of 10,000. If non-protected employment creation is added to this, then there may be some compatibility with the Daly figure.

38. Ferguson to Leydon, 19 August 1931; UCDA, McGilligan Papers, P35A/19.
39. Draft manuscript, Sean Lemass; no date from internal evidence, possibly 1929. NLI, Gallagher Papers MS.18339.
40. Minute prepared by T.J. Barrington 18 October 1928. Memorandum 'Laws Governing Rights and Liabilities of Foreign Companies in Various Countries', UCDA, McGilligan Papers, P35B/14.
41. 'Effects of Tariffs on Prices in the Saorstat', no date; UCDA, McGilligan Papers, P35/28.
42. Campbell to Ferguson, 15 July 1930; UCDA, McGilligan Papers, P35/153.Blythe Papers, P24/321. Industry and Commerce memorandum 14 April 1931 for statistics on employment and imports.
43. Ferguson to Campbell, 16 July 1930; UCDA, McGilligan Papers, P35/153; unattributed quotations below are from this memorandum.
44. Statistical tables contained in UCDA, McGilligan Papers, P35/153.
45. *Irish Trade Journal* 2 No. 2 (1927), pp.171–72. *Census of Industrial Production 1926 and 1929*, pp.1–2, 24.
46. Campbell to McGilligan, 20 May 1930. McGilligan to Campbell, 15 July 1930; UCDA, McGilligan Papers, P35/153.
47. McGilligan to McElligott, 25 October 1930. McElligott to Blythe, 1 November 1930. McElligott to Hogan, 13 November 1930; Department of Finance, F100/3/30.
48. McElligott to McGilligan, 13 November 1930. Department of President to Finance, 17 November 1930; Department of Finance, F100/3/30. Tariff Commission Act (Amendment) 1930; SPO, S.2494.
49. 'Mr Leydon on State Enterprise', 31 August 1929; UCDA, McGilligan Papers, P35B/18.
50. Ronan Fanning, *The Irish Department of Finance* (Dublin, 1978), p.205.
51. D.W. Harkness, *The Restless Dominion* (London,1969) for details of his activities as Minister for External Affairs.
52. 'Dependence on British Market', unsigned memorandum. Marked read 13 August 1931; UCDA, McGilligan Papers, P35B/27.
53. 'Statistics on Taxation and Expenditure', 2 October 1930; UCDA, McGilligan Papers, P35A/28.
54. Ronan Fanning, *Independent Ireland* (Dublin, 1983), pp.77–8.
55. Hogan to McGilligan, 22 October 1929; UCDA, McGilligan Papers, P35C/166.
56. Typescript 'Fianna Fáil Economic Policy', no date, from internal evidence 1929/30; UCDA, McGilligan Papers, P35C/166.
57. Note by McGilligan, from internal evidence 1931/32; UCDA, McGilligan Papers, P35B/29.

58. 'A Brief Outline of the Aims and Programme of Fianna Fáil' published prior to June 1927 election. SPO, S.12882B.
59. 'Draft History of Fianna Fáil'; no date NLI, Gallagher Papers MS 18339.
60. Draft manuscript, Sean Lemass; NLI, Gallagher Papers MS 18339.
61. Details can be found in 'Economic Committee' 1928–29 SPO, S.5768A-C.
62. See in particular 'Economic Committee' files C and B op.cit.
63. Draft manuscript, Sean Lemass; NLI, Gallagher Papers MS 18339.
64. All references contained in ibid.
65. 'Dependence on British Market'; UCDA, McGilligan Papers, P35B/27.
66. Sean Lemass, reported in *Irish Times*, 7 September 1931.
67. Report in *Irish Independent*, 24 October 1931.
68. Report in *Irish Independent*, 28 October 1931.
69. 'Fianna Fáil Economic Policy', op.cit.

Chapter 4:
The Drive to Industrialise: Fianna Fáil and Protectionism 1932–39
(pp.88–130)

1. For a comparative study of this period cf. John A. Garraty, *The Great Depression* (New York, 1987).
2. Draft manuscript, Sean Lemass (no date; from internal evidence, possibly 1929); NLI, Gallagher Papers MS 18339.
3. W.O. Henderson, *Friedrich List: Economist and Visionary, 1789–1846* (London, 1983). List excluded small nations from his model, believing that they would be subordinated to larger ones. For the post-1945 period Gavin Kitching, *Development and Underdevelopment in Historical Perspective* (London, 1982).
4. Even the Department of Finance was not immune to this process. Ronan Fanning, *The Irish Department of Finance* (Dublin,1978), pp.216–23.
5. V.O. Key, 'A Theory of Critical Elections' in *Journal of Politics*, 17 (1955), pp.3–18.
6. Raymond Crotty, *Irish Agricultural Production* (Cork, 1966), pp.126–30. Brian Girvin 'Nationalism, Democracy, and Irish Political Culture', in Brian Girvin and Roland Sturm (eds), *Politics and Society in Contemporary Ireland* (Aldershot, 1986), pp.3–28.
7. Draft history of Fianna Fáil, NLI, Gallagher Papers MS 18376. Liam Skinner, *Politicians by Accident* (Dublin, 1946), pp.58–68.
8. David Johnson, *The Interwar Economy in Ireland* (Dundalk, 1985) p.26.
9. Draft manuscript, Sean Lemass; NLI, Gallagher Papers MS 18339.
10. Kitchen, op.cit., pp.152–7, 179.
11. Draft history of Fianna Fáil op.cit. C.S. Andrews, *Man of No Property* (Dublin and Cork, 1982), pp.118–19 for a similar view.

12. Brian Farrell, *Sean Lemass* (Dublin, 1983), pp.30–34.
13. Fanning, op.cit., pp.218–20, 251–8.
14. Industry and Commerce, 'Board for External Trade', 1 November 1932; SPO, Economic Committee of the Cabinet, S6274.
15. Sean Lemass, 'Present Economic Situation in Saorstat', 7 November 1932; SPO, Economic Committee of the Cabinet, S6274.
16. By 1936 Lemass was one of those within the Cabinet willing to seriously consider an end to the economic war: 'Trade Relations with Great Britain', 4 December, 1936; SPO, Great Britain: Trade Relations with Saorstat, S.9420
17. Minutes of Cabinet meeting Cab.6/10, 5 December, 1932; SPO, Economic Committee of the Cabinet, S.6274. Fanning, op. cit., pp.244–51.
18. Detailed memoranda and exchange of correspondence are contained in SPO, Unemployment-Relief Payments. Proposals 1933, S.6242A.
19. Industry and Commerce, 'Flour Milling Industry', 6 June 1930; SPO, Flour Milling Reorganisation, 1932, S.6045. *Census of Industrial Production, 1931*, (Dublin, 1934), p.xiv. PDDE, vol. 38. c.845, cf. 6th May 1931 for exchange.
20. Jon S. Cohen 'Fascism and Agriculture in Italy: Policies and Consequences', in *Economic History Review* xxxii (February 1979), pp.70–87.
21. 'Attitude to the Rank Interests', 22 March 1932. Department of President to Industry and Commerce, 9 April 1932. Cab. 6/5, 18 March 1932; Cab.6/8, 24 March 1932; Cab.6/19, 25 April 1932; SPO, Flour Milling Reorganisation, 1932, S.6045.
22. For details cf 'Flour Milling Reorganisation, 1932' and Agricultural Produce (Cereals) Act 1932.
23. Evidence by Irish Bakers' Confectioners' and Allied Workers' Amalgamated Union; NLI, Commission on Vocational Organisation, MS.924, Q.6656. Evidence of Irish Flour Millers Association; NLI, Commission on Vocational Organisation, MS.925, Q.6690–92, 6714, 6717.
24. 'Cement Manufacture in the Saorstat', 30 March 1931; SPO, Cement Manufacture 1929–34, S.6137 A-B.
25. Letter circulated by Gordon Campbell, 14 October 1929. McGilligan to Department of President, 26 February 1931 'Cement Manufacture in Saorstat'. Cab.5/76, 6 August 1931; SPO, Cement Manufacture 1929–34, S.6137 A-B.
26. McElligott to Campbell, memorandum 22 April 1931; UCDA, Blythe Papers, P24/115.
27. Details in SPO, Cement Manufacture 1929–34 S.6137 A-B.
28. Geoffrey Jones, 'The Growth and Performance of British Multinational Firms Before 1939: the Case of Dunlop', in *Economic History*

Review xxxvii, no.1 (1984), pp.50–51. Memorandum 11 June 1934; SPO, Proposed Rubber Factory, S.6560A. The insurance industry was also reorganised in the interests of the state and along lines determined by Lemass. Department of Industry and Commerce, TIA 834, Insurance Act, 1936.

29. Albert Hirschman, *Exit Voice and Loyalty: Responses to Decline in Firms, Organisations, and States* (Cambridge, Mass., 1970).
30. For change in approach cf. Report on Meat Meals and Bone Meals, 15 September 1933; SPO, Tariff Commission, S.2491. For abolition; SPO, Tariff Commission Abolition, 1938, S.10919. In his evidence to the Banking Commission, John Leydon emphasised that the Department explicitly rejected the cautious and consultative approach of the Tariff Commission. Commission of Inquiry into Banking, Currency and Credit, *Memoranda and Minutes of Evidence* (Dublin: 2 vols., 1937), 11 p.1417 (hereafter, *Memoranda*).
31. Mary Daly, 'An Irish-Ireland for Business?: The Control of Manufactures Acts 1932 and 1934', in *Irish Historical Studies*, xxiv, 94 (1984), pp.266–72.
32. The main instruments used are contained in *The Emergency Imposition of Duties Act 1932, The Control of Imports Act 1934*, and *The Control of Manufactures Acts 1932 and 1934.*
33. 'Establishment of Industrial Development Branch' approved by Cabinet, 27 May 1932; SPO, Development of Protected Industries, S.6283.
34. Fanning, op.cit., pp.256–7.
35. *Memoranda* 1, pp.2–3, 15, 23–4. Mary Daly, 'Government Finance for Industry in the Irish Free State: the Trade Loans (Guarantee) Acts in *Irish Economic and Social History,* xi (1984), pp.73–93.
36. Dudley Seers, *The Political Economy of Nationalism* (Oxford, 1983), for a detailed discussion of this theme.
37. Skinner, op.cit., p.62.
38. 'Present Economic Situation in Saorstat', 7 November 1932; SPO, Economic Committee of the Cabinet, 1932. S.6274.
39. 'Industrial Financing', 24 May, 1932; SPO, Industrial Credit, S.6467.
40. Fanning, op.cit., p.253.
41. Smiddy to de Valera, 8 March 1933. Report of Committee, 16 March 1933. Cabinet decision, Cab.7/14, 20 March 1933; SPO, Industrial Credit, S.6467.
42. Commission of Inquiry into Banking, Currency and Credit, *Report* (Dublin, 1938), p.p84–7. Hereafter *Report. Memoranda* 2, p.1431.
43. *Memoranda* 2, pp.1370, 1375.
44. Evidence of Industrial Credit Company; NLI, Commission on Vocational Organisation, MS.923, Q.4682, 4475–6.
45. ibid, Q.4889–94, 4908.

46. *Report*, pp.69–70. The possibility of further industrial expansion within a protected economy is discussed in Chapters 6 and 7.
47. Cab.6/51, 21 August 1932; SPO, Emergency Imposition of Duties (No. 1) Order 1932, S.6315A.
48. Department of Industry and Commerce, TID 1207/421. British United Shoe Machines, 26 June 1934; Department of Industry and Commerce, TID 1207/579.
49. *Memoranda*, 3 May 1935. Revised views 23 October 1935; SPO, Control of Manufactures (No. 1) Order, S.7751.
50. Irish Structural Steel and Ironworkers Association, 21 May 1938; Department of Industry and Commerce, TID,41/25. Irish Aluminium Ltd, 16 June 1938; Department of Industry and Commerce, TID, 1207/601.
51. R.C. Ferguson to Commission on Vocational Organisation, 5 September 1941; NLI, Commission on Vocational Organisation, MS 940 Document 171.
52. *Memoranda* 2, p.1399. Report of meeting, 14 September 1937; Department of Industry and Commerce, TID, 1207/465.
53. *Report*, 106–7.
54. Census of Industrial Production, 1936 (Dublin, 1938), pp.vi–vii. Calculated from tables in Census for 1929, 1931, 1936, 1938–44.
55. *Memoranda*, 2 p.1378.
56. Tables can be found in SPO, Employment in Protected Industries, S.11219A.
57. Skinner, op.cit.; James Meenan, 'Irish Industrial policy 1921–43' in *Studies*, xxxii (1943), pp.209–18.
58. 'Statistical Summary' 2 February 1940; UCDA, McGilligan Papers P35A/30.
59. Johnson, op.cit., p.29.
60. ibid., p.30. Garret Fitzgerald, 'Mr. Whitaker and Industry' in *Studies*, xlvii (1959), pp.138–50.
61. ibid., p.28.
62. Statistical data collected by Industry and Commerce, late 1920s. 'Effect of Tariffs on Prices', 14 April 1931; UCDA, McGilligan Papers, P35/153. Blythe Papers, P24/321. Other calculations from CIP, 1926 and 1929.
63. CIP, 1936 p.vii, Table 10, pp.30–1.
64. Johnson, op.cit., p.30. Data calculated from information collected by Industry and Commerce 'Information Relating to Industries Established in 1932 and onwards ...' No date but from internal evidence 1947. SPO, Establishment of Industries, S.11987B.
65. ibid., p.29 for his reference to the Soviet Union and the comparison with the Free State.
66. *Memoranda*, 2, pp.1375–8, 1384.
67. Federation of Irish Manufacturers; NLI, Commission on Vocational Organisation, MS.924 Q.6445.

68. Johnson, op.cit.,p.43.
69. L. M. Cullen, *An Economic History of Ireland Since 1660* (London, 1972), pp.175–87.
70. James Meenan, *The Irish Economy Since 1922* (Liverpool, 1970), pp.321–23.
71. Raymond Crotty, *Ireland in Crisis* (Dingle, 1986), pp.73–5.
72. Fanning, op.cit., pp.244–75. Andrew Orridge, 'The Blueshirts and the 'Economic War': A Study of Ireland in the Context of Dependency Theory' in *Political Studies*, 31 no.3 (1983), pp.351–69.
73. Deirdre McMahon, *Republicans and Imperialists* (New Haven and London,1984) *passim* for an assessment of de Valera's concern with sovereignty.
74. Fanning, op.cit., p.269.
75. Memoranda 2, pp1385–6, 1423.
76. Federation of Saorstat Industries (FSI), 27 August 1937. FIM, oral evidence; NLI, Commission on Vocational Organisation, MS.924 Q.9370.
77. Federation of Irish Industries, Minute Book, 11 January 1933, hereafter FII. FII delegation to Minister, 7 March 1933; Dept. of Industry and Commerce, TID 1207/278.
78. Ferguson to Commission on Vocational Organisation, 5 September 1941; NLI, MS.940 Document 171.
79. FII, 23 June 1933.
80. FII to Industry and Commerce 7 March 1933; FII to Industry and Commerce, 22 March 1933, Memoranda on Act forwarded to Department, 16 October 1933. Department of Industry and Commerce; TID, 1207/178 and 1207/199. FII, 16 March 1934.
81. Exchange of correspondence during 1936 can be found in Department of Industry and Commerce; TID, 1207/969.
82. Federation of Irish Manufacturers, oral evidence. Linen and Cotton Textile Manufacturers' Association, oral evidence; NLI, Commission on Vocational Organisation, MS 924, Q.6355. MS 925 Q.6906–58.
83. FSI, 21 January 1938. The FII changed its name to FSI in 1935 and subsequently to FIM in January 1938.
84. FSI, 25 October 1937.
85. FSI, 27 January 1938 for report.
86. FIM, ibid. Memorandum Irish Motor Traders' Association, NLI, Commission on Vocational Organisation, MS 924, Q.6458. MS 939 for memo.
87. FIM, ibid., NLI MS 924 Q.6435.
88. FIM, memorandum, 8 March 1940; NLI, Commission on Vocational Organisation, MS 937. Document 92.
89. FIM, oral evidence NLI, MS 924, Q.6448–59.
90. FIM, memorandum, 8 March 1940 NLI, MS397. Document 92.

91. Albert Hirschman, *The Strategy of Economic Development* (New Haven, 1958), pp.11–28, 50–75.
92. Erskine Childers to Commission, 17 July 1940; NLI, Commission on Vocational Organisation, MS 937.
93. FIM supplementary evidence supplied by Childers; NLI, Commission on Vocational Organisation, MS 931 Q.20464, for discussion Q.20457–60.
94. ibid.; NLI, MS 931, Q.20499–20500.
95. Commission on Vocational Organisation, *Report* (Dublin, 1943), pp.351–62.
96. FIM, op.cit., MS 924 Q.6412–14, 6439–44. FSI, 29 October 1937 for details. 14 January 1938, for report on meeting with Lemass.
97. Irish Trade Union Congress, *Thirty-Ninth Annual Report* (Dublin, 1933), p.145.
98. Industry and Commerce to ITUC, 29 January 1937 in ITUC, *Forty-Third Annual Report* (Dublin, 1936), pp.68–9.
99. ITUC, *Forty-Second Annual Report* (Dublin, 1936), p.162.
100. Department of Labour: Trade Union Bill 1941, TIW 766. 'Loss of Production Due to Inter-Union Disputes', 30 June 1941. Industry and Commerce to ITUC, 9 January 1937, ITUC to Industry and Commerce, 3 May 1937.
101. Parliamentary Debates Seanad Éireann, 24 April 1940, cc.1132–39; the debate can be found at cc.1085–1151.
102. McMahon, op.cit., p.138 for quotation.
103. Finance memorandum 23 August 1936, SPO, S.6315/3; Lemass memorandum 4 December 1936, SPO, S.9420.
104. McMahon, op cit., pp.237–284.
105. Minute of meeting, 25 February 1938. BT11/2833.
106. The changes in the drafting of the agreement can be found in BT11/2834.
107. Industry and Commerce memorandum, 12 June 1939, SPO, S.10633.

Chapter 5:
The Failure of Radical Alternatives: Policy Formation 1939–48 (pp.131–168)

1. John Maynard Keynes, 'National Self Sufficiency' in *Studies*, xxii (1933), pp.177–93.
2. Alfred O'Rahilly, *Money* (Cork, 1942) pp.xix–xxi.
3. J.J. Lee and M.A.G. Ó Tuathaigh, *The Age of de Valera* (Dublin, 1983) p.141.
4. Richard N. Gardner, *Sterling-Dollar Diplomacy in Current Perspective* (New York, 1980).
5. Lee and Ó Tuathaigh, op. cit., p.141.
6. 'Present Position of Outstanding Proposals for the Establishment of Certain Industries', 10 July 1940; SPO, Establishment of Industries, S.11987A.

7. 'Department of Supplies Record of Activities'; Department of Industry and Commerce, E37/578, p.1 (hereafter cited as Dept. of Supplies).
8. 'Control of Industry', 25 April 1942; SPO, Emergency Powers Order 1939, S.12811.
9. 'Dept. of Supplies', pp.19–24; cf. Robert Fisk, *In Time of War* (London,1983) for a comprehensive discussion of issues throughout the war period.
10. 'Dept. of Supplies', pp.13–14.
11. 'Dept. of Supplies', pp.4, 33.
12. 'Labour Policy', June 1942. G2/372; SPO, Planning for Post War Situation, S.12882A. For a discussion of the 1941 Trade Union Act see Brian Girvin, *Protectionism and Economic Development in Independent Ireland* (Ph.D. National University of Ireland,1986) Chapter 4, pp.146–98.
13. 'Labour Policy', ibid.
14. Copy of speech in SPO, Planning for Post War Situation, S.12882A.
15. Reported in *Irish Times*, 29 October 1942.
16. 'Labour Policy' op.cit.
17. ibid.
18. Memorandum on Industrial Relations, 23 October 1944; Department of Labour, Labour Court, IR. 19. The evolution of this policy will be discussed in the next chapter.
19. Raymond J. Raymond, 'De Valera, Lemass and Irish Economic Development: 1933–48' in J.P. O'Carroll and John A. Murphy (eds), *De Valera and His Times* (Cork, 1983), p.120.
20. De Valera to Lemass, 8 July 1942, Lemass to de Valera 16 July 1942; SPO, Planning for Post War Situation: Industry and Commerce, S.12886. For details of Committee; SPO, Cabinet Committee on Economic Planning, S.13645 A and B.
21. Minutes of Committee; SPO, Cabinet Committee on Economic Planning: Proceedings, S.13026 A-B.
22. cf. minutes of proceedings: 34th meeting, 20 March, 1944. 41st meeting, 22 November 1944 in ibid. De Valera's biographer T.P.O'Neill has stressed that de Valera never obstructed Lemass's policy making, although he may not have played and active part himself in the policy formation. I am grateful to Professor O'Neill for discussing this matter with me.
23. cf. de Valera's contribution to Dáil debate on estimates, PDDE, Vol. 97, 6 July 1945, cc.2082–88.
24. Albert Hirschman, *The Strategy of Economic Development* (New Haven, 1958). Andrew Shonfield, *Modern Capitalism* (London, 1965).
25. Estimates for projects, January to July 1944; SPO, Planning for Post War Situation, S.12882B.

26. For a recent analysis of planning in France, R.F. Kuisel, *Capitalism and the State in Modern France* (Cambridge, 1981).
27. Brian Farrell, *Sean Lemass* (Dublin, 1983), pp.66–7, 68, 70.
28. 'General Industrial Development', 1 December 1942; SPO, Planning for Post War Situation, S.12886.
29. 5th meeting, 7 Jan. 1943; SPO, Cabinet Committee on Economic Planning: Proceedings, S.13026A-B.
30. 'General Industrial Development', 3 April 1943; SPO, Establishment of Industries, S.11987A.
31. Industry and Commerce memorandum to Dept. of Taoiseach, 29 November, 1943; SPO, Establishment of Industries, S.11987A.
32. All references to memorandum cited in footnote 31.
33. Evidence of Association of Wholesale Grocers, Importers and Distributors; NLI, Commission on Vocational Organisation, MS 924.Q.5402–08.
34. Industry and Commerce memorandum to Dept. of Taoiseach, 29 November 1943; SPO, Establishment of Industries, S.11987A.
35. 'Progress Report', May 1944, Taoiseach to Industry and Commerce, 2 November 1944; SPO, Post-War Planning. Progress Reports, S.13526.
36. Industry and Commerce to Taoiseach, 5 March 1945, in ibid.
37. Memorandum on White Papers, 12 April 1945; SPO, Government Policy, S.13481.
38. 3rd meeting, 16 December 1942; 42nd meeting, 6 December 1944; SPO, Cabinet Committee on Economic Planning: Proceedings, S.13026 A-B.
39. *Irish Press*, 13 February 1943.
40. Alan Booth, 'The "Keynesian Revolution" in Economic Policy-Making' in *Economic History Review*, xxxvi, no.1 (1983), pp.103–23.
41. Department of Finance, memorandum, 31 October 1944; SPO, Full Employment, S.13101A.
42. Lemass, to Maurice Moynihan, 21 November 1944; SPO, Full Employment, S.13101A.
43. 'Memorandum on Full Employment Policy', 17 January 1945. All quotations from this memo unless otherwise stated.
44. Minister for Agriculture, Full Employment, 14 March 1945 in ibid. Fianna Fáil had received a shock and a warning at the 1944 general election. Although receiving a majority of seats its vote slumped in the west due mainly to the success of Clann na Talmhan, an agrarian protest party.
45. There is now an extensive literature on corporatism. Philippe C. Schmitter, 'Still the Century of Corporatism?' in *Review of Politics*, 36 (1974), pp.85–131; J.J.Lee, 'Aspects of Corporatist Thought in Ireland: The Commission on Vocational Organisation,1939–43' in

Art Cosgrove and Donal McCartney (eds), *Studies in Irish History* (Dublin, 1979), pp.324–46.
46. Farrell, op cit., pp.73–4.
47. Paul Bew and Henry Patterson, *Sean Lemass and the Making of Modern Ireland* (Dublin, 1982), p.16.
48. T.K. Whitaker, 'Capital Formation, Saving and Economic Growth' in Basil Chubb and Patrick Lynch (eds) *Economic Development and Planning* (Dublin,1969). p.50. Herman van der Wee, *Prosperity and Upheaval* (Harmondsworth, 1987), p.50.
49. Alan Milward, *The Reconstruction of Europe* (London,1984), pp.462–504. Van der Wee, ibid., pp.25–47.
50. Industry and Commerce to Department of Taoiseach, 2 July 1945; SPO, Establishment of Industries, S.11987B.
51. Bew and Patterson op.cit, pp.18–20. The authors rely heavily on a newspaper interview with a former official of the Department of Industry and Commerce. His rather general remarks are not borne out by the archives of the Department. Kevin McCourt, who is described as a stalking horse for Lemass at this time did not even know him; moreover McCourt remained a protectionist until well into the 1950s (interview with Kevin McCourt).
52. PPDE, Vol.101, 24 May 1946, cc.832–3.
53. Mary Daly, 'An Irish Ireland for Business?: The Control of Manufactures Acts, 1932 and 1934' in *Irish Historical Studies*, xxiv, no.94 (1984), pp.246–72; cf. pp.271–2, 259.
54. Department of Industry and Commerce, *Minutes of Departmental Conferences* (hereafter *Departmental Conferences*): No.6, 8 October 1945; No.9, 19 October 1945; No.8, 15 October 1945; No.22, 19 December 1945; No.25, 7 January 1946; No.27, 17 January 1946 for details of these developments.
55. *Departmental Conferences*: No.85, 16 September 1947.
56. Department of Industry and Commerce, TID, 1207/2254. *Departmental Conferences*: No.53, 24 October 1946.
57. *Departmental Conferences*: No.41, 14 May 1946; No. 94, 14 January 1948; Memoranda on hosiery sector, 13 August 1948; 10 October 1948; SPO. Suspension of Customs, S.120652 A-D.
58. Exchanges contained in SPO. Taxation of Industry, S.13776A.
59. There is an extensive literature on the importance of international trade in the recovery process: cf. Milward and Van der Wee, op.cit. for discussion.
60. The exchanges are contained in SPO. Foreign Trade Development and Assistance to Industry, S.13765A. The departmental conferences contain numerous references to Industry and Commerce's approach.
61. The draft legislation and exchanges are contained in Department of Labour, Industrial Relations Bill,1946 IR19,IR39. Charles McCarthy,

Trade Unions in Ireland 1894–1960 (Dublin, 1977) contains the most extensive discussion of this period available.

62. A Note on Irish Industry; 13 October 1947. SPO. Cost of Living, S.13965B. This was prepared by Lemass for de Valera's use.
63. SPO. Control of Prices and Promotion of Industrial Efficiency 1947. S.13814A.

Chapter 6:
The Crisis of the Traditional Economy 1948–61 (pp.169–201)

1. Tom Garvin, *The Evolution of Irish Nationalist Politics* (Dublin,1981); Peter Mair, *The Changing Irish Party System* (London,1987) for comprehensive analysis.
2. Ronan Fanning, *The Irish Department of Finance* (Dublin, 1978), p.456–60.
3. Richard Kuisel, *Capitalism and the State in Modern France* (Cambridge,1981); Herman van der Wee, *Prosperity and Upheaval* (Harmondsworth,1987).
4. Cited in Fanning, op.cit.,p.406.
5. Noel Browne, *Against The Tide* (Dublin,1986),pp.122–25; Paul Bew and Henry Patterson, *Sean Lemass and the Making of Modern Ireland 1945–66* (Dublin,1982), pp.54–5.
6. Department of Industry and Commerce, *Minutes of Departmental Conferences*: No. 134, 22 December 1948; No.137, 15 January 1949. No. 149, 11 May 1949; No. 140, 5 February 1949; No. 151, 27 May 1949. (Hereafter: *Departmental Conferences.*)
7. *The European Recovery Programme* (Dublin, 1948), pp.133–39.
8. *Departmental Conferences*: No. 185, 10 July 1950; J.E. Corrigan to Sean MacBride, 7 December 1949; Department of Industry and Commerce. Establishment of Dollar Exports Advisory Committee, FT. 135. J.A. Costello to first meeting of Dollar Exports Advisory Committee, 16 June 1950; SPO, Dollar Exports Advisory Committee, S.14818.
9. Interim Report of the Industrial Development Authority Regarding Industrial Exports, 27 September 1949; SPO, Foreign Trade, S.11752A.
10. Note for Minister for Finance, 18 October 1949; UCDA, McGilligan Papers, P35B/55.
11. The reports are contained in SPO, Dollar Exports Advisory Committee, S.14818. Interview with Patrick Lynch, 5 October 1983. Professor Lynch was a member of the Dollar Export Advisory Committee and the Foreign Trade Committee at this time.
12. Lemass to Automac Co. Ltd, 30 January 1952; Department of Industry and Commerce. Establishment of Dollar Exports Advisory Committee, FT. 135.
13. Van der Wee, op.cit., pp.258–62.

14. The discussion contained in the foregoing paragraphs has been influenced by the comments of Alan Milward on an earlier draft in a letter to author 18 February 1987. A version of this chapter was read at the Seminar on the Mixed Economy, Institute of Historical Research, London 28 October 1987. The discussion at the seminar was of considerable benefit to the development of this chapter.
15. PDDE, vol. 119, 9 March 1950, c.1585.
16. Mary E. Daly, *Social and Economic History of Ireland since 1800* (Dublin, 1981) p.164.
17. Draft statement for the Government, 6 January 1949; UCDA McGilligan Papers, P35B/47. *Report in Irish Independent*, 2 February 1949.
18. Memorandum by Department of Finance with McGilligan's remarks, 7 January 1949; UCDA McGilligan Papers, P35B/47. Cabinet decision G.C.5/68, 11 February 1949; SPO, Industrial Development Authority, S.14474.
19. Draft Bill circulated by Industry and Commerce, 31 May 1949. John Leydon to Department of the Taoiseach, 26 January 1950; SPO, Industrial Development Authority, S.14474.
20. Memorandum by MacBride, 9 November 1950, which refers to meeting between IDA and government, 20 October 1950, in ibid.
21. PDDE, vol. 119, 9 March 1950, cc. 1595–1618. Interview with John Walsh, 6 December 1983. Mr. Walsh was one of the four appointees to the IDA in 1949 and later became its Chairman. For an example of the IDA's role in the examination of tariffs cf. SPO, Imposition of a Customs Duty ... 1951, S.14935.
22. Bew and Patterson, op.cit., pp.57–8.
23. IDA memorandum on Havana Charter, March 1950. Industry and Commerce, memorandum on ITO and GATT, 6 April 1950; SPO, United Nations Organisation/ITO, S.13915 A and B. *Departmental Conferences*: No. 179, 23 March, 1950. No. 185, 10th July 1950, where the IDA recommends opposition to the Stikker Plan on the grounds that it would involve further liberalisation of trade. Milward, *The Reconstruction of Western Europe*, pp.446–7, 453–4, 492.
24. Interview with John Walsh, 6 December 1983. Interview with Kevin McCourt, 26 July 1984. Mr. McCourt was one of the original appointees in 1949. Lemass's official reasons for retaining the IDA can be found in PDDE, vol. 126, 12 July 1951, c.1515.
25. Interview with John Walsh, 6 December 1983. *Survey of Grant-aided Industry* (Dublin, 1967). The IDA records for the period remain closed to researchers because of their sensitive nature.
26. Interview with John Walsh, 6 December 1983.
27. *Departmental Conferences*: No. 297, 4 May 1953.
28. Interview with Sean O'Gorman, 12 December 1985. Mr. O'Gorman

was an official of the Department of Industry and Commerce attached to the IDA at this time.

29. IBEC Technical Services Corporation, *An Appraisal of Ireland's Industrial Potential* (Dublin and New York, 1952).
30. Stacy May Report: Observations of Department of Industry and Commerce, 13 November 1953; SPO, Industrial Potentialities of Ireland, S.15389.
31. Industry and Commerce Memorandum on Industrial Taxation, 13 April 1953. Memorandum by Department of Finance, 20 April 1953. Note by Lemass, 17 August 1953. Memorandum by Finance, 22 August 1953. Memorandum by Finance, 22 August 1953. Leydon to Lemass, 21 August 1953. G.C.6/205, 8 September 1953; SPO, Taxation of Industry, S.13776B. For outcome of Commission of Inquiry into Taxation on Industry, *Report* (Dublin, 1956). The report drew attention to some of the difficulties facing industry in this area, but there is little evidence that the problem was addressed by the government.
32. Fanning, op.cit., pp.461–500. T.K. Whitaker continues to maintain that this approach was correct; interview 10 December 1982.
33. cf. exchanges contained in SPO, Industrial Potentialities of Ireland, S.15389.
34. Kieran A. Kennedy and Brendan R. Dowling, *Economic Growth in Ireland* (Dublin, 1975), p.216.
35. *Departmental Conferences*: No. 225, 15 October 1951; No. 239, 28 January 1952.
36. *Departmental Conferences*: No. 256, 9 June 1952.
37. Minute, de Valera, 5 February 1953. Memorandum by John Leydon, 7 February 1953. Industry and Commerce Progress Reports, 1 October 1952, 3 December 1952 and February 1953; SPO, Full Employment, S.13101B.
38. Record of meeting by de Valera and Lemass with the Irish Trade Union Congress and the Labour Party, 27 July 1953. Memorandum by Lemass, 28 July 1953 in ibid.
39. MacEntee, observations on Lemass, memorandum 31 July 1953. F. Aiken, memorandum 11 August 1953; SPO, National Development Fund, S.15551A.
40. Department of Finance, National Development Fund, 18 August 1953. The Central Bank, National Development Fund, 24 August 1953, in ibid.
41. Lemass to Leydon, 14 August 1953. Department of Industry and Commerce, Cabinet Committee on Provision of Employment, E26/1/21, *Departmental Conferences*: No. 389, 22 February 1955.
42. Provision of Superphosphates at World Prices, 5 November 1956, UCDA McGilligan Papers, P35B/66. Development of Forest Products, 29 September 1956, UCDA McGilligan Papers, P35B/74.

43. Fanning, op.cit., pp.500–08. Department of Finance: memorandum, 8 May 1954; Emergency Imposition of Duties, 24 July 1956; Trade and Payments Position, 2 October 1956. UCDA, McGilligan Papers, P35B/48; for Board of Trade cf. BT11/4410, minute 27 June 1951.
44. Industry and Commerce, liberalisation of trade, 4 March 1955; UCDA, McGilligan Papers, P35B/153.
45. Inter-departmental memorandum on European Free Trade Area, 15 January 1957; UCDA, McGilligan Papers, P35B/154.
46. John W. O'Hagan and Kyran P. McStay, *The Evolution of Manufacturing Industry in Ireland* (Dublin, 1981) p.23. Daly, op.cit., pp.165–7.
47. *Economic Development* (Dublin, 1958). For the conventional view, Fanning, op.cit., pp.509–19. This approach has been criticised by Paul Bew and Henry Patterson, op.cit., pp.94–117.
48. Interview with T.K. Whitaker, 10 December, 1982.
49. PDDE, vol. 165, 20 February 1958, cc. 531–81. *Survey of Grant Aided Industry*, op.cit.
50. Kennedy and Dowling, op.cit., p.227.
51. Sean F. Lemass, 'The Organisation Behind the Economic Programme' (1961) reprinted in Basil Chubb and Patrick Lynch (eds), *Economic Development and Planning* (Dublin, 1969) pp.203–12, for quote pp.203–04.
52. T.K. Whitaker, 'Capital Formation, Saving and Economic Progress (1956) reprinted in Chubb and Lynch (eds.), op.cit., pp.48–76.
53. Garret FitzGerald, *Planning in Ireland* (Dublin, 1968), pp.7–13. Dermot McAleese, 'Political Independence, Economic Growth and the Role of Economic Policy' in P.J. Drudy (ed.), *Ireland: Land, Politics and People* (Cambridge, 1982) p.285.
54. Ronan Fanning, 'Transition to Economics of Independence', *Irish Times*, 19 January 1985. The concept is also discussed in Patrick Lynch, 'The Economics of Independence: Some Unsettled Questions of Irish Economics' (1959), reprinted in Chubb and Lynch (eds), op.cit., pp.128–44.
55. O'Hagan and McStay, op.cit., pp.18–22. J.W. O'Hagan and P.J. Kelly, 'Growth Performance' in J.W. O'Hagan (ed.), *The Economy of Ireland* (Dublin, 1978) p.138.
56. For questionable use of statistics cf. Daly, op.cit., pp.163–65. O'Hagan and McStay, op.cit., pp.19–20.
57. Kennedy and Dowling, op.cit., pp.74, 46.
58. Data derived from ibid., pp.12–26 and O'Hagan and McStay, op.cit., pp.58–9.

Chapter 7:
Towards an Industrial Economy (pp.202–211)

1. Committee on Industrial Organisation, *Final Report*, (Dublin, 1965).

2. Committee on Industrial Progress, *General Report*, (Dublin, 1973).
3. Albert O.Hirschman, 'The Political Economy of Import-Substituting Industrialisation in Latin America', in *The Quarterly Journal of Economics*, lxxxii, no. 1 (1968), pp 1–32, quotation at p.28.
4. Peter J. Katzenstein, 'The Small European States in the International Economy: Economic Dependence and Corporatist Politics', in John Gerrard Ruggie (ed.), *The Antinomies of Interdependence* (New York, 1983), pp.91–130, quotation at p.94.
5. Brian Girvin, 'Industrialisation and the Irish Working Class Since 1922' in *Saothar*, 10 (1984), pp.31–42.
6. Survey of Grant Aided Industry, *Report* (Dublin, 1967), pp.21–3.
7. National Economic and Social Council, *An Analysis of Job Losses* in Irish Manufacturing Industry (Dublin, 1983), Report No. 67.
8. Alan Matthews, 'The State and Irish Agriculture, 1950–80' in P. J. Drudy (ed.), Ireland: *Land Politics and People* (Cambridge, 1982), pp.241–69.
9. Mancur Olson, *The Rise and Decline of Nations* (New Haven and London, 1982).
10. Brian Girvin, 'Government Intervention and the Nature of Interdependence', paper delivered at Europen Consortium for Political Research Workshops, Freiburg, West Germany, March 1983, and 'Consensus and Change in a Recessionary Environment', paper delivered at European Consortium for Political Research Workshops at Salzburg, Austria, April 1984, for discussion.
11. Joseph Lee, 'Society and Culture' in Frank Litton (ed.) *Unequal Achievement*, (Dublin 1982), pp. 1–20, quotation at p.14.
12. David Rottman and Phillip O'Connell, 'The Changing Social Structure of Ireland', in Litton (ed.) op.cit. pp. 63–88, p.70 for table.
13. White Paper, *Industrial Policy* (Dublin 1984) for details.

Bibliography

Official Sources

State Paper Office Dublin
Department of the Taoiseach (S. files)
Dáil Éireann (DE. files)

Department of Finance
F. Files

Department of Industry, Trade, Commerce, and Tourism
TIA Files
TID Files
Minutes of Departmental Conferences:1945 to 1955.

Department of Labour
TIW Files

Private Collections

Commission on Vocational Organisation (National Library of Ireland).
Ernest Blythe Papers (Archives Department, University College Dublin).
Federation of Irish Industries, Minutes (Confederation of Irish Industry).
Frank Gallagher Papers (National Library of Ireland).
Patrick McGilligan Papers (Archives Department, University College Dublin).

Interviews

Patrick Lynch
Kevin McCourt
Sean O'Gorman
J.J. Walsh
T.K. Whitaker

Secondary Works

Andrews, C.S., *Man of No Property* (Dublin and Cork: Mercier, 1982).
Ashworth, William. 'Typologies and Evidence: Has Nineteenth- Century Europe a Guide to Economic Growth?' in *Economic History Review*, xxx, no.1 (1977), pp.140–58.
Ballance, Robert and Stuart Sinclair, *Collapse and Survival Industrial Strategies in a Changing World* (London: George Allen and Unwin, 1983).
Banking Commission, *Final Report* (Dublin: Stationery Office, 1926).

Baran, Paul, *The Political Economy of Growth* (New York: Monthly Review Press, 1957).

Berg, Maxine, *The Machine Question and the Making of Political Economy* (Cambridge: Cambridge University Press, 1980).

Bew, Paul, and Henry Patterson, *Sean Lemass and the Making of Modern Ireland* (Dublin: Gill and Macmillan, 1982).

Booth, Alan, 'The "Keynesian Revolution" in Economic Policy-Making' in *Economic History Review*, xxxvi, no.1 (1983), pp.103-23.

Browne, Noel, *Against the Tide* (Dublin: Gill and Macmillan,1986).

Browne, Vincent (ed.), *The Magill Book of Irish Politics* (Dublin: Magill, 1981).

Census of Industrial Production (Dublin: Stationery Office, 1926–44).

Chubb, Basil and Patrick Lynch (eds), *Economic Development and Planning* (Dublin: Institute for Public Administration, 1969).

Cipolla, C.M., (ed.), The Fontana Economic History of Europe: The Emergence of Industrial Societies (Glasgow: Collins, 1973).

Cipolla, C. M., (ed.), *The Fontana Economic History of Europe: Contemporary Economics* (Glasgow: Collins, 1976).

Cochran, Thomas, *Frontiers of Change* (New York: Oxford University Press, 1981).

Cohen, Jon S., 'Fascism and Agriculture in Italy: Policies and Consequences' in *Economic History Review*, xxxii, no.1 (1979), pp.70–87.

Commission of Inquiry into Banking, Currency and Credit, *Memoranda and Minutes of Evidence*, 2 vols (Dublin: Stationery Office, 1938).

Commission of Inquiry into Banking, Currency and Credit, *Reports* (Dublin: Stationery Office, 1938).

Commission of Inquiry into Taxation on Industry, *Report* (Dublin: Stationery Office, 1956).

Commission on Emigration, *Reports* (Dublin: Stationery Office, 1955).

Committee on Industrial Organisation, *Final Report* (Dublin: Stationery Office, 1965).

Committee on Industrial Progress, *General Report* (Dublin: Stationery Office,1973).

Cosgrave, Art, and Donal McCartney (eds.), *Studies in Irish History*, (Dublin: UCD, 1979)

Corkery, Daniel, *Synge and Anglo-Irish Literature* (Cork: Cork University Press, 1931).

Crotty, Raymond, *Irish Agricultural Production* (Cork: Cork University Press, 1966).

Crotty, Raymond, *Ireland in Crisis* (Dingle: Brandon,1986).

Cullen, L.M., *An Economic History of Ireland since 1660* (London: Batsford,1972).

Curzon, Gerard, *Multilateral Commercial Diplomacy* (London: Michael Joseph, 1965).

Daly, Mary E., *Social and Economic History of Ireland since 1800* (Dublin: Educational Company, 1981).

Daly, Mary, 'An Irish Ireland for Business?: The Control of Manufactures Acts, 1932 and 1934' in *Irish Historical Studies*, xxiv, 94 (1984), pp.246–72.

Daly, Mary, 'Government Finance for Industry in the Irish Free State: The Trade Loans (Guarantee) Acts', in *Irish Economic and Social History*, xi (1984), pp.73–93.

Daniel, T.K., 'Griffith on his Noble Head: the Determinants of Cumann na nGaedheal's Economic Policy 1922–32' in *Irish Economic History*, iii (1976), pp.55–65.

Drudy, P.J. (ed.), *Ireland: Land, Politics and People* (Cambridge: Cambridge University Press, 1982).

Economic Development (Dublin: Stationery Office, 1958).

The European Recovery Programme (Dublin: Stationery Office, 1948).

Fanning, Ronan, *The Irish Department of Finance* (Dublin: Institute of Public Administration, 1978).

Fanning, Ronan, *Independent Ireland* (Dublin: Helicon, 1983).

Fanning, Ronan, 'Transition to Economics of Independence', *Irish Times* 19 January 1985.

Farrell, Brian, *The Founding of Dáil Éireann* (Dublin: Gill and Macmillan, 1971).

Farrell, Brian, *Sean Lemass* (Dublin: Gill and Macmillan, 1983).

Ferguson, R.C., 'Industrial Policy and Organisation' in King (ed.), pp.27–54.

Fiscal Inquiry Committee, *Reports* (Dublin: Stationery Office, 1923).

FitzGerald, Garret, *Planning in Ireland* (Dublin: Institute for Public Administration, 1968).

FitzGerald, Garret, 'Mr Whitaker and Industry', *Studies*, xlviii (1959), 138–50.

Frank, Andre Gunder, *Capitalism and Underdevelopment in Latin America* (New York: Monthly Review Press, 1967).

Gardner, Richard N., *Sterling-Dollar Diplomacy in Current Perspective* (New York: Columbia University Press, expanded ed. 1980, orig. ed. 1956).

Garvin, Tom, *The Evolution of Irish Nationalist Politics* (Dublin: Gill and Macmillan, 1981).

Garvin, Tom, *Nationalist Revolutionaries in Ireland 1895-1928* (Oxford: Oxford University Press,1987).

Garvin, Tom, 'The Sociology of a Nationalist Revolution: Ireland 1858-1928' (unpublished manuscript: Dept. of Politics, UCD, April 1984).

Genovene, Eugene, *The Political Economy of Slavery* (New York: Vintage Books, 1967).

Gibbins, John (ed.), *Politics and Contemporary Culture: New and Old Politics* (London: Sage, forthcoming 1989).

Girvin, Brian, 'The Dominance of Fianna Fáil and the Nature of Political Adaptability in Ireland' in *Political Studies*, xxxii, no.4 (1984), pp.461–70.

Girvin, Brian, 'Industrialisation and the Irish Working Class Since 1922' in *Saothar,* 10 (1984), pp.31–42.
Girvin, Brian, 'Nationalism, Democracy, and Irish Political Culture', in Girvin and Sturm (eds), pp.3–28.
Girvin, Brian and Roland Sturm (eds), *Politics and Society in Contemporary Ireland* (Aldershot: Gower, 1986).
Girvin, Brian, 'Change and Continuity in Liberal Democratic Culture', in Gibbins, (ed.).
Grantham, D.W., *The Life and Death of the Solid South* (Lexington, Kentucky: University of Kentucky Press, 1988).
Greaves, C. Desmond, *The Irish Transport and General Workers Union,* (Dublin: Gill and Macmillan, 1982).
Hall, John A., *Powers and Liberties* (Harmondsworth: Penguin, 1986).
Hannan, Damien, *Displacement and Development: Class Kinship and Social Change in Irish Rural Communities* (Dublin: ESRI, 1979).
Harkness, D.W., *The Restless Dominion* (London: Macmillan, 1969).
Harris, Nigel, *The End of the Third World* (Harmondsworth: Penguin,1986).
Henderson, W.O., *Friedrich List: Economist and Visionary 1789–1846* (London: Frank Cass, 1983).
Hirschman, Albert O., *National Power and the Structure of Foreign Trade* (Berkeley: University of California Press, 1980. orig. ed. 1945).
Hirschman, Albert O., *The Strategy of Economic Development* (New Haven: Yale University Press, 1958).
Hirschman, Albert O., Exit, Voice and Loyalty: *Responses to Decline in Firms* (Cambridge, Mass.: Harvard University Press, 1970).
Hirschman, Albert O., *Essays in Trespassing* (Cambridge: Cambridge University Press, 1981).
Hirschman, Albert O., 'The Political Economy of Import-Substituting Industrialisation in Latin America' in *The Quarterly Journal of Economics,* lxxxii, no.1 (1968), pp.1-32.
Hirschman, Albert O., 'Rival Interpretations of Market Societies: Civilising, Restrictive, or Feeble?' in *Journal of Economic Literature,* xx (1982), pp.1463–84.
Hobsbawm, Eric, *The Age of Revolution* (New York: Mentor,1962).
IBEC Technical Services Corporation, *An Appraisal of Ireland's Industrial Potential* (Dublin and New York: Stationery Office, 1952).
Industrial Policy White Paper (Dublin: Government Publications Office,1984).
Industry and Commerce, Department of, *Agricultural Statistics 1928–33* (Dublin: Stationery Office, 1935).
Irish Trade Journal, 1926-subsequently *Irish Trade Journal and Statistical Bulletin.*
Irish Trade Union Congress, *Annual Conference* (1931–48).
Johanson, Hans Christian, *The Danish Economy in the Twentieth Century* (London and Sydney: Croom Helm, 1987).

Johnson, David, *The Interwar Economy in Ireland* (Dundalk: Economic and Social History Society of Ireland, 1985).
Johnson, Harry (ed.), *Economic Nationalism in Old and New States* (London: George Allen and Unwin, 1968)
Johnson, Harry, 'The Ideology of Economic Policy in the New States' in Johnson (ed.), pp.124–41.
Jones, Geoffrey, 'The Growth and Performance of British Multinational Firms Before 1939: The Case of Dunlop' in *Economic History Review*, xxxvii, no.1 (1984), pp.35–53.
Jorberg, Lennart, 'The Nordic Countries 1950-1914', in Cipolla (ed.), 1973, pp.375–485.
Jorberg, Lennart and Olle Krantz, 'Scandinavia 1914–1970', in Cipolla (ed.) 1976, pp.377–459.
Katzenstein, Peter J., 'The Small European States in the International Economy: Economic Dependence and Corporatist Politics' in Ruggie (ed.), pp.91–130.
Katzenstein, Peter J., *Corporatism and Change: Switzerland and Austria and the Politics of Industrialisation* (Ithaca: Cornell University Press, 1984).
Kennedy, Kieran A., *Productivity and Industrial Growth: The Irish Experience* (Oxford: Clarendon Press, 1971).
Kennedy, Kieran A. and Brendan R. Dowling, *Economic Growth in Ireland* (Dublin: Gill and Macmillan, 1975).
Kennedy, Liam and Philip Ollerenshaw (eds), *An Economic History of Ulster 1820–1939* (Manchester: Manchester University Press, 1985).
Key, V.O., 'A Theory of Critical Elections' in *Journal of Politics*, 17 (1955), pp.3–18.
Keynes, John Maynard, 'National Self Sufficiency' in *Studies*, xxii (1933), pp.177–93.
King, F.C. (ed.), *Public Administration in Ireland* (Dublin: Parkside Press, 1945).
Kitching, Gavin, *Development and Underdevelopment in Historical Perspective* (London: Methuen, 1982).
Koblik, Steven (ed.), *Sweden's Development from Poverty to Affluence 1950–70* (Minneapolis: University of Minnesota Press, 1975).
Kuisel, R.F., *Capitalism and the State in Modern France* (Cambridge: Cambridge University Press, 1981).
Lahiff, Eddie, *Industry and Labour in Cork 1890–1921* (Unpublished M.A. thesis, National University of Ireland, 1988)
Lee, Joseph, 'Aspects of Corporatist Thought in Ireland: the Commission on Vocational Organisation, 1939-43' in Cosgrave and McCartney (eds), pp.324–46.
Lee, J.J. and M.A.G. Ó Tuathaigh, *The Age of de Valera* (Dublin: Ward River Press, 1983).
Lee, Joseph, 'Society and Culture' in Litton (ed.) pp.1–20.

Leff, Nathaniel, *Underdevelopment and Development in Brazil*, 2 vols (London: George Allen and Unwin, 1982).

Lemass, Sean F., 'The Organisation Behind the Economic Programme' published 1961, reprinted in Chubb and Lynch (eds), pp.203-12.

Litton, Frank (ed.), *Unequal Achievement* (Dublin:Institute of Public Administration, 1982)

Lynch, Patrick, 'The Economics of Independence: Some Unsettled Questions of Irish Economics', published 1959, reprinted in Chubb and Lynch (eds), pp.128–44.

McAleese, Dermot, 'Political Independence, Economic Growth and the Role of Economic Policy', in Drudy (ed.), pp.271–95.

Macardle, Dorothy, *The Irish Republic* (London: Corgi, 1968, orig. ed., 1937).

Mair, Peter, 'Labour and the Irish Party System re-visited: Party Competition in the 1920s' in *Econonomic and Social Review*, 9, no.1 (1977), pp.59–70.

Mair, Peter, *The Changing Irish Party System* (London: Frances Pinter, 1987).

Mandel, Ernest, *Late Capitalism* (London: New Left Books, 1978).

Matthews, Alan, 'The State and Irish Agriculture 1950–80' in Drudy (ed.), pp.241–69.

McCarthy, Charles, *Trade Unions in Ireland 1894–1960* (Dublin: Institute of Public Administration, 1977).

McClelland, D.C., *The Achieving Society* (Princeton: Princeton University Press, 1961)

McKenzie, Robert B. and Gordon Tullock, *Modern Political Economy* (Tokyo: McGraw-Hill Kogakusha, 1978).

McManus, Francis (ed.), *The Years of the Great Test 1926–1939* (Cork: Mercier, 1967).

Meenan, James, 'Irish Industrial Policy 1921–43', *Studies* xxxii (1943), pp.209–18.

Meenan, James, 'From Free Trade to Self-Sufficiency', in McManus (ed.), pp.69–79.

Meenan, James, *The Irish Economy since 1922* (Liverpool: Liverpool University Press, 1970).

Milward, Alan S., *The Reconstruction of Western Europe 1945–51* (London: Methuen, 1984).

Mitchell, Arthur, *Labour in Irish Politics 1890–1930* (Dublin: Irish University Press, 1974).

Mokyr, Joel, *Why Ireland Starved* (London:George Allen and Unwin, 1983).

Moss, Warner, *Political Parties in the Irish Free State* (New York: Columbia University Press, 1933).

Mouzelis, Nicos, 'Capitalism and the Development of the Greek State',in Scase (ed.), pp.241-73.

Mouzelis, Nicos P., *Politics in the Semi-Periphery* (London: Macmillan,1986).

Moynihan, Maurice (ed.), *Speeches and Statements by Eamon de Valera 1917–73* (Dublin: Gill and Macmillan, 1980).

National Economic and Social Council, *An Analysis of Job Losses in Irish Manufacturing Industry* (Dublin: Government Publications Office,1983).

O'Brien, George, *The Economic History of Ireland from the Union to the Famine* (London:Longmans Green,1921).

O'Carroll, J.P. and John A. Murphy (eds), *De Valera and his Times* (Cork: Cork University Press, 1983).

O'Hagan, J.W. (ed.), *The Economy of Ireland* (Dublin: IMI, 1978 2nd ed.).

O'Hagan, J.W. and P.J. Kelly, 'Growth Performance', in O'Hagan (ed.), pp.137–49.

O'Hagan, J.W. and Kyran P. McStay, *The Evolution of Manufacturing Industry in Ireland* (Dublin: Helicon, 1981).

O'Leary, Cornelius, *Irish Elections 1918–77* (Dublin: Gill and Macmillan,1979).

O'Malley, Eoin, 'The Decline of Irish Industry in the Nineteenth Century' in *Economic and Social Review*, 13, no.1 (1981), pp.21–42.

O'Rahilly, Alfred, *Money* (Cork: Cork University Press, 1942).

Ó Tuathaigh, M.A.G., 'De Valera and Sovereignty', in O'Carroll and Murphy (eds), pp.62–73.

Olson, Mancur, *The Rise and Decline of Nations* (New Haven and London: Yale University Press,1982).

Orridge, Andrew, 'The Blueshirts and the "Ecomomic War": a Study of Ireland in the Context of Dependency Theory' in *Political Studies*, 31, no.3 (1983), pp.351–69.

Owen, Roger and Bob Sutcliffe, *Studies in the Theory of Imperialism* (London: Longman, 1972).

Patterson, Henry, 'Industrial Labour and the Labour Movement 1820-1914' in Kennedy and Ollerenshaw (eds), pp.158–83.

Pearse, Padraig, *Political Writings and Speeches* (Dublin: Talbot, 1966).

Pelaez, Carlos, 'The Theory and Reality of Imperialism in the Coffee Economy of Nineteenth Century Brazil' in *Economic History Review*, xxix, no.2 (1976), pp.276–90.

Pollard, Sidney, *Peaceful Conquest* (Oxford: Oxford University Press, 1981).

The Programme for Economic Expansion, (Dublin: Stationery Office, 1958).

Raymond, Raymond J., 'De Valera, Lemass and Irish Economic Development: 1933–1948', in O'Carroll and Murphy (eds), pp.113–33.

Rottman, David and Phillip O'Connell, 'The Changing Social Structure in Ireland' in Litton (ed.), pp. 63–88.

Ruggie, John Gerard, *The Antinomies of Interdependence* (New York: Columbia University Press, 1983).

Scase, Richard (ed.), *The State in Western Europe* (London: Croom Helm, 1980).

Schmitter, Philippe C., 'Still the Century of Corporatism?', *Review of Politics*, 36 (1974), pp.85–131.

Schmitter, Philippe and Gerhart Lehmbruch (eds), *Trends Towards Corporatist Intermediation* (London: Sage, 1979).

Seers, Dudley, *The Political Economy of Nationalism* (Oxford: Oxford University Press, 1983).

Shonfield, Andrew, *Modern Capitalism* (London: Oxford University Press, 1965).

Sinnott, Richard, 'Interpretations of the Irish Party System' in *European Journal of Political Research*, 12 (1984), pp.289—07.

Skinner, Liam, *Politicians by Accident* (Dublin: Metropolitan Publishers, 1946).

Solow, Barbara, *The Land Question and the Irish Economy, 1870–1903* (Cambridge, Mass.: Harvard University Press, 1971).

Soderplan, Sven Anders, 'The Crisis Agreement and the Social Democratic Road to Power', in Koblik (ed.), pp.258–78.

Survey of Grant-Aided Industry (Dublin, Stationery Office, 1967).

Sutcliffe, Bob, 'Imperialism and Industrialisation in the Third World' in Owen and Sutcliffe (eds) pp.171–92.

Tivey, Leonard, 'States, Nations and Economies' in Tivey (ed.), pp.59–81.

Tivey, Leonard (ed.), *The Nation State* (Oxford: Martin Robertson, 1981).

Varley, Tony and Chris Curtin, 'The Political Negotiation of State Agricultural Policy: Ireland 1922–1939', paper presented at annual conference, Irish Sociological Association, Magee College, Derry, April 1980.

de Vere White, Terence, *Kevin O' Higgins* (Tralee: Anvil Press, 1966, orig.ed. 1948).

Warren, Bill, *Imperialism: Pioneer of Capitalism* (London: New Left Books, 1980).

Whitaker, T.K., 'Capital Formation, Saving and Economic Progress'; published 1956, reprinted in Chubb and Lynch (eds), pp.48–76.

Index

PROPERTY OF
ST. MARY'S COLLEGE
STRAWBERRY HILL

3M

before

ST. MARY'S COLLEGE
00180537